DATE DUE

~~MY 26 '98~~			
~~DE 7 '98~~			
~~NO 28 '01~~			
~~APR 1 9 2007~~			
~~MY 2 1 '09~~			
~~DE 1 0 '09~~			
DE 1 8 '09			

PRINCETON SERIES ON THE MIDDLE EAST

Bernard Lewis and Heath W. Lowry, Editors

JIHAD IN CLASSICAL AND MODERN ISLAM:

An early 14th c. miniature of a siege of a town by a Muslim army using a mangonel. The use of mangonels is expressly allowed in the legal literature. See chapter 4, § 3.

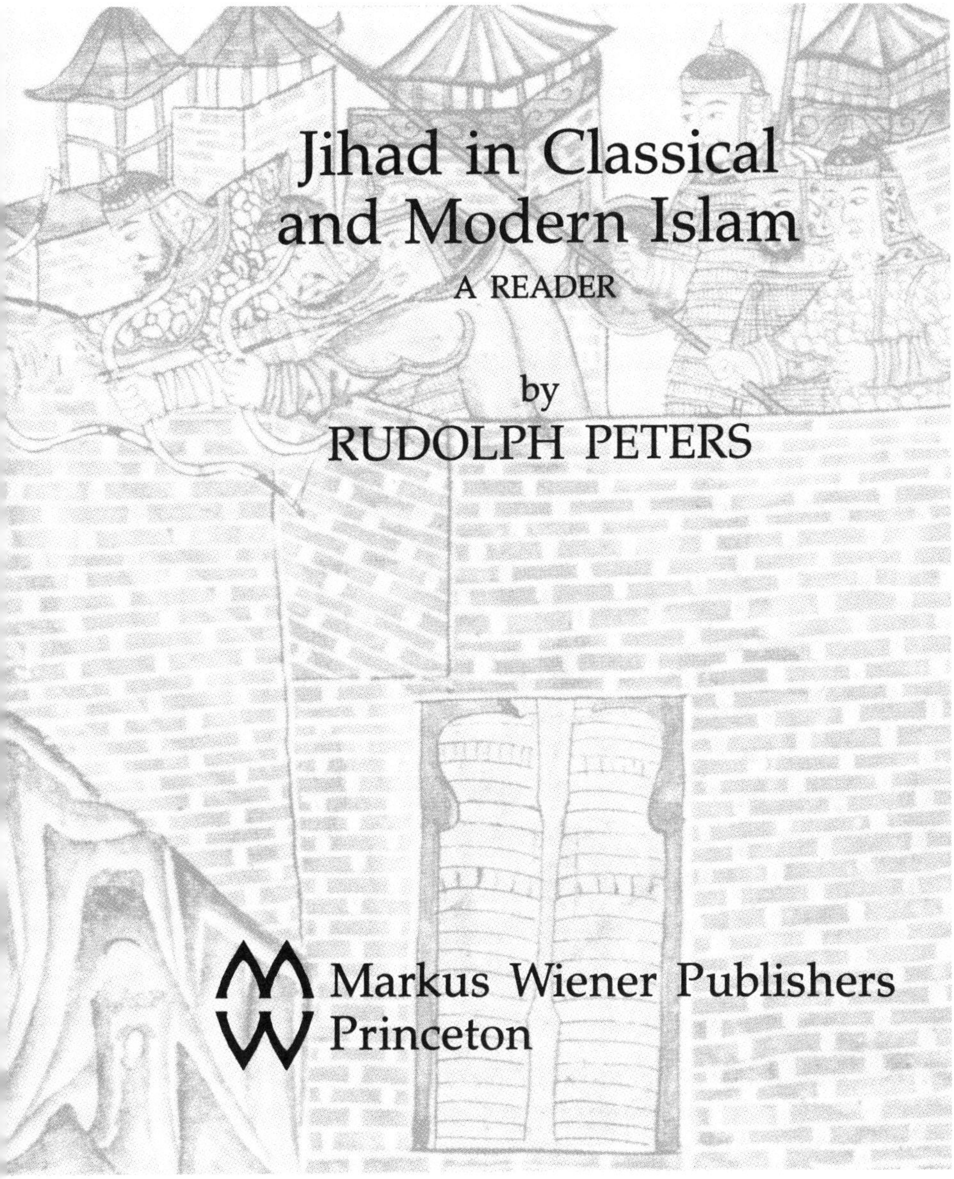

Jihad in Classical and Modern Islam

A READER

by

RUDOLPH PETERS

Markus Wiener Publishers
Princeton

For information write to:
Markus Wiener Publishers
114 Jefferson Road, Princeton, NJ 08540

Library of Congress Cataloging-in-Publication Data

Peters, Rudolph.
The jihad in classical and modern times / Rudolph Peters.
Includes bibliographical references.
ISBN 1-55876-108-X (alk. paper)
ISBN 1-55876-109-8 (pbk. : alk. paper)
1. Jihad. 2. Islam—Doctrines. I. Title.
BP182.P48 1995
297'.72—dc20 95-20943
CIP

Cover design by Cheryl Mirkin
Cover Illustration: Parts of A 16th century Ottoman representation of the Battle of Uhud.

This book has been composed in Palatino
by Coghill Book Typesetting Company.

Markus Wiener Publishers books are printed on acid-free paper, and meet the guidelines for permanence and durability of the committee on production guidelines for book longevity of the council on library resources.

Printed in the United States of America

Contents

Preface vii

1 ♦ JIHAD, AN INTRODUCTION
Page 1

2 ♦ THE PROPHET'S LESSONS ON CONDUCT IN WAR:
Ḥadīths on Jihad From the *Ṣaḥīḥ* of Muslim ibn Ḥajjāj
Page 9

3 ♦ EXHORTATIONS TO JIHAD:
Passages on Jihad and Martyrdom from Mālik's *al-Muwaṭṭa'*
Page 19

4 ♦ THE LEGAL DOCTRINE OF JIHAD:
The Chapter on Jihad from Averroes' Legal Handbook *al-Bidāya*
Page 27

5 ♦ THE RELIGIOUS AND MORAL DOCTRINE OF JIHAD:
Ibn Taymiyya on Jihad
Page 43

6 ♦ JIHAD AND WAR PROPAGANDA:
The Ottoman Jihad Fatwa of November 11th, 1914
Page 55

7 ♦ A MODERNIST INTERPRETATION OF JIHAD:
Maḥmûd Shaltût's Treatise *Koran and Fighting*
Page 59

8 ♦ THE DOCTRINE OF JIHAD IN MODERN ISLAM
Page 103

9 ♦ THE RELEVANCE OF THE JIHAD DOCTRINE
IN SADAT'S EGYPT
Page 149

Notes 171

Bibliography 197

Acknowledgements 203

Cover of the book "The Trial of Pharaoh: The Secrets of the Trial of Sadat's Murderers", written by one of the lawyers of the Jihad Organization that was responsible for President Sadat's assassination. See chapter 9.

Preface

Jihad is one of those Arabic words that has become familiar to the educated public in the West. The reason, of course, is that the notion is very much alive in the Islamic world and plays a prominent political role. There are many Islamist groups nowadays who define their struggle against their adversaries as jihad. And at the moment that this is being written, the blind Egyptian preacher ʿUmar ʿAbd al-Rahmān stands trial in New York for being the leader of a violent jihad group. The word jihad is capable of evoking intense emotions. When the Palestinian leader Yasir ʿArafat recently used the word in a speech to South African Muslims, there were emotional reactions, especially on the part of those who accused him of mobilizing religious fanaticism in spite of the peace treaty between the PLO and Israel, and also heated debates as to the real significance of the word jihad. Jihad is a word that is frequently mentioned in the media. However, its precise meaning is not well known, except that it is usually translated as "Holy War." In this book we want to give some background information about jihad.

The present book contains six Islamic texts, translated from the Arabic and Turkish, and two articles on jihad. With the exception of the translation of Ibn Taymiyya's chapter on jihad, all of them have appeared earlier and, save the passages from Muslim's *Ṣaḥīḥ* and Mālik's *al-Muwaṭṭa*ʾ, they were translated or written by the author and compiler of this book.

The aim of the present book is to provide basic reading material on the doctrine of jihad and to highlight the various aspects of jihad (in the sense of struggle) through the ages. The first text consists of a number of *ḥadīths*, sayings and deeds of the Prophet Mohammed, containing prescriptions for proper conduct during warfare. Together with the Koran they form the raw material from which Islamic law was elaborated and in the texts on jihad included in this book, many of the *ḥadīths* presented here are quoted or referred to. The second text, taken from the *al-Muwaṭṭa*ʾ of

Mālik ibn Anas (d. 795), consists of two passages containing sayings of the Prophet Mohammed or his Companions, exhorting the Muslims to participate in jihad and expounding the ultimate happiness of the martyrs, i.e. those slain in performing jihad. This text is followed by an exposé of the legal doctrine of jihad taken from the legal handbook *Bidāyat al-Mujtahid wa-Nihāyat al-Muqtaṣid* ("The beginning for him who interprets the sources independently and the end for him who wishes to limit himself"), written by the famous philosopher, physician and judge Averroes (Arabic: Abū al-Walīd Muḥammad ibn Muhammad Ibn Rushd; d. 1198). Averroes' book contains a discussion of the doctrines of the four legal schools *(madhhab,* plural *madhāhib)* with an explanation of the arguments brought forward in support of their points of view by the theoreticians of each school. The text selected here, therefore, offers a comprehensive overview of the rules concerning jihad, as interpreted by the various legal schools.

The fourth text, a passage from Ibn Taymiyya's (d. 1328) *al-Siyāsa al-sharʿiyya fī iṣlāḥ al-rāʿī wa-al-raʿiyya* ("Governance according to God's Law in reforming both the ruler and his flock"), focuses not so much on the legal as on the religious and moral aspects of jihad. It quotes a number of Koranic verses and sayings of the Prophet on jihad, and deals with the meritoriousness of participating in it and with the definition of the enemy. The text shows clearly that Ibn Taymiyya's concern was the struggle against deviant and heretical Muslims in the Territory of Islam, as much as warfare against the unbelievers in the Territory of War.

The next brief text illustrates how the doctrine of jihad can be used for war propaganda. It is the fatwa that was issued by the highest religious authority in the Ottoman Empire on 11 November 1914 and accompanied the official declaration of war against the Allied Powers. The last translated text I have included is a treatise on jihad in which the author, Maḥmûd Shaltūt (d. 1963), who, from 1958 until his death, was Rector of the famous Azhar University in Cairo, argues for a modernist and peaceful interpretation of jihad. The following chapter presents recent currents of thought on jihad. In it both the modernist and the fundamentalist interpretations are analysed. The final chapter is a case study of the political role the jihad doctrine has played in Egypt in the

1970s, and especially its importance for the emerging Islamist groups.

In order to achieve a measure of editorial unity in the book, the transliteration has been adapted according to the system of the *International Journal of Middle East Studies*. For the same reason, the Koran is quoted in the translation of Arberry,[1] except, of course, in the chapters that were not translated or written by me.

RUDOLPH PETERS
Amsterdam, May 1995

A 16th century Ottoman miniature shows how, during the Battle of Badr (624), the angel Jibrîl or Gabriel informs the Prophet Mohammed that a host of angels (depicted on top, with white turbans) will assist the Muslims.

1

Jihad, an Introduction

The Arabic word *jihād* (verbal noun of the verb *jāhada*) means to strive, to exert oneself, to struggle. The word has a basic connotation of an endeavour towards a praiseworthy aim. In a religious context it may express a struggle against one's evil inclinations or an exertion for the sake of Islam and the *umma,* e.g. trying to convert unbelievers or working for the moral betterment of Islamic society ("jihad of the tongue" and "jihad of the pen"). In the books on Islamic law, the word means armed struggle against the unbelievers, which is also a common meaning in the Koran. Sometimes the "jihad of the sword" is called "the smaller jihad," in opposition to the peaceful forms named "the greater jihad." Nowadays, it is often used without any religious connotation, more or less equivalent to the English word crusade ("A crusade against drugs"). If used in a religious context, the adjective "Islamic" or "holy" is currently added to it *(al-jihād al-Islāmī* or *al-jihād al-muqaddas).*

The origin of the concept of jihad goes back to the wars fought by the Prophet Mohammed and their written reflection in the Koran. It is clear that the concept was influenced by the ideas of war among the pre-Islamic Northern Arabic tribes. Among these, war was the normal state, unless two or more tribes had concluded a truce. War between tribes was regarded as lawful and if the war was fought as a defence against aggression, the fighting had an additional justification. Ideas of chivalry forbade warriors to kill non-combatants like children, women and old people. These rules have become incorporated into the doctrine of jihad which was fixed in the latter half of the second century of the Hijra era.

The Koran frequently mentions jihad and fighting *(qitāl)* against the unbelievers. K. 22:39 (*"Leave is given to those who fight because they were wronged—surely God is able to help them—who were expelled from their habitations without right, except that they say 'Our Lord is God.'"*), revealed not long after the Hijra, is traditionally considered to be the first verse dealing with the fighting of the unbelievers. Many verses exhort the believers to take part in the fighting "with their goods and lives" *(bi-amwālihim wa-anfusihim)*, promise reward to those who are killed in the jihad (K. 3:157–158, 169–172) and threaten those who do not fight with severe punishments in the hereafter (K. 9:81–82, 48:16). Other verses deal with practical matters such as exemption from military service (K. 9:91, 48:17), fighting during the holy months (K. 2:217), and in the holy territory of Mecca (K. 2:191), the fate of prisoners of war (K. 47:4), safe conduct (K. 9:6) and truce (K. 8:61).

It is not clear whether the Koran allows Muslims to fight the unbelievers only as a defense against aggression or under all circumstances. In support of the first view a number of verses can be quoted justifying fighting as a reaction against aggression or perfidy on the part of the unbelievers (e.g. *"And fight in the way of God with those who fight you, but aggress not: God loves not the aggressors,"* (K. 2:190) and *"But if they break their oaths after their covenant and thrust at your religion, then fight the leaders of unbelief."* [K. 9:12]). In those verses that seem to order the Muslims to fight the unbelievers unconditionally, the general condition that fighting is only allowed by way of defense could be said to be understood (e.g. *"Then, when the sacred months are drawn away, slay the idolaters wherever you find them, and take them, and confine them, and lie in wait for them at every place of ambush."* (K. 9:5) and *"Fight those who believe not in God and the Last Day and do not forbid what God and His Messenger have forbidden—such men as practise not the religion of truth, being of those who have been given the Book—until they pay the tribute out of hand and have been humbled."* [K. 9:29]). Classical Muslim Koran interpretation, however, did not go into this direction. It regarded the Sword Verses, with the unconditional command to fight the unbelievers, as having abrogated all previous verses concerning the intercourse with non-Muslims. This idea is no doubt connected with the pre-Islamic concept that war between tribes was allowed, unless there existed a truce between them, whereby the Islamic *umma* took the place of a tribe.

During the second half of the eighth century the first comprehensive treatises on the law of jihad were written by al-Awzāʿī (d. 774) and Muḥammad al-Shaybānī (d. 804). The legal doctrine of jihad was the result of debates and discussions that had been going on since the Prophet's death and through which the doctrine had been developed. The period in which the doctrine of jihad was gradually formulated coincided with the period of the great conquests, in which the Muslim conquerors were exposed to the cultures of the conquered peoples. With regard to the doctrine of jihad, there may have been some influence from the Byzantine Empire, where the idea of religious war and related notions were very much alive. It is, however, very difficult to identify these influences. If there are similarities, they are not necessarily the result of borrowing and may be due to parallel developments.

The doctrine of jihad, as laid down in the works on Islamic law, developed out of the Koranic prescriptions and the example of the Prophet and the first caliphs, which is recorded in the *ḥadīth*. The crux of the doctrine is the existence of one single Islamic state, ruling the entire *umma*. It is the duty of the *umma* to expand the territory of this state in order to bring as many people under its rule as possible. The ultimate aim is to bring the whole earth under the sway of Islam and to extirpate unbelief: *"Fight them until there is no persecution (or: seduction) and the religion is God's (entirely)."* (K. 2:193 and 8:39). Expansionist jihad is a collective duty *(farḍ ʿalā al-kifāya)*, which is fulfilled if a sufficient number of people take part in it. If this is not the case, the whole *umma* is sinning. Expansionist jihad presupposes the presence of a legitimate caliph to organize the struggle. After the conquests had come to an end, the legal specialists laid down that the caliph had to raid enemy territory at least once a year in order to keep the idea of jihad alive.

Sometimes jihad becomes an individual duty. This is the case when the caliph appoints certain persons to participate in a raiding expedition or when someone takes an oath to fight the unbelievers. Moreover, jihad becomes obligatory for all people capable of fighting in a certain region if this region is attacked by the enemy. In this case, jihad is defensive.

Sunnite and Shiʿite theories of jihad are very similar. However, there is one crucial difference. The Twelver Shiʿites hold that jihad can only be waged under the leadership of the rightful *Imām*. After the Occultation of the last one in 873, theoretically no lawful jihad can be fought. This is true for expansionist jihad. However, as defence against attacks remains obligatory and the 'ulamā' are often regarded as the representatives of the Hidden *Imām*, several wars between Iran and Russia in the 19th century have been called jihad.

War against unbelievers may not be mounted without summoning them to Islam or submission before the attack. A *ḥadīth* lays down the precise contents of the summons:

> Whenever the Prophet appointed a commander to an army or an expedition, he would say: "(. . .) When you meet your heathen enemies, summon them to three things. Accept whatsoever they agree to and refrain then from fighting them. Summon them to become Muslims. If they agree, accept their conversion. In that case summon them to move from their territory to the Abode of the Emigrants [i.e. Medina]. If they refuse that, let them know that then they are like the Muslim bedouins and that they share only in the booty, when they fight together with the [other] Muslims. If they refuse conversion, then ask them to pay poll-tax *(jizya)*. If they agree, accept their submission. But if they refuse, then ask God for assistance and fight them. (. . .)" (*Ṣaḥīḥ* Muslim)

This *ḥadīth* also neatly sums up the aims of fighting unbelievers: conversion or submission. In the latter case, the enemies were entitled to keep their religion and practice it, against payment of a poll-tax *(jizya)* (cf. K. 9:29, quoted above). Although the Koran limits this option to the People of the Book, i.e. Christians and Jews, it was in practice extended to other religions, such as the Zoroastrians *(Majūs)*.

Whenever the caliph deems it in the interest of the *umma*, he may conclude a truce with the enemy, just as the Prophet did with the Meccans at al-Ḥudaybiyya. According to some law schools a truce must be concluded for a specified period of time, no longer than ten years. Others hold that this is not necessary, if the caliph stipulates that he may resume war whenever he wishes to do so. The idea behind it is that the notion of jihad must not fall into oblivion.

The books on law contain many practical rules concerning warfare, dealing e.g. with exemptions from the obligation to fight, the protection of the lives of noncombatants, lawful methods of warfare, treatment of prisoners of war, safe-conduct to enemy persons and the division of the spoils.

The most important function of the doctrine of jihad is that it mobilizes and motivates Muslims to take part in wars against unbelievers, as it is considered to be the fulfillment of a religious duty. This motivation is strongly fed by the idea that those who are killed on the battlefield, called martyrs *(shahīd,* plur. *shuhadāʾ),* will go directly to Paradise. At the occasion of wars fought against unbelievers, religious texts would circulate, replete with Koranic verses and *ḥadīths* extolling the merits of fighting a jihad and vividly describing the reward waiting in the hereafter for those slain during the fighting.

Another function was to enhance the legitimation of a ruler. After the year 750, the political unity of the *umma* was lost, never to be restored again. Several rulers would govern different regions of the Muslim world. One of the ways to acquire greater legitimacy was to wage jihad against unbelievers, which is one of the main tasks of the lawful caliph.

A final function of the jihad doctrine was that it provided a set of rules governing the relationship with the unbelieving enemies and behaviour during actual warfare. Muftis could invoke this set of rules and give fatwas showing that a ruler's foreign policy was in conformity with the rules of Islamic law. These rules could be moulded to fit the circumstance. A case in point is that, due to the collapse of Islamic political unity, often two Muslim states would be at war with one another. In such situations muftis would usually find cause to label the enemies either as rebels or as heretics, thus justifying the struggle against them.

During Islamic history, but especially in the 18th and 19th centuries, radical movements striving for a purification of Islam and the establishment of a purely Islamic society proclaimed jihad against their opponents, both Muslims and non-Muslims. To justify the struggle against their Muslim adversaries, they would brand them as unbelievers for their neglect to adhere to and enforce the strict rules of Islam.

For some Muslim intellectuals the colonial experience affected their outlook on jihad. Some would argue that in view of the military superiority of the colonizer, jihad was not obligatory anymore on the strength of K. 2:195 (". . . and cast not yourselves by your own hands into destruction . . ."). Others, however, elaborated new interpretations of the doctrine of jihad.

The first one to do so was the Indian Muslim thinker Sayyid Aḥmad Khān (1817–1898). When after the Mutiny of 1857 the British, arguing that the Muslims wanted to restore Moghul rule and that the doctrine of jihad made them fight the British, began favouring the Hindus in the army and in government service, Sayyid Aḥmad Khan wanted to show that Islam did not forbid cooperation with the British colonial government. In this he was motivated by his desire to safeguard employment for the young Muslims from the middle and higher classes. In order to demonstrate that the Indian Muslims were not obliged to fight the British and could be loyal subjects, he gave a new interpretation of the jihad doctrine. On the basis of a new reading of the Koran, he asserted that jihad was obligatory for Muslims only in the case of "positive oppression or obstruction in the exercise of their faith (. . .) impair[ing] the foundation of some of the pillars of Islam." Since the British, in his opinion, did not interfere with the practising of Islam, jihad against them was not allowed.

Middle Eastern Muslim reformers like Muḥammad ʿAbduh (1849–1905) and Muḥammad Rashīd Riḍā (1865–1935) did not go as far as Sayyid Aḥmad Khān. On the strength of those Koranic verses that make fighting against the unbelievers conditional upon their aggression or perfidy, they argue that peaceful coexistence is the normal state between Islamic and non-Islamic territories, and that jihad is only allowed as defensive warfare. This, however, left the way open to proclaim jihad against colonial oppression, as the colonial enterprise was clearly an attack on the territory of Islam. A recent development in this line of thinking is the presentation of the jihad doctrine as a form of Muslim international law and the equation of jihad with the concept of *bellum justum*. Those who have elaborated this theory proudly point out that Muḥammad al-Shaybānī (d. 804) had formulated a doctrine of international public law more than eight centuries before Hugo Grotius.

Present-day thinking about jihad, however, offers a wider spectrum than only the modernist interpretation mentioned here. Apart from the conservatives, who adhere to the interpretation as given in the classical books on Islamic law, there are the ideologues of the radical Islamic opposition, who call for jihad as a means to spread their brand of Islam. Some of these radical groups call for the use of violence in order to defeat the established governments. However, they are faced with a serious doctrinal problem, as they preach an armed revolution against Muslim rulers, whereas Islamic law allows revolt only in very rare circumstances. One of these is when a ruler abandons his belief. Since the apostate deserves capital punishment, fighting against him is allowed. Throughout Islamic history, governments and opposition movements have declared their Muslim adversaries to be heretics or unbelievers (*takfīr*, declaring someone to be a *kāfir*, unbeliever) in order to justify their struggle against them. It is this line of reasoning that is used by contemporary radical Islamic groups to give legitimacy to their use of arms against rulers who are to all appearances Muslims. In modern times these views were first propagated by fundamentalists like Sayyid Quṭb (d. 1966) and Abū ʾl-Aʿlā al-Mawdūdī (1903–1979).

The most eloquent and elaborate statement of this view can be found in a pamphlet published by the ideologue of the Jihad Organization, whose members, in 1981, assassinated President Sadat of Egypt. It is called *al-Farīḍa al-Ghāʾiba*, or "the Absent Duty," referring to the duty to wage jihad, which, according to the author, ʿAbd al-Salām Faraj, is not fulfilled anymore. The author borrows his arguments from two fatwas issued by the fundamentalist author Ibn Taymiyya (1263–1328), whose opinion was sought regarding the legitimacy of Mongol rule in the Middle East. The prop of Ibn Taymiyya's reasoning is the fact that they apply their own law instead of the Sharīʿa. This, in his opinion,

This miniature of a fight between rival clans is one of the earliest depictions of Islamic warfare.

is sufficient cause to regard them as unbelievers, even if they pronounce the profession of faith. However, even if this argument is not accepted, then they still have forfeited their right to demand the obedience of their Muslim subjects and they may be fought.

The author of "The Absent Duty" argues that the situation Ibn Taymiyya describes is very similar to the Egyptian situation, as Egyptian law, with the exception of family law and the law of succession, is based on codes of Western inspiration. Observing that in spite of the vocal demands of the Islamist groups the government has always refused to introduce the Sharīʿa, the author concludes that such a government cannot be regarded as Islamic and that it is an individual duty of all Muslims to rise in armed rebellion against this heathen regime in order to replace it with an Islamic one.

2

The Prophet's Lessons on Conduct in War:

ḤADĪTHS ON JIHAD FROM THE *ṢAḤĪḤ* OF MUSLIM IBN ḤAJJĀJ

Introduction

After the Koran, Muslims regard the words and deeds of the Prophet Mohammed as an authoritative source of religious law and doctrine. These words and deeds have been transmitted in the form of *ḥadīth,* a usually short account of these sayings or acts and sometimes the circumstances surrounding them, preceded by the names of the transmitters of this account, which guarantees its authenticity. To give an example:

> Qutayba ibn Saʿīd has told us (=the compiler, al-Bukhārī): al-Layth has told us on the authority of Bukayr, on the authority of Sulaymān ibn Yasār on the authority of Abū Hurayra, may God be pleased with him, that he (=Abū Hurayra) said: "The Messenger of God, Peace be upon him, once sent us on an expedition and said: 'If you find so-and-so and so-and-so, burn them with fire.' Then, when we wanted to leave, the Messenger, Peace be upon him, said 'I have ordered you to burn so-and-so and so-and-so, but [I just realized that] only God may punish with fire [i.e. the fire of Hell], so if you find them both, just kill them.'"[1]

Such accounts were already circulating during the first century of Islam. They were passed on from generation to generation, but in the process many forgeries were introduced. Muslim scholars were aware of that and they tried to sift the vast material

[1] Bukhārī, *Ṣaḥīḥ* (Cairo, Dār Iḥyāʾ al-Turāth al-ʿArabī, II), p. 172.

in order to weed out the false *ḥadīth*. The main criterion applied by them was the scrutiny of the reliability of the chains of transmitters. During the third/ninth century the traditions that had passed the test were collected in compilations that in the course of time were canonized. Whether the *ḥadīth* included in these collections really represent the Prophet's sayings and deeds is controversial. Many Western scholars have expressed skepticism and regard the bulk of the *ḥadīth* on legal topics as later forgeries. But be that as it may, these collections are of the greatest importance for the study of Islam as Muslims regard them as constituting the second source of Islam after the Koran.

The *ḥadīths* given here deal mainly with conduct during warfare. They are taken from the collection *al-Ṣaḥīḥ* (the Sound one) compiled by Muslim ibn Hajjāj al-Qushayrī al-Naysabūrī (d. 261/875) and presented in the translation of 'Abdul Hamīd Ṣiddīqī (*Ṣaḥīḥ Muslim,* rendered into English by ʿAbdul Ḥamīd Ṣiddīqī. 4 vols. Lahore; Sh. Muhammad Ashraf, vol. III, pp. 942–947, 960–962 and 1001–1002). In this translation the chains of authorities have been omitted and only the person who heard the Prophet speak or saw him act is mentioned, and in some cases the person who transmitted the *ḥadīth* from him. The notes in the text are the translator's, but the numbering has been changed for editorial reasons.

Regarding Permission to Make a Raid, Without an Ultimatum, Upon the Disbelievers Who Have Already Been Invited to Accept Islam

(4292) Ibn ʿAun reported: I wrote to Nāfiʾ inquiring from him whether it was necessary to extend (to the disbelievers) an invitation to accept (Islam) before engaging them in fight. He wrote (in reply) to me that it was necessary in the early days of Islam. The Messenger of Allah (may peace be upon him) made a raid upon Banū Muṣṭaliq while they were unaware and their cattle were having a drink at the water. He killed those who fought and imprisoned others.[1] On that very day, he captured Juwairīya bint al-Ḥārith. Nāfiʾ said that this tradition was related to him by ʿAbdullah b. ʿUmar who (himself) was among the raiding troops.

Appointment of the Leaders of Expeditions by the Imām and His Advice to Them on Etiquettes of War and Related Matters

(4294) It has been reported from Sulaimān b. Buraid through his father that when the Messenger of Allah (may peace be upon him) appointed anyone as leader of an army or detachment[2] he would especially exhort him to fear Allah and to be good to the Muslims who were with him. He would say: Fight in the name of Allah and in the way of Allah. Fight against those who disbelieve in Allah. Make a holy war; do not embezzle the spoils; do not break your pledge; and do not mutilate (the dead) bodies; do not kill the children. When you meet your enemies who are polytheists, invite them to three courses of action. If they respond to any one of these, you also accept it and withold yourself from doing them any harm. Invite them to (accept) Islam; if they respond to you, accept it from them and desist from fighting against them. Then invite them to migrate from their lands to the land of Muhājirs[3] and inform them that, if they do so, they shall have all the privileges and obligations of the Muhājirs. If they refuse to migrate, tell them that they will have the status of Bedouin Muslims and will be subjected to the Commands of Allah like other Muslims, but they will not get any share from the spoils of war or Faiʾ[4] except when they actually fight with the Muslims (against the disbelievers). If they refuse to accept Islam, demand from them the Jizya.[5] If they agree to pay, accept it from them and hold off your hands. If they refuse to pay the tax, seek Allah's help and fight them. When you lay siege to a fort and the besieged appeal to you for protection in the name of Allah and His Prophet, do not accord to them the guarantee of Allah and His Prophet, but accord to them your own guarantee and the guarantee of your companions for it is a lesser sin that the security given by you or your companions be disregarded than that the security granted in the name of Allah and His Prophet be violated. When you besiege a fort and the besieged want you to let them out in accordance with Allah's Command, do not let them come out in accordance with His Command, but do so at your (own) command, for you do not know whether or not you will be able to carry out Allah's behest with regard to them.

Justification for the Use of Stratagem in War

(4311) It is narrated on the authority of Jābir that the Messenger of Allah (may peace be upon him) said: War is a strategem.

One Should Not Desire an Encounter with the Enemy, but it is Essential to Show Patience During the Encounter

(4313) It has been narrated on the authority of Abū Huraira that the Messenger of Allah (may peace be upon him) said: Do not desire an encounter with the enemy; but when you encounter them, be firm.

(4314) It is narrated by Abū Naḍr that he learnt from a letter sent by a man from the Aslam tribe, who was a Companion of the Holy Prophet (may peace be upon him) and whose name was ʿAbdullah b. Abū Aufā, to ʿUmar b. ʿUbaidullah when the latter marched upon Ḥarūrīyya (Khawārij) informing him that the Messenger of Allah (may peace be upon him) in one of those days when he was confronting the enemy waited until the sun had declined. Then he stood up (to address the people) and said: O ye men, do not wish for an encounter with the enemy. Pray to Allah to grant you security; (but) when you (have to) encounter them, exercise patience, and you should know that Paradise is under the shadows of the swords. Then the Messenger of Allah (may peace be upon him) stood up (again) and said: O Allah, Revealer of the Book, Disperser of the clouds, Defeater of the hordes, put our enemy to rout and help us against them.

Desirability of Praying for Victory at the Time of Confrontation with the Enemy

(4315) It is narrated on the authority of Ibn Abū Aufā that the Messenger of Allah (may peace be upon him) cursed the tribes (who had marched upon Medina with a combined force in 5 H) and said: O Allah, Revealer of the Book, swift in (taking) account, put the tribes to rout. O Lord, defeat them and shake them.

(4318) It is narrated on the authority of Anas that the Messenger of Allah (may peace be upon him) said on the day of the Battle of Uḥud: O Allah, if Thou wilt (defeat Muslims), there will be none on the earth to worship Thee.

Prohibition of Killing Women and Children in War

(4319) It is narrated on the authority of ʿAbdullah that a woman was found killed in one of the battles fought by the Messenger of Allah (may peace be upon him). He disapproved of the killing of women and children.

(4320) It is narrated by Ibn ʿUmar that a woman was found killed in one of these battles; so the Messenger of Allah (may peace be upon him) forbade the killing of women and children.

Permissibility of Killing Women and Children in the Night Raids, Provided it is not Deliberate

(4321) It is reported on the authority of Ṣaʾb b. Jaththāma that the Prophet of Allah (may peace be upon him), when asked about the women and children of the polytheists being killed during the night raid, said: They are from them.[6]

Justification for Cutting Down the Trees and Burning Them

(4324) It is narrated on the authority of ʿAbdullah that the Messenger of Allah (may peace be upon him) ordered the date-palms of Banū Naḍīr to be burnt and cut. These palms were at Buwaira. Qutaibah and Ibn Rumḥ in their versions of the tradition have added: So Allah, the Glorious and Exalted, revealed the verse: "Whatever trees you have cut down or left standing on their trunks, it was with the permission of Allah so that He may disgrace the evil-doers" (lix. 5).[7]

The Help with Angels in Badr and the Permissibility of the Spoils of War

(4360) It has been narrated on the authority of ʿUmar b. al-Khaṭṭāb who said: When it was the day on which the Battle of Badr was fought, the Messenger of Allah (may peace be upon him) cast a glance at the infidels, and they were one thousand while his own Companions were three hundred and nineteen. The Holy Prophet (may peace be upon him) turned (his face) towards the Qibla. Then he stretched his hands and began his supplication to his Lord: "O Allah, accomplish for me what Thou hast promised to me. O Allah, bring about what Thou hast promised to me. O Allah, if this small band of Muslims is destroyed, Thou wilt not be worshipped on this earth."[8] He continued his supplication to his Lord, stretching his hands, facing the Qibla, until his mantle slipped down from his shoulders. So Abū Bakr came to him, picked up his mantle and put it on his shoulders. Then he embraced him from behind and said: Prophet of Allah, this prayer of yours to your Lord will suffice you, and He will fulfil for you what He has promised you. So Allah, the Glorious and Exalted, revealed (the Qurʾānic verse): "When ye appealed to your Lord for help, He responded to your call (saying): I will help you with one thousand angels coming in succession."[9] So Allah helped him with angels.

Abū Zumail said that the ḥadīth was narrated to him by Ibn ʿAbbās who said: While on that day a Muslim was chasing a disbeliever who was going ahead of him, he heard over him the swishing of the whip and the voice of the rider saying: Go ahead, Ḥaizūm! He glanced at the polytheist who had (now) fallen down on his back. When he looked at him (carefully he found that) there was a scar on his nose and his face was torn as if it had been lashed with a whip, and had turned green with its poison. An Anṣārī came to the Messenger of Allah (may peace be upon him) and related this (event) to him. He said: You have told the truth. This was the help from the third heaven. The Muslims that day (i.e. the day of the Battle of Badr) killed seventy persons and captured seventy. The Messenger of Allah (may peace be upon him) said to Abū Bakr and ʿUmar (Allah be pleased with them): What is your opinion about these captives? Abū Bakr said: They are our kith and kin. I think you should release them after getting from them a ransom. This will be a source of strength to us against the infidels. It is quite possible that Allah may guide them to Islam. Then the Messenger of Allah (may peace be upon him) said: What is your opinion, Ibn Khaṭṭāb? He said: Messenger of Allah, I do not hold the same opinion as Abū Bakr. I am of the opinion that you should hand them over to us so that we may cut off their heads. Hand over ʿAqīl to ʿAlī that he may cut off his head, and hand over such and such relative to me that I may cut off his head. They are leaders of the disbelievers and veterans among them. The Messenger of Allah (may peace be upon him) approved the opinion of Abū Bakr and did not approve what I said. The next day when I came to the Messenger of Allah (may peace be upon him), I found that both he and Abū Bakr were sitting shedding tears. I said: Messenger of Allah, why are you and your Companion shedding tears? Tell me the reason. For I will weep and, if not, I will at least pretend to weep in sympathy with you. The Messenger of Allah (may peace be upon him) said: I weep for what has happened to your companions for taking ransom (from the prisoners). I was shown the torture to which they were subjected. It was brought to me as close as this tree. (He pointed to a tree close to him.) Then God revealed the verse: "It is not befitting for a prophet that he should take prisoners until the force of the disbelievers has been crushed . . ." to the end of the verse: "so eat ye the spoils of war, (it is) lawful and pure. So Allah made booty lawful for them."[10]

Fighting of Women Side by Side With Men

(4453) It has been narrated on the authority of Anas that, on the Day of Ḥunain, Umm Sulaim took out a dagger she had in her possession. Abū Ṭalḥa saw her and said: Messenger of Allah, this is Umm Sulaim. She is holding a dagger. The Messenger of Allah (may peace be upon him) asked (her): What for are you holding this dagger? She said: I took it up so that I may tear open the belly of a polytheist who comes near me. The Messenger of Allah (may peace be upon him) began to smile (at these words). She said: Messenger of Allah, kill all those people—other than us—whom thou hast declared to be free (on the day of the Conquest of Mecca). (They embraced Islam because) they were defeated at your hands (and as such their Islam is not dependable). The Messenger of Allah (may peace be upon him) said: Umm Sulaim, God is sufficient (against the mischief of the polytheists) and He will be kind to us (so you need not carry this dagger).

(4454) It has been narrated on the authority of Anas b. Mālik who said that the Messenger of Allah (may peace be upon him) allowed Umm Sulaim and some other women of the Anṣār to accompany him when he went to war; they would give water (to the soldiers) and would treat the wounded.

(4455) It has been narrated on the authority of Anas b. Mālik who said: On the Day of Uḥud some of the people, being defeated, left the Holy Prophet (may peace be upon him), but Abū Ṭalḥa stood before him covering him with a shield. Abū Ṭalḥa was a powerful archer who broke two or three bows that day. When a man would pass by carrying a quiver containing arrows, he would say: Spare them for Abū Ṭalḥa. Whenever the Holy Prophet (may peace be upon him) raised his head to look at the people, Abū Ṭalḥa would say: Prophet of Allah, may my father and my mother be thy ransom, do not raise your head lest you be struck by an arrow shot by the enemy. My neck is before your neck. The narrator said: I saw ʿĀʾisha bint Abū Bakr and Umm Sulaim. Both of them had tucked up their garments, so I could see the anklets on their feet. They were carrying water-skins on their backs and would pour water into the mouths of the people.

They would then go back (to the well), would fill them again and would return to pour water into the mouths of the soldiers. (On this day), Abū Ṭalḥa's sword dropped down from his hands twice or thrice because of drowsiness.

A 16th century Ottoman representation of the Battle of Uhud (625).
Top right a Muslim warrior, killed during the battle,
is being washed by angels before being admitted to Paradise
as a martyr. For the reward of martyrs, see chapter 3.

3

Exhortations to Jihad:

PASSAGES ON JIHAD AND MARTYRDOM FROM MĀLIK'S *AL-MUWAṬṬAʾ*

Introduction

About the life of the author of the text, Mālik ibn Anas (ca. 710–796), very little is known with certainty. A religious scholar specializing in Islamic law, he lived most of his life in Medina and is regarded as the founder of the Malikite school of law *(madhhab).* His great work, from which we here present a fragment in translation, is *al-Muwaṭṭaʾ*, "the smoothed path," one of the oldest works of Islamic jurisprudence. Mālik's aim was to codify and systematize the customary law of Medina and thus further its practical application. There were various recensions of the text, two of which have survived: the one by Yaḥyā ibn Yaḥyā al-Maṣmūdī (d. 848) and the one by Muḥammad al-Shaybānī (d. 805), in which Mālik's opinions are discussed and contrasted with Hanafite views. Our text is taken from Yaḥyā's recension. It contains hortative sayings of the Prophet and the first Caliphs.

The text has been reprinted from Malik ibn Anas, *Al-Muwatta of Imam Malik ibn Anas: The First Formulation of Islamic Law.* Translated by Aisha Abdurrahman Bewley. London and New York: Kegan Paul International, 1989, pp. 173–174 and 180–182.

Literature:
J. Schacht, "Mālik ibn Anas," in: Encyclopaedia of Islam. 2nd ed. Leiden: E. J. Brill, 1960—Vol. VI, pp. 262–5.
N. Calder, *Studies in Early Muslim Jurisprudence,* Oxford: Oxford University Press, 1993, ch. 2 "The *Muwaṭṭaʾ of Mālik.*"

Stimulation of Desire for Jihad

Yahya related to me from Malik from Abu'z-Zinad from al-Aʿraj from Abu Hurayra that the Messenger of Allah, may Allah bless him and grant him peace, said, "Someone who does *jihad* in the way of Allah is like someone who fasts and prays constantly and does not slacken from his prayer and fasting until he returns."

Yahya related to me from Malik from Abu'z-Zinad from al-Aʿraj from Abu Hurayra that the Messenger of Allah, may Allah bless him and grant him peace, said, "Allah guarantees either the Garden or a safe return to his home with whatever he has obtained of reward or booty for the one who does *jihad* in His way, if it is solely *jihad* and trust in his promise that brings him out of his house."

Yahya related to me from Malik from Zayd ibn Aslam from Abu Salih as-Samman from Abu Hurayra that the Messenger of Allah, may Allah bless him and grant him peace, said, "Horses are a reward for one man, a protection for another, a burden for another. The one for whom they are a reward is the one who dedicates them for use in the way of Allah, and tethers them in a meadow or grassland. Whatever the horse enjoys of the grassland or meadow in the length of its tether are good deeds for him. If it breaks its tether and goes over a hillock or two, its tracks and droppings are good deeds for him. If it crosses a river and drinks from it while he did not mean to allow it to drink it, that counts as good deeds for him, and the horse is a reward for him. Another man uses his horse to gain self reliance and upstandingness and does not forget Allah's right on their necks and backs. Horses are a protection for him. Another man uses them out of pride to show them off and in hostility to the people of Islam. They are a burden on that man.

The Messenger of Allah, may Allah bless him and grant him peace, was asked about donkeys, and he said, "Nothing has been revealed to me about them except this single all-inclusive *ayat*, 'Whoever does an atom of good will see it, and whoever does an atom of evil will see it' (*Sura* 99 *ayats* 7,8).

Yahya related to me from ʿAbdullah ibn ʿAbd ar-Rahman ibn

Maᶜmar al-Ansari that ᶜAtaᵓ ibn Yasar said that the Messenger of Allah, may Allah bless him and grant him peace, "Shall I tell you who has the best degree among people? A man who takes the rein of his horse to do *jihad* in the way of Allah. Shall I tell you who has the best degree among people after him? A man who lives alone with a few sheep, performs the prayer, pays the *zakat*, and worships Allah without associating anything with Him."

Yahya related to me from Malik that Yahya ibn Saᶜid said, "ᶜUbayda ibn al-Walid ibn ᶜUbada ibn as-Samit informed me from his father that his grandfather (ᶜUbada) said, "We made a contract with the Messenger of Allah, may Allah bless him and grant him peace, to hear and obey in ease and hardship, enthusiasm and reluctance, and not to dispute with people in authority and to speak to establish the truth wherever we were without worrying about criticism.'"

Yahya related to me from Malik that Zayd ibn Aslam had said that ᶜUbayda ibn al-Jarrah had written to ᶜUmar ibn al-Khattab mentioning to him a great array of Byzantine troops and the anxiety they were causing him. ᶜUmar ibn al-Khattab wrote in reply to him, "Whatever hardship befalls a believing slave, Allah will make an opening for him after it, and a hardship will not overcome two eases. Allah the Exalted says in His Book, 'O you who trust, be patient, and vie in patience! Be steadfast and fear Allah, perhaps you will profit.'" (*Sura* 3 *ayat* 200)

The Martyrs in the Way of Allah

Yahya related to me from Malik from Abuᵓz-Zinad from al-Aᶜraj from Abu Hurayra that the Messenger of Allah, may Allah bless him and grant him peace, said, "By He in whose hand my self is! I would like to fight in the way of Allah and be killed, then be brought to life again so I could be killed, and then be brought to life again so I could be killed."

Abu Hurayra said three times, "I testify to it by Allah!"

Yahya related to me from Malik from Abuᵓz-Zinad from al-Aᶜraj from Abu Hurayra that the Messenger of Allah, may Allah bless him and grant him peace, said, "Allah laughs at two men.

One of them kills the other, but each of them will enter the Garden; one fights in the way of Allah and is killed, then Allah turns (in forgiveness) to the killer, so he fights (in the way of Allah) and also becomes a martyr."

Yahya related to me from Malik from Abu'z-Zinad from al-Aʿraj from Abu Hurayra that the Messenger of Allah, may Allah bless him and grant him peace, said, "By He in whose hand my self is! None of you is wounded in the way of Allah—and Allah knows best who is wounded in His way, but that when the Day of Rising comes, blood will gush forth from his wound. It will be the colour of blood, but its scent will be that of musk."

Yahya related to me from Malik from Zayd ibn Aslam that ʿUmar ibn al-Khattab used to say, "O Allah! Do not let me be slain by the hand of a man who has prayed a single prostration to You with which he will dispute with me before You on the Day of Rising!"

Yahya related to me from Malik from Yahya ibn Saʿid from Saʿid al-Maqburi from ʿAbdullah ibn Abi Qatada that his father said that a man came to the Messenger of Allah, may Allah bless him and grant him peace, and said, "O Messenger of Allah! If I am killed in the way of Allah, expecting the reward, sincere, advancing, and not retreating, will Allah pardon my faults?" The Messenger of Allah, may Allah bless him and grant him peace, said, "Yes." When the man turned away, the Messenger of Allah, may Allah bless him and grant him peace, called him—or sent an order to him and he was called to him. The Messenger of Allah, may Allah bless him and grant him peace, said to him, "What did you say?" He repeated his words to him, and the Prophet, may Allah bless him and grant him peace, said to him, "Yes, except for debts. Jibril said that to me."

Yahya related to me from Malik from Abuʿn-Nadr, the *mawla* of ʿUmar ibn ʿUbaydullah that he had heard that the Messenger of Allah, may Allah bless him and grant him peace, said over the martyrs of Uhud, "I testify for them." Abu Bakr as-Siddiq said, "Messenger of Allah! Are we not their brothers? We entered Islam as they entered Islam and we did *jihad* as they did *jihad*." The Messenger of Allah, may Allah bless him and grant him peace, said, "Yes, but I do not know what you will do after me." Abu

Bakr wept profusely and said, "Are we really going to out-live you!"

Yahya related to me from Malik that Yahya ibn Sa'id said, "The Messenger of Allah, may Allah bless him and grant him peace, was sitting by a grave which was being dug at Madina. A man looked into the grave and said, 'An awful bed for the believer.' The Messenger of Allah, may Allah bless him and grant him peace, said, 'Evil? What you have said is absolutely wrong.'

The man said, 'I didn't mean that, Messenger of Allah. I meant being killed in the way of Allah.' The Messenger of Allah, may Allah bless him and grant him peace, said, 'Being killed in the way of Allah has no like! There is no place on the earth where I would prefer my grave to be than here (meaning Madina).' He repeated it three times."

Things in which Martyrdom Lies

Yahya related to me from Malik from Zayd ibn Aslam that ʿUmar ibn al-Khattab used to say, "O Allah! I ask You for martyrdom in Your way and death in the city of Your Messenger!"

Yahya related to me from Malik from Yahya ibn Sa'id that ʿUmar ibn al-Khattab said, "The nobility of the believer is his *taqwa*. His *deen* is his noble descent. His manliness is his good character. Boldness and cowardice are but instincts which Allah places wherever He wills. The coward shrinks from defending even his father and mother, and the bold one fights for the sake of the combat not for the spoils. Being slain is but one way of meeting death, and the martyr is the one who gives himself, expectant of reward from Allah."

How to Wash the Martyr

Yahya related to me from Malik from Nafiʿ from ʿAbdullah ibn ʿUmar that ʿUmar ibn al-Khattab was washed and shrouded and prayed over, yet he was a martyr, may Allah have mercy on him.

Yahya related to me from Malik that he had heard the people

of knowledge say that martyrs in the way of Allah were not washed, nor were any of them prayed over. They were buried in the garments in which they were slain.

Malik said, "This is the *sunna* for someone who is killed on the battleground and is not reached until he is already dead. Someone who is carried off and lives for as long as Allah wills after it, is washed and prayed over as was ᶜUmar ibn al-Khattab."

What is Disliked to be Done with Something Given in the Way of Allah

Yahya related to me from Malik from Yahya ibn Saᶜid that ᶜUmar ibn al-Khattab in one year gave 40,000 camels as war-mounts. Sometimes he would give one man a camel to himself. Sometimes he would give one camel between two men to take them to Iraq. A man from Iraq came to him and said, "Give Suhaym and I a mount." ᶜUmar ibn al-Khattab said to him, "I demand from you, by Allah! is Suhaym a water-skin?" He said, "Yes."

Stimulation of Desire for Jihad

Yahya related to me from Malik from Ishaq ibn ᶜAbdullah ibn Abi Talha that Anas ibn Malik had said that when the Messenger of Allah, may Allah bless him and grant him peace, arrived at Quba, he visited Umm Haram bint Milhan and she fed him. Umm Haram was the wife of ᶜUbada ibn as-Samit. One day the Messenger of Allah, may Allah bless him and grant him peace, had called on her and she had fed him, and sat down to delouse his hair. The Messenger of Allah, may Allah bless him and grant him peace, had dozed and woke up smiling. Umm Haram said, "What is making you smile, Messenger of Allah?" He said, "Some of my community were presented to me, riding in the way of Allah. They were riding in the middle of the sea, kings on thrones, or like kings on thrones." (Ishaq wasn't sure). She said, "O Messenger of Allah! Ask Allah to put me among them!" So he made a *duᶜa᾿* for her, and put his head down and slept. Then he had woken up smiling, and she said to him, "Messenger of Allah, why are you smiling?" He said, "Some of my community were presented to me, raiding in the way of Allah. They were kings on thrones or like kings on thrones," as he had said the first time. She said, "O Messenger of Allah! Ask Allah to let me be among them!" He said, "You are among the first."

Ishaq added, "She travelled on the sea in the time of Muʿawiya, and when she landed, she was thrown from her mount and killed."

Yahya related to me from Malik from Yahya ibn Saʿid from Abu Salih as-Samman from Abu Hurayra that the Messenger of Allah, may Allah bless him and grant him peace, said, "Had I not been concerned for my community, I would have liked never to stay behind a raiding party going out in the way of Allah. However, I do not have the means to carry them to it, nor can they find for themselves anything on which to ride out and it is grievous for them to have to stay behind from me. I would like to fight in the way of Allah and be killed, then brought to life so I could be killed and then brought to life so I could be killed."

Yahya related to me from Malik that Yahya ibn Saʿid said, "On the Day of Uhud, the Messenger of Allah, may Allah bless him and grant him peace, said, 'Who will bring me news of Saʿid ibn ar-Rabiʿ al-Ansari?' A man said, 'Me, Messenger of Allah!' So the man went around among the slain, and Saʿid ibn ar-Rabiʿ said to him, 'What are you doing?' The man said to him, 'The Messenger of Allah, may Allah bless him and grant him peace, sent me to bring him news of you.' He said, 'Go to him, and give him my greetings, and tell him that I have been stabbed twelve times, and am mortally wounded. Tell your people that they will have no excuse with Allah if the Messenger of Allah, may Allah bless him and grant him peace, is slain while one of them is still alive.'"

Yahya related to me from Malik from Yahya ibn Saʿid that the Messenger of Allah, may Allah bless him and grant him peace, was stimulating people to do *jihad,* mentioning the Garden. One of the Ansar was eating some dates he had in his hand, and said, "Am I so desirous of this world that I should sit until I finish them?" He threw aside what was in his hand and took his sword and fought until he was slain.

Portrayal of Muslim soldiers in a 13th century manuscript of the Cantigas de Santa María by Alfons X of Castile.

Yahya related to me from Malik from Yahya ibn Saʿid that Muʿadh ibn Jabal said, "There are two military expeditions. There is one military expedition in which valuables are spent, things are made easy for a fellow, the authorities are obeyed, and corruption is avoided. That military expedition is all good. There is a military expedition in which valuables are not spent, things are not made easy, the authorities are not obeyed, and corruption is not avoided. The one who fights in that military expedition does not return with reward."

4

The Legal Doctrine of Jihad:

THE CHAPTER ON JIHAD FROM AVERROES' LEGAL HANDBOOK *AL-BIDĀYA*

Introduction

Averroes (Ar.: Abū al-Walīd Muḥammad Ibn Muḥammad Ibn Rushd) was born of a family of lawyers, in the then Arabic town of Córdoba, in 1126 A.D. His grandfather and namesake had written a number of works on Islamic law which enjoyed great popularity and it was as a matter of course that Averroes followed in the footsteps of his ancestors. He held the post of judge *(qāḍī)* in Sevilla and in his native town Córdoba, but he also became known as a physician—he was the court-physician of the Almohad prince Abū Yaʿqūb (who reigned from 1162 until 1184)—and as a philosopher. It is in this latter quality that he achieved fame in Europe, especially through his comments on the works of Aristotle. In the Islamic world, on the other hand, he remained famous chiefly as a lawyer. He died in Marrakesh (Morocco) in 1198.

His best known legal handbook is *Bidāyat al-Mujtahid wa-Nihāyat al-Muqtaṣid* (lit.: The beginning for him who interprets the sources independently and the end for him who wishes to limit himself). With the exception of the chapter on pilgrimage *(ḥadjdj)*, which he did not finish until 1188, he wrote the work around the year 1167, when he accepted the post of *qāḍī*. The book belongs to the genre of *ikhtilāf*-works. These are treatises in which the opinions of the different schools are juxtaposed and in which the controversies *(ikhtilāf)* between the early lawyers are discussed. Although traditional as far as contents are concerned, the manner of presentation of the *Bidāya* is original. In his treatment of each controversy, Averroes enters deeply into the different arguments underlying it. Usually, he reduces the controversy to a disagreement about the question of how two conflicting Koran-verses or Traditions are related to each other. This often boils down to the question whether the one rule is a general one and the other an exception, or whether the one rule has abrogated the other. However ingenious these reasonings may be, it is to be kept well in mind that this is a matter of *hineininterpretieren.* The prescriptions of Islamic Law had already been formulated soon after Mohammed's death, the theoretical foundations with Koran-verses and Traditions followed later. Averroes was an adherent of the Malikite School, the ruling one in Islamic Spain. Nevertheless he juxtaposes the opinions of the different Schools with impartiality and refrains from passing judgements on the validity of the arguments brought forward. The only indication that he is a Malikite might be found in the fact that he sometimes expatiates a little longer on the controversies within this school.

For the translation of the *Bidāya* I used two nearly identical Cairo editions: Muṣṭafā al-Bābī al-Ḥalabī, 1960 and Dār al-Fikr / Maktabat Khānjī, n.d. The points wherein they differ are of minor importance and mainly due to printing errors. The present translation appeared originally in *Jihad in Mediaeval and Modern Islam: The Chapter on Jihad from Averroes' Legal Handbook 'Bidāyat al-Mudjtahid' and the Treatise 'Koran and Fighting' by the Late Shaykh al-Azhar, Maḥmūd Shaltūt.* Translated and annotated by Rudolph Peters. Leiden: E. J. Brill, 1977, pp. 9–25, 80–84.

Literature:

Dominique Urvoy, *Ibn Rushd (Averroes).* Tr. from the French. London: Routledge, 1991.

L. Bercher, "Averroës "Bidāyat al-Mudjtahid," *Revue Tunisienne de Droit,* 1955, no. 3/4, pp. 34–37 (translation of the introduction to the *Bidāya,* in which Averroes expounds his method).

R. Brunschvig, "Averroës juriste," in *Études d'Orientalisme, dédiées à la mémoire de Lévi-Provençal.* Paris: Maisonneuve, 1962. Vol. I, pp. 35–68.

The Jihad

The most important rules concerning this subject will be dealt with in two chapters. The first will contain the most important regulations as regards warfare, the second the rules pertaining to the enemy's property when it is captured by the Muslims.[1]

The first chapter consists of seven paragraphs:

1. The legal qualification *(ḥukm)* of this activity and the persons who are obliged to take part in it.
2. The enemy.
3. The damage allowed to be inflicted upon the different categories of enemies.
4. The prerequisites for warfare.
5. The maximum number of enemies against which one is obliged to stand one's ground.
6. Truce.
7. The aims of warfare.

Par. 1. The Legal Qualification *(Ḥukm)* of this Activity and the Persons Obliged to Take Part in It.

Scholars agree that the jihad is a collective not a personal obligation. Only ʿAbd Allāh Ibn al-Ḥasan[2] professed it to be a recommendable act. According to the majority of scholars, the compulsory nature of the jihad is founded on [2:216]: *"Prescribed for you is fighting, though it be hateful to you."*[3] That this obligation is a collective and not a personal one, i.e. that the obligation, when it can be properly carried out by a limited number of individuals, is cancelled for the remaining Muslims, is founded on [9:122]: *"It is not for the believers to go forth totally,"*[4] on [4:95]: *"Yet to each God has promised the reward most fair"*[5] and, lastly, on the fact that the Prophet never went to battle without leaving some people behind. All this together implies that this activity is a collective obligation. The obligation to participate in the jihad applies to adult free men who have the means at their disposal to go to war and who are healthy, that is, not ill or suffering from chronic diseases. There is absolutely no controversy about the latter restriction because of [48:17]: *"There is no fault in the blind, and there is no fault in the lame, and there is no fault in the sick"*[6] and because of [9:91]: *"There is no fault in the weak and the sick and those who find nothing to expend."*[7] Nor do I know of any dissentient views as regards the rule that this obligation applies only to free men. Nearly all scholars agree that this obligation is conditional on permission granted by the parents. Only in the case that the obligation has become a personal one, for instance because there is nobody else to carry it out, can this permission be dispensed with.[8] This prerequisite of permission is based on the following authentic Tradition: *"Once a man said to the Messenger of God: 'I wish to take part in the jihad.' The Messenger said to him: 'Are both your parents still alive?' When he answered in the affirmative, the Messenger said: 'Then perform the jihad for their sake.'"* Scholars are not agreed whether this permission is also required of parents who are polytheists. There is controversy, too, about the question whether the creditor's permission has to be asked when a person has run into debt. An argument in favour of this can be found in the following Tradition: *"A man said to the Prophet: 'Will God forgive me my sins if I shall sacrifice myself patiently and shall be killed in the way of God (i.e. by taking part in the jihad)?' The Prophet said: 'Yes, with the exception of your debts. This Jibrīl has told me before.'"*[9] The majority of scholars do not consider it obligatory, especially not when the debtor leaves enough behind to serve as payment for his debts.

Par. 2. The Enemy.

Scholars agree that all polytheists should be fought. This is founded on [8:39]: *"Fight them until there is no persecution and the religion is God's entirely."*[10] However, it has been related by Mālik[11] that it would not be allowed to attack the Ethiopians and the Turks on the strength of the Tradition of the Prophet: *"Leave the Ethiopians in peace as long as they leave you in peace."* Questioned as to the authenticity of this Tradition, Mālik did not acknowledge it, but said: "People still avoid attacking them."

Par. 3. The Damage Allowed to be Inflicted Upon the Different Categories of Enemies.

Damage inflicted upon the enemy may consist in damage to his property, injury to his person or violation of his personal liberty, i.e. that he is made a slave and is appropriated. This may be done, according to the *Consensus (ijmāʿ)* to all polytheists: men, women, young and old, important and unimportant. Only with regard to monks do opinions vary; for some take it that they must be left in peace and that they must not be captured, but allowed to go unscathed and that they may not be enslaved. In support of their opinion they bring forward the words of the Prophet: *"Leave them in peace and also that to which they have dedicated themselves,"*[12] as well as the practice of Abū Bakr.[13]

Most scholars are agreed that, in his dealings with captives, various policies are open to the Imam [head of the Islamic state, caliph]. He may pardon them, enslave them, kill them, or release them either on ransom or as *dhimmī* [non-Moslem subject of the Islamic state], in which latter case the released captive is obliged to pay poll-tax *(jizya).* Some scholars, however, have taught that captives may never be slain. According to al-Ḥasan Ibn Muḥammad al-Tamīmī,[14] this was even the *Consensus (ijmāʿ)* of the *Ṣaḥāba* [contemporaries of Mohammed that have known him]. This controversy has arisen because, firstly, the Koran-verses contradict each other in this respect; secondly, practice [of the Prophet and the first caliphs] was inconsistent; and lastly, the obvious interpretation of the Koran is at variance with the Prophet's deeds. The obvious interpretation of [47:4]: *"When you meet the unbelievers, smite their necks, then, when you have made wide slaughter among them, tie fast the bonds"*[15] is that the Imam is only entitled to pardon captives or to release them on ransom. On the other hand, [8:67]: *"It is not for any Prophet to have prisoners until he make wide slaughter in the land,"*[16] as well as the occasion when this verse was revealed [viz. the captives of Badr] would go to prove that it is better to slay captives than to enslave them. The Prophet himself would in some cases slay captives outside the field of battle, while he would pardon them in others. Women he used to enslave. Abū ʿUbayd[17] has related that the Prophet never enslaved male Arabs.

After him, the *Ṣaḥāba* reached unanimity about the rule that the People of the Book *(ahl al-kitāb),* both male and female, might be enslaved. Those who are of the opinion that the verse which prohibits slaying [K 47:4] abrogates the Prophet's example, maintain that captives may not be slain. Others profess, however, that this verse does not concern itself with the slaughter of captives and that it was by no means intended to restrict the number of policies possible with regard to captives. On the contrary, they say, the fact that the Prophet used to slay captives adds a supplementing rule to the verse in question [K 47:4] and thus removes the occasion for the complaint that he omitted to kill the captives of Badr. These, now, do profess that the killing of captives is allowed.

It is only allowed to slay the enemy on the condition that *amān* [safe-conduct] has not been granted. There is no dissension about this among the Muslims. There is controversy, however, concerning the question who is entitled to grant *amān*. Everyone is agreed that the Imam is entitled to this. The majority of scholars are of the opinion that free Muslim males are also entitled to grant it, but Ibn Mājishūn[18] maintains that in this case, it is subject to authorization by the Imam. Similarly, there is controversy concerning the *amān* granted by women and slaves. Ibn Mājishūn and Saḥnūn[19] hold that *amān* granted by a woman is also subject to authorization by the Imam. Abū Ḥanīfa[20] has taught that the *amān* granted by a slave is only valid when the slave is allowed to join in the fighting.[21] The source of the controversy is that a general rule is in conflict with the analogous interpretation of another rule. The general rule is founded on the words of the Prophet: *"The blood(money) of all Muslims is equal. Even the humblest strives for their protection. Together, they make up a unity against the others."* These words, in their universality, imply that *amān* granted by a slave is valid. The conflicting analogy is that in order to be able to grant *amān,* full legal capacity is required. Now, a slave has only partial legal capacity by the very fact of his being a slave. By analogy, the fact that he is a slave should counteract the validity of his *amān,* as it does with regard to numerous other legal acts. The general rule, then, should be restricted by analogy.

The controversy about the validity of *amān* granted by a

woman owes its origin to two different readings of the words of the Prophet: *"We grant protection to those to whom you have granted protection, Umm Hāniʾ"* as well as to the question whether women are to be put on a par with men by analogy. Some read in the words of the Prophet an authorization of the *amān* granted by Umm Hāniʾ, not a confirmation of its validity, and they infer that her *amān* would have had no legal effects had the Prophet not authorized it. Consequently, they maintain that *amān* granted by a woman is only valid when the Imam has authorized it. Others hold that the Prophet confirmed the *amān* granted by Umm Hāniʾ in the sense that he approved something which already existed and had legal effects, not in the sense that the act was only validated by his authorization. Thus, the latter group maintains that a woman is entitled to grant valid *amān*. This view finds also favour with those who, in this respect, put women on a par with men and feel that there is no difference between them here. Others, who are of the opinion that a woman is inferior to a man, consider an *amān* granted by her invalid. Anyhow, *amān* does not afford protection against enslavement but only against death.[22] The controversy [about the validity of *amān* granted by women] might also be explained by the divergent opinions about the use of the male plural: does this include women or not? All this, of course, according to legal usage.

As regards injury to the person, that is, the slaying of the enemy, the Muslims agree that in times of war, all adult, able-bodied, unbelieving males may be slain. As to the question whether the enemy may also be slain after he has been captured, there is the above-mentioned controversy. There is no disagreement about the rule that it is forbidden to slay women and children, provided that they are not fighting, for then women, in any case, may be slain. This rule is founded on the fact that, according to authoritative Traditions, the Prophet prohibited the slaughter of women and children and once said about a woman who had been slain: *"She was not one who would have fought."*[23]

There is controversy about the question whether it is allowed to slay hermits who have retired from the world, the blind, the chronically ill and the insane, those who are old and unable to fight any longer, peasants, and serfs. Mālik professes that neither the blind, nor the insane, nor hermits may be slain and that of their property not all may be carried off, but that enough should be left for them to be able to survive. Neither is it allowed, according to him, to slay the old and decrepit. Of the same opinion are Abū Ḥanīfa and his pupils. Thawrī[24] and Awzāʿī,[25] however, have taught that of these groups, only the aged may not be slain. On the other hand, Awzāʿī had also taught that this prohibition is also valid with regard to peasants. According to the most authoritative opinion of Shāfiʿī,[26] all of these categories may be slain. The source of this controversy is to be found in the fact that in a number of Traditions, rules are given which are at variance with the general rule from the Book [i.e. the Koran] as well as with the general rule of the authentic Tradition: *"I have been commanded to fight the people until they say: 'There is no God but God.'"*[27] [9:5]: *"Then, when the sacred months are drawn away, slay the idolaters wherever you find them"*[28] as well as the above-mentioned Tradition give as a general rule that every polytheist must be slain, whether he is a monk or not. Nevertheless, the following Traditions, among others, are brought forward in support of the prescription that the lives of the categories mentioned must be saved: 1. Dāwūd Ibn al-Haṣīn[29] has related on the authority of ʿIkrima[30] on the authority of Ibn ʿAbbās[31] that the Prophet used to say, whenever he sent out his armies: *"Do not slay hermits."* 2. On the authority of Anas Ibn Mālik[32] it has been related that the Prophet said: *"Do not slay the old and decrepit, children, or women. Do not purloin what belongs to the spoils."* Abū Dāwūd[33] included this Tradition in his compilation. 3. Mālik has related that Abū Bakr said: *"You will find people who will profess that they have dedicated themselves entirely to God. Leave them in peace and also that to which they have dedicated themselves."* 4. *"Do not slay women, nor infants, nor those worn with age."* However, it seems to me that the chief source for the controversy about this question is that [2:190]: *"And fight in the way of God with those who fight you, but aggress not: God loves not the aggressors"* is in conflict with [9:5]: *"Then, when the sacred months are drawn away, slay the idolaters wherever you find them."*[34] Some maintain that K 9:5 has abrogated K 2:190, because at the outset it was only allowed to slay people who were able-bodied.[35] Consequently, the latter take it that K 9:5 gives a rule without exceptions. Others are of the opinion that K 2:190 has not been abrogated and that it is valid with regard to all those categories which do not take part in the fighting. According to these, K 2:190 gives an exceptive regulation as regards K 9:5. Shāfiᶜī, in support of his interpretation, argues that it has been related on the authority of Sumra[36] that the Prophet commanded: *"Slay the polytheists but spare their children."* The only motive why the enemy should be put to death, according to him, is their unbelief. This motive, then, goes for all unbelievers. Those who maintain that peasants are not to be slain argue that Zayd Ibn Wahb[37] has related: *"We received a letter from ᶜUmar,[38] saying: Do not purloin what belongs to the spoils, do not act perfidiously, do not slay babies and be god-fearing with regard to peasants."*[39] The prohibition to slay polytheist serfs is based on the Tradition of Rabāḥ Ibn Rabīᶜa: *"Once, when Rabāḥ Ibn Rabīᶜa sallied forth with the Messenger of God, he and (the) companions of the Prophet passed by a woman who had been slain. The Messenger halted and said: 'She was not one who would have fought.' Thereupon he looked at the men and said to one of them: 'Run after Khālid Ibn al-Walīd (and tell him) that he must not slay children, serfs or women.'"* Basically, however, the source of their controversy is to be found in their divergent views concerning the motive why the enemy may be slain. Those who think that this is because they are unbelieving do not make exceptions for any polytheist. Others, who are of the opinion that this motive consists in their capacity for fighting, in view of the prohibition to slay female unbelievers, do make an exception for those who are unable to fight or who are not as a rule inclined to fight, such as peasants and serfs. Enemies must not be tortured nor must their bodies be mutilated. The Muslims agree that they may be slain with weapons. Controversy exists, however, concerning the question whether it is allowed to burn them by fire. Some consider it reprehensible to burn or to assail them with fire. This is also the opinion of ᶜUmar. It has been related that Mālik held a similar view. Sufyān al-Thawrī, on the other hand, considered it admissible. Others allow it only in case the enemy has started it. The source of this controversy is again in the fact that a general rule and a particular rule are at variance. The general rule is given by [9:5]: *"Slay the idolaters wherever you find them."* [40] This does not preclude any manner of slaying. The particular rule is founded on an authoritative Tradition, according to which the Prophet said to a certain man: *"If ye should seize him, then slay him, yet do not burn him. No one is free to punish by means of fire, save the Lord of the (Hell) fire (i.e. God)."* Most scholars agree that fortresses may be assailed with mangonels, no matter whether there are women and children within them or not. This is based on the fact that the Prophet used mangonels against the population of al-Ṭāʾif. Some, among whom is Awzāʿī, have taught that mangonels should not be resorted to when Muslim captives or children are within the [walls of the] fortress. Layth,[41] on the other hand, considered it admissible. The argument of those who do not allow it, reads [48:25]: *"Had they been separated clearly, then We would have chastised the unbelievers among them with a painful chastisement."*[42] Those who do allow it do so, as it were, with a view to the general interest. So much for the extent to which injury may be inflicted upon the person of the enemy.

Opinions vary as to the damage that may be inflicted on their property, such as buildings, cattle and crops. Mālik allowed the felling of trees, the picking of fruits and the demolishing of buildings, but not the slaughter of cattle and the burning of date-palms. Awzāʿī disapproved of the felling of fruit-trees and the demolishing of buildings, regardless of whether the buildings in question were churches or not. According to Shāfiʿī, dwellings and trees may be burnt as long as the enemy have the disposal of fortresses. When that is not the case, he considers it reprehensible to demolish buildings and to fell trees. The reason why there is this divergence of opinions is that the practice of Abū Bakr was at variance with that of the Prophet. According to an authoritative Tradition, the Prophet set fire to the palmtrees of Banū Naḍīr. On the other hand, it has been related as an irrefutable fact that Abū Bakr said: *"Do not fell trees and do not demolish buildings."* Some are of the opinion that Abū Bakr could only have spoken thus because he knew the practice of the Prophet to have been abrogated, since he would of course not have been at liberty to act in defiance of this practice had he known it. There are also those who take it that this policy of the prophet [did not give a general rule but] had reference only to Banū Naḍīr, since it was them who attacked him. Those who bring forward all these arguments adhere to the view of Abū Bakr. Others, however, go entirely by the practice of the Prophet. They maintain that it is impossible that anybody's words or deeds could be put forward as an argument against his practice and they consider it lawful to burn trees. Mālik makes a distinction between cattle and trees. According to him, the slaughter of cattle is torture, which is prohibited. Moreover, the Prophet is not related ever to have slain animals. So much for the extent to which it is allowed to inflict damage to the lives and property of the unbelievers.

Par. 4. The Prerequisites for Warfare.

According to all scholars, the prerequisite for warfare is that the enemy must have heard the summons to Islam. This implies that it is not allowed to attack them before the summons has reached them. All Muslims are agreed about this because of [17:15]:"*We never chastise, until We send forth a Messenger.*"[43] However, there is controversy about the question whether the summons should be repeated when the war is resumed. Some hold that this is obligatory, others consider it merely recommendable, while according to a third group it is neither obligatory nor recommendable [and therefore a matter of indifference]. The source of this controversy is that the words and the deeds of the Prophet are at variance. According to an authoritative Tradition, the Prophet, when he sent out his armies, used to say to the leader: *"When ye will encounter your polytheist foes, then summon them to three things. Accept that which they consent to and refrain from [attacking] them. Summon them to conversion to Islam. If they consent to that, accept it and refrain from [attacking] them. Summon them thereupon to sally forth from their territory to the Abode of the Emigrants (muhādjirūn) [i.e. Medina] and impart to them that, if they do so, they will have the same rights and duties as the Emigrants. If they are unwilling to do so, however, and prefer to remain in their own territory, impart to them thereupon that they will be like the converted Bedouins, who are subject to the same supreme authority of God as the [other] believers, but who are not entitled to a share in the spoils, unless they join the*

Muslims in the war. If they refuse that, then summon them to the payment of poll-tax. If they consent to that, accept it and refrain from [attacking] them. But if they refuse it, then invoke the help of God and attack them." Nevertheless it has been related irrefutably that the Prophet repeatedly made sudden attacks upon the enemy at night or at dawn. Some, consequently, maintain, and they are in the majority, that the practice of the Prophet has abrogated his words. According to the latter, the relevant dictum dates back from an early period of Islam, before the summons had been propagated, because it contains a summons to emigration *(hijra)*.[44] Others are of the opinion that more weight should be attached to the Prophet's words than to his deeds, because the latter are to be interpreted in the light of the particular circumstances. Those, lastly, who consider it recommendable, do so in order to reconcile both views.[45]

Par. 5. The Maximum Number of Enemies Against Which One is Obliged to Stand One's Ground.

The maximum number of enemies against which one is obliged to stand one's ground is twice the number [of one's own troops]. About this, everybody agrees on account of [8:66]: *"Now God has lightened it for you, knowing that there is weakness in you."*[46] Ibn Mājishūn maintains, on the authority of Mālik, that the actual force, rather than the number, is to be considered and that it might be allowed for a single man to flee before another if the latter should possess a superior horse, superior weapons and superior physical strength.

Par. 6. Truce.

The conclusion of truce is considered by some to be permitted from the very outset and without an immediate occasion, provided that the Imam deems it in the interest of the Muslims. Others maintain that it is only allowed when the Muslims are pressed by sheer necessity, such as a civil war and the like. As a condition for truce, it may be stipulated that the enemy pay a certain amount of money to the Muslims. This is not poll-tax *(jizya),* because for that it would be required that they come under Islamic rule [which is not the case here]. Such a stipulation [the payment of a tribute], however, is not obligatory. Awzāʿī even considered it admissible that the Imam should conclude a truce with the stipulation that the Muslims pay a certain amount to the enemy, should this be forced upon them by emergency, such as a civil war and the like. Shāfiʿī's opinion is that the Muslims may never give anything to the unbelievers, unless they are in mortal fear of being extinguished, on account of the enemy's superiority or because they are being harrassed by disasters. Among those who profess that the Imam is entitled to conclude a truce when he considers it in the interest [of the Muslims] are Mālik, Shāfiʿī and Abū Ḥanīfa. Shāfiʿī maintains that a truce may not be concluded for a period longer than that of the truce which the Prophet concluded with the unbelievers in the year of Ḥudaybiyya.[47] The controversy about the question whether the conclusion of truce is also allowed without a compulsive reason, is rooted in the fact that the obvious interpretation of [9:5]: *"Slay the idolaters wherever you find them,"*[48] and that of [9:29]: *"Fight those who believe not in God and the Last Day,"*[49] contradict that of [8:61]: *"And if they incline to peace, do thou incline to it."*[50] Some hold that the verse which commands the Muslims to fight the polytheists until they have been converted or until they pay poll-tax *(jizya)* [K 9:29] abrogates the Peace-verse [K 8:61]. Consequently, they maintain that truce is only admissible in cases of necessity. Others are of the opinion that the Peace-verse [K 8:61] supplements the other two verses and they consider the concluding of truce allowed if the Imam deems it right. They also argue, in support of their view, that the Prophet acted accordingly, as the truce of Ḥudaybiyya had not been concluded from necessity. According to Shāfiʿī, the principle is that polytheists must be fought until they have been converted or until they are willing to pay poll-tax *(jizya).* The acts of the Prophet in the year of Ḥudaybiyya are an exception to this [principle]. Therefore, says Shāfiʿī, a truce may never exceed the period for which the Prophet concluded truce in the case of Ḥudaybiyya. Still, there is controversy about the duration of this period. According to some it amounts to four years, but according to others three or ten years. Shāfiʿī opts for the latter. As to the view of some, that in cases of emergency such as civil war and the like, the Muslims may conclude a truce on the stipulation that they pay the enemy a certain amount of money, this is based on the Prophet's example, for it has been related that he was seriously contemplating to bestow a third of the date-harvest of Medina upon a group of polytheists belonging to the Confederates with a view to induce them to move off. However, before he had had time to reach an agreement on the basis of the quantity of dates he had been allowed [by the people of Medina] to give away, God granted him the victory.[51] The opinion of those who profess that a truce may only be concluded when the Muslims are in mortal fear of extinction, is founded on analogous application of the rule that Muslim captives may be ransomed; for when Muslims have been reduced to such a state they are in the position of captives.

Par. 7. The Aims of Warfare.

The Muslims are agreed that the aim of warfare against the People of the Book, with the exception of those belonging to the Quraysh-tribe and Arab Christians, is twofold: either conversion to Islam, or payment of poll-tax *(jizya)*. This is based on [9:29]: *"Fight those who believe not in God and the Last Day and do not forbid what God and His Messenger have forbidden—such men as practise not the religion of truth, being of those who have been given the Book—until they pay the tribute out of hand and have been humbled."* Most lawyers likewise agree that poll-tax *(jizya)* may also be collected from Zoroastrians *(madjūs)* on the strength of the words of the Prophet: *"Treat them like the People of the Book."* There is, however, controversy with regard to polytheists who are not People of the Book: is it allowed to accept poll-tax *(jizya)* from them or not? Some, like Mālik, have taught that it may be collected from any polytheist. Others make an exception for the polytheist Arabs. Shāfiʿī, Abū Thawr[52] and a few others maintain that poll-tax *(jizya)* may only be accepted from People of the Book and Zoroastrians. The controversy is again brought about by the fact that a general rule conflicts with a particular one. The general rule is derived from [2:193 and 8:39]: *"Fight them until there is no persecution and the religion is God's (entirely),"*[53] and from the Tradition: *"I have been commanded to fight the people until they say: 'There is no god but God.' When they say that, then their lives and property are inviolable to me, except* [*in the case when*] *the* [*law of*] *Islam allows it* [*to take them*]. *They will be answerable to God."* The particular rule is founded on the Tradition mentioned earlier,[54] viz. that Mohammed used to say to the leaders of troops which he sent out to the polytheist Arabs: *"When ye will encounter your polytheist foes, then summon them to three things,"* etc. In this Tradition, poll-tax *(jizya)* is also mentioned. Now, some scholars hold that a general rule cancels a particular one if the general rule was revealed at a later date. These do not accept poll-tax *(jizya)* from others than People of the Book, since the verses prescribing, in general terms, to fight them are of a more recent date than the Tradition mentioned; for the general command to fight the polytheists is to be found in the *Sūrat Barāʾa*[55] which was revealed in the year of the conquest of Mecca.[56] The Tradition in question, on the other hand, dates back from before the conquest of Mecca, in view of the fact that it contains a summons to emigration.[57] Others, however, maintain that general rules should always be interpreted in association with the particular rules, no matter whether the one is more recent than the other or whether this is unknown. The latter group, accordingly, accepts poll-tax *(jizya)* from any polytheist. The People of the Book are in an exceptional position with respect to the other polytheists because they have been excluded from the general rule just mentioned, on the strength of the particular rule given in [9:29]: *". . . being of those who have been given the Book—until they pay the tribute out of hand and have been humbled."*[58] The poll-tax *(jizya)* itself and the rules related to it will be dealt with in the next chapter. So much for the principles of warfare. One famous question remains to be touched upon in this connection: that whether it is prohibited to march into hostile territory carrying a copy of the Koran. Most scholars do not consider it allowed because an authoritative rule to this effect has been handed down from the Prophet in an authentic Tradition. Abū

Great mosque in Córdoba (961-966 A.D.)

Ḥanīfa, on the other hand, has taught that it is allowed, provided that it is done under the protection of a strong and safe army. The source of this controversy is the question: was this prohibition put in general terms in order that it might hold good universally and without exceptions, or was the prohibition put in general terms while it was nevertheless intended as a particular rule?

5

The Religious and Moral Doctrine of Jihad:

IBN TAYMIYYA ON JIHAD

Introduction

Taqī al-Dīn Aḥmad Ibn Taymiyya (1263–1328) was a Syrian Hanbalite theologian and jurist. His approach towards religion and law was fundamentalist, in the sense that he emphasized that the example of the pious ancestors *(al-salaf al-ṣāliḥ)* was the highest authority. His intransigent stances brought him several times into conflict with the religious establishment and the political authorities of his era, and he spent many years in prison because of his beliefs. His concern for the purity of Islam was not only academic as he is known to have participated in several military expeditions against heretics. This, however, did not detract him from producing an immense body of works consisting of books, treatises and fatwas.

In his *al-Siyāsa al-sharʿiyya fī iṣlāḥ al-rāʿī wa-al-raʿiyya* ("Governance according to God's Law in reforming both the ruler and his flock"), he developed a political theory that on the one hand legitimized the political system prevailing after the fall of the Caliphate in 1258 and on the other emphasized the necessity for the ruler to wield his power in accordance with the *Sharīʿa.* The main function of government, in his view, is to maintain order through coercion, but coercion exercised in a correct way, i.e. by enforcing God's law. In this treatise he sketches a broad outline of the ideal principles of government.

The passages on jihad deal more with the religious and moral than the purely legal aspects. Quoting a host of Koranic verses and sayings of the Prophet he underlines the excellence and meritoriousness of the jihad duty. Then he deals briefly with the position of non-combatants among the enemies and the fate of prisoners of war. A great part of the text is devoted to the legitimacy of waging jihad against Muslims who revolt against the established political authorities or refuse to abide by the rules of the *Sharīʿa,* and therefore compromise the pure religion. Finally he discusses the difference between war waged at the initiative of the Muslims and defensive warfare.

The translation is based on the edition by Muḥammad Ibrāhīm al-Bannā and Muḥammad Aḥmad ʿĀshūr, published in Cairo by Dār al-Shaʿb in 1971.

Literature:
H. Laoust, *Essai sur les doctrines sociales et politiques d'Ibn Taimiyya.* Cairo: IFAO, 1939.
H. Laoust, *Le traité de droit public d'Ibn Taimīya. Tr. ann. de la Siyāsah Šarʿiyya.* Beirut: Institut Français de Damas, 1948.

Jihad

The penalties that the *Sharīʿa* has introduced for those who disobey God and His Messengers are of two kinds: the punishment of those who are under the sway [of the imam], both individuals and collectivities, as has been mentioned before [in the chapter on criminal law], and, secondly, the punishment of recalcitrant groups, such as those that can only be brought under the sway of the Imam by a decisive fight. That then is the jihad against the unbelievers *(kuffār),* the enemies of God and His Messenger. For whoever has heard the summons of the Messenger of God, Peace be upon him, and has not responded to it, must be fought, *"until there is no persecution and the religion is God's entirely."* (K. 2:193, 8:39)

When God sent his Prophet and ordered him to summon the people to His religion, He did not permit him to kill or fight anyone for that reason before the Prophet emigrated to Medina.

Thereafter He gave him and the Muslims permission with the words:

> Leave is given to those who are fought[1] because they were wronged—surely God is able to help them—who were expelled from their habitations without right, except that they say 'Our Lord is God.' Had God not driven back the people, some by the means of others, there had been destroyed cloisters and churches, oratories and mosques, wherein God's name is much mentioned. Assuredly God will help him who helps Him—surely God is all-strong, all-mighty—who, if We establish them in the land, perform the prayer, and pay the alms, and bid to honour, and forbid dishonour; and unto God belongs the issue of all affairs. *(K. 22:39–41)*

Then, after that, He imposed fighting to them with the following words:

> Prescribed for you is fighting, though it be hateful to you. Yet it may happen that you will hate a thing which is better for you; and it may happen that you will love a thing which is worse for you. God knows and you know not. *(K. 2:216)*

He has emphasized this command and glorified jihad in many of the Medinese suras. He has criticized those who fail to participate in it and called them hypocrites and sick in their hearts. God has said:

> Say: 'If your fathers, your sons, your brothers, your wives, your clan, your possessions that you have gained, commerce you fear may slacken, dwellings you love—if these are dearer to you than God and His Messenger, and to struggle in His way, then wait till God brings His command; God guides not the people of the ungodly. *(K. 9:24)*

And:

> The believers are those who believe in God and His Messenger, then have not doubted, and have struggled with their posses-

> sions and their selves in the way of God; those—they are the truthful ones. *(K. 49:15)*

And:

> Then, when a clear sura is sent down, and therein fighting is mentioned, thou seest those in whose heart is sickness looking at thee as one who swoons of death; but better for them would be obedience and words honourable. Then when the matter is resolved, if they were true to God, it would be better for them. *(K. 47: 20–21)*

There are numerous similar verses in the Koran and equally frequent is the glorification of jihad and those who participate in it, [for instance] in Surat The Ranks *(al-ṣaff):*

> O believers, shall I direct you to a commerce that shall deliver you from a painful chastisement? You shall believe in God and His Messenger, and struggle in the way of God with your possessions and your selves. That is better for you, did you but know. He will forgive you your sins and admit you into gardens underneath which rivers flow, and to dwelling places goodly in Gardens of Eden; that is the mighty triumph; and other things you love, help from God and a nigh victory. Give thou good tidings to the believers. *(K. 61:10–13)*

And [elsewhere] He has said:

> Do you reckon the giving of water to pilgrims and the inhabiting of the Holy Mosque as the same as one who believes in God and the Last Day and struggles in the way of God? Not equal are they in God's sight; and God guides not the people of the evildoers. Those who believe, and have emigrated, and have struggled in the way of God with their possessions and their selves are mightier in rank with God; and those—they are the triumphant; their Lord gives them good tidings of mercy from Him and good pleasure; for them await gardens wherein is lasting bliss, therein to dwell forever and ever; surely with God is a mighty wage. *(K. 9: 19–21)*

And:

> O believers, whosoever of you turns from his religion, God will assuredly bring a people He loves, and who love Him, humble towards the believers, disdainful towards the unbelievers, men who struggle in the path of God, not fearing the reproach of any reproacher. That is God's bounty; He gives it unto whom He will. *(K. 5:54)*

And He has said:

> That is because they are smitten neither by thirst, nor fatigue, nor emptiness in the way of God, neither tread they any tread enraging the unbelievers, nor gain any gain from any enemy, but a righteous deed is thereby written to their account; God leaves not to waste the wage of the good-doers. Nor do they expend any sum, small or great, nor do they traverse any valley, but it is written to their account, that God may recompense them the best of what they were doing. *(K. 9:120–121)*

Thus He has mentioned [the reward] resulting from their deeds and the deeds they must practice.

The command to participate in jihad and the mention of its merits occur innumerable times in the Koran and the Sunna. Therefore it is the best voluntary [religious] act that man can perform. All scholars agree that it is better than the *ḥajj* (greater pilgrimage) and the *ʿumra* (lesser pilgrimage), than voluntary *ṣalāt* and voluntary fasting, as the Koran and Sunna indicate. The Prophet, Peace be upon him, has said: *"The head of the affair is Islam, its central pillar is the ṣalāt and its summit is the jihad."* And he has said: *"In Paradise there are a hundred grades with intervals as wide as the distance between the sky and the earth. All these God has prepared for those who take part in jihad."* There is unanimity about the authenticity of this Tradition. Al-Bukhārī[2] has transmitted that he has said: *"Him whose feet have become dusty in the way of God [i.e. jihad] will God save from hellfire."* And, as related by Muslim[3], he has said:

> A day and a night in spent in ribāṭ[4] are better than one month spent in fasting and vigils. If he dies [in the fulfillment of this task], he will receive the recompense of his deeds and subsistence, and he will be protected from the Angel of the Grave[5].

It is related in the *Sunan* that *"a day spent in ribāṭ in the way of God is better than thousand days spent elsewhere."* He has said: *"Two eyes will not be touched by the fire: the eye that has wept out of fear for God and the eye that has spent the night on the watch in the way of God."* Al-Tirmidhī[6] has said about this tradition that it is good *(ḥasan).*[7] In the *Musnad* of Aḥmad ibn Ḥanbal[8] we find: *"A night spent on the watch in the way of God is better than a thousand nights and days spent in nightly vigils and fasting."* In the *Ṣaḥīḥ* of al-Bukhārī as well as in the *Ṣaḥīḥ* of Muslim we find:

> A man said: 'O Messenger of God, tell me of an act that equals jihad in the way of God.' He answered: 'You will not be capable of it." The man said: 'Tell me anyway.' The Messenger of God said: 'Can you, when a jihad warrior has gone out on expedition, fast without interruption and spend the night in continuous prayer?' The man said: 'No.' Then the Messenger of God said: 'This then is what equals jihad.'

In the *Sunan* we find that Mohammed has said: *"Every community has its devotional journeys and the devotional journey of my community is jihad in the way of God."*

This is a vast subject, unequalled by other subjects as far as the reward and merit of human deeds is concerned. This is evident upon closer examination. The [first] reason is that the benefit of jihad is general, extending not only to the person who participates in it but also to others, both in a religious and a temporal sense. [Secondly,] jihad implies all kinds of worship, both in its inner and outer forms. More than any other act it implies love and devotion for God, Who is exalted, trust in Him, the surrender of one's life and property to Him, patience, asceticism, remembrance of God and all kinds of other acts [of worship]. Any individual or community that participates in it, finds itself between two blissful outcomes: either victory and triumph or martyrdom and Paradise. [Thirdly,] all creatures must live and die. Now, it is in jihad that one can live and die in ultimate happiness, both in this world and in the Herafter. Abandoning it means losing entirely or partially both kinds of happiness. There are people who want to perform religious and temporal deeds full of hardship, in spite of their lack of benefit, whereas actually jihad is religiously and temporally more beneficial than any other deed full of hardship. Other people [participate in it] out of a desire to make things easy for themselves when death meets them, for the death of a martyr is easier than any other form of death. In fact, it is the best of all manners of dying.

Since lawful warfare is essentially jihad and since its aim is that the religion is God's entirely[9] and God's word is uppermost,[10] therefore, according to all Muslims, those who stand in the way of this aim must be fought. As for those who cannot offer resistance or cannot fight, such as women, children, monks, old people, the blind, handicapped and their likes, they shall not be killed, unless they actually fight with words [e.g. by propaganda] and acts [e.g. by spying or otherwise assisting in the warfare]. Some [jurists] are of the opinion that all of them may be killed, on the mere ground that they are unbelievers, but they make an exception for women and children since they constitute property for Muslims. However, the first opinion is the correct one, because we may only fight those who fight us when we want to make God's religion victorious. God, Who is exalted, has said in this respect: *"And fight in the way of God with those who fight you, but aggress not: God loves not the aggressors."* (K. 2:190). In the *Sunan* it is reported from the Messenger of God, Peace be upon him:

> That he once passed by a woman who had been slain. The Messenger of God halted and said: 'She was not one who would have fought.' Then he said to one of [his companions]: 'Catch up with Khālid ibn al-Walīd and tell him not to kill women, children and serfs.'"

It is also reported in the *Sunan* that he used to say: *"Do not kill very old men, nor small children or women."* The reason is that God has [only] permitted to shed blood if that is necessary for the welfare of the creation. He has said: *"Persecution is more grievous than slaying."* (K. 2:191). This means that, although there is evil and abomination in killing, there is greater evil and abomination in the persecution by the unbelievers. Now, the unbelief of those who do not hinder the Muslims from establishing God's religion, is only prejudicial to themselves. In the same vein, the jurists have said that the one who propagates innovations *(bidaᶜ)* that are contrary to the Koran and the *Sunna* must be punished much more severely than the person [who holds such beliefs but] remains silent. *"A mistake that is kept secret,"* says a Tradition, *"only harms the person who has committed it, but if it becomes public and is not denounced, it harms the community."*

The *Sharīᶜa* enjoins fighting the unbelievers, but not the killing of those who have been captured. If a male unbeliever is taken captive during warfare or otherwise, e.g. as a result of a shipwreck, or because he lost his way, or as a result of a ruse, then the head of state *(imām)* may do whatever he deems appropriate: killing him, enslaving him, releasing him or setting him free for a ransom consisting in either property or people. This is the view of most jurists and it is supported by the Koran and the *Sunna*. There are, however, some jurists who hold that the options of releasing them or setting them free for a ransom have been abrogated. As for the People of the Book and the Zoroastrians *(Majūs)*, they are to be fought until they become Muslims or pay the tribute *(jizya)* out of hand and have been humbled.[11] With regard to the others, the jurists differ as to the lawfulness of taking tribute from them. Most of them regard it as unlawful to accept it from [heathen] Arabs.

If a rebellious group, although belonging to Islam, refuses to comply with clear and universally accepted commands, all Muslims agree that jihad must be waged against them, in order that the religion will be God's entirely.[12] Thus Abū Bakr al-Ṣiddīq[13] and other Companions, may God be pleased with them, have fought those who refused to pay *zakāt*. Initially some of the Companions hesitated in fighting them, but eventually they all agreed. ᶜUmar ibn al-Khaṭṭāb[14] said to Abū Bakr, may God be pleased with them: "How can you fight these people? Has the Messenger of God, Peace be upon him, not said: 'I have been ordered to fight people until they profess that there is no god but God and that Mohammad is God's Messenger. If they say that, their lives and properties will be inviolable for me, unless there is a rule of law that allows taking them. [For their actions] they must render account to God.' Abū Bakr then said: 'The [obligation to pay] *zakāt* is such a rule. By God, if they refuse to give me one she-kid which they used to give to the Messenger of God, Peace be upon him, I shall fight them for this refusal.' ᶜUmar said: 'Then I realized immediately that God had opened his heart for fighting and I knew that that was right.'"

There are various authentic Traditions according to which the Prophet, Peace be upon him, has ordered to fight the Kharijites.[15] In the *ṣaḥīḥ* of al-Bukhārī as well as in the *ṣaḥīḥ* of Muslim it is reported on the authority of ᶜAlī ibn Abī Ṭālib,[16] may God be pleased with him, that he said:

> I have heard the Messenger of God, Peace be upon him, saying: 'Towards the end of time a group of people will emerge, young of age and simple of minds, who will speak the most beautiful words, but whose faith does not go deeper than their throats. They will abandon the religion just like an arrow pierces and then abandons a game animal. Wherever you find them you must kill them since those who kill them will be rewarded on the Day of Resurrection.'

Muslim has reported that ᶜAlī, may God be pleased with him, said:

> I have heard the Messenger of God, Peace be upon him, saying: 'A group of people will emerge from amongst my community, who will recite the Koran [very well]. Your recitation is nothing compared to theirs. Likewise your way of performing salāt and your way of fasting are nothing compared with theirs. They will recite the Koran believing that it[s text] supports them, whereas [in reality] it condemns them. Their recitation does not go deeper than their collarbones. They will abandon the religion just like an arrow pierces and then abandons a game animal. If the army that reaches them would know how much [reward] the Prophet has promised them, they would rely on this deed [alone and not worry about other good deeds].

In another version of this Tradition, transmitted on the authority of Abū Saᶜīd from the Prophet, Peace be upon him, we find the following words: *"They will fight the people of faith and leave the idolaters. If I live long enough to meet them, I shall kill them in the manner the tribe of ᶜĀd*[17] *was killed."* There is unanimity about the authenticity of this Tradition.

In another Tradition reported by Muslim it is said: *"My community will fall apart into two parties. From amongst them there will emerge heretics (māriqa). The party that is closest to truth will be in charge of killing them."* These were the people that were killed by the Commander of the Faithful ᶜAlī, when the breach between the people of Iraq and the people of Syria took place. They were called *ḥarūriyya.*[18] The Prophet, Peace be upon him, has made it clear that both parties into which the community had fallen apart, belonged to his community and that the partisans of ᶜAlī were closer to the truth. He incited to fight only those heretics that had abandoned Islam and had left the community and that had permitted the taking of the lives and properties of the other Muslims. It has been established on the authority of the Koran, the *Sunna,* and the Consensus of the Community, that those who depart from the law of Islam must be fought, even if they pronounce the two professions of faith.

The jurists disagree about the permissibility to fight rebellious groups that abandon an established supererogatory act of worship *(sunna rātiba),* such as the two [extra] *rakᶜas*[19] of dawn prayer. There is, however, unanimity that it is allowed to fight people for [not observing] unambiguous and generally recognized obligations and prohibitions, until they undertake to perform the explicitly prescribed prayers, to pay *zakāt,* to fast during the month of Ramaḍān, to make the pilgrimage to Mecca and to avoid what is prohibited, such as marrying women in spite of legal impediments, eating impure things, acting unlawfully against the lives and properties of Muslims and the like. It is obligatory to take the initiative in fighting those people, as soon as the Prophet's summons with the reasons for which they are fought has reached them. But if they first attack the Muslims, then fighting them is even more urgent, as we have mentioned when dealing with the fighting against rebellious and aggressive bandits.

The most serious type of obligatory jihad is the one against the unbelievers and against those who refuse to abide by certain prescriptions of the *Sharīᶜa,* like those who refuse to pay *zakāt,* the

Kharijites and the like. This jihad is obligatory if it is carried out on our initiative and also if it is waged as defence. If we take the initiative, it is a collective duty, [which means that] if it is fulfilled by a sufficient number [of Muslims], the obligation lapses for all others and the merit goes to those who have fulfilled it, just as God, He is exalted, has said:

> Such believers as sit at home—unless they have an injury—are not the equals [of those who struggle in the path of God with their possessions and their selves. God has preferred in rank those who struggle in the path of God with their possessions and their selves over the ones who sit at home; yet to each God has promised the reward most fair; and God has preferred those who struggle over the ones who sit at home for the bounty of a mighty wage, in ranks standing before Him, forgiveness and mercy.] (K. 4:95–96)

But if the enemy wants to attack the Muslims, than repelling him becomes a duty for all those under attack and for the others in order to help them. God, He is exalted, has said: *"Yet if they ask you for help, for religion's sake, it is your duty to help them."* (K. 8:72) In the same vein the Prophet has ordered Muslims to help fellow Muslims. The assistance, which is obligatory both for the regular professional army and for others, must be given, according to everybody's possibilities, either in person, by fighting on foot or on horseback, or through financial contributions, be they small or large. When the Muslims were attacked by the enemy in the year of the Trench,[20] God did not permit anybody to abandon jihad, although He did allow them not to take part in jihad [after the siege was lifted] in order to pursue the enemy. At that occasion He divided them into two categories, those who sat at home and those who marched out, and He criticized those who were asking the Prophet for leave [not to take part in jihad]: *"[And a part of them were asking leave of the Prophet,] saying, 'Our houses are exposed'; yet they were not exposed; they desired only to flee."* (K. 33:13)

So the latter [form of jihad] consists in defense of the religion, of things that are inviolable, and of lives. Therefore it is fighting

Christian captives being marched to Istanbul (German, 16th century)

out of necessity. The former [type of jihad], however, is voluntary fighting in order to propagate the religion, to make it triumph and to intimidate the enemy, such as was the case with the expedition to Tabūk and the like.[21] Now, this form of punishment [i.e. jihad] must be administered to rebellious groups. As for inhabitants of the territory of Islam who are not rebellious [but refuse to carry out religious duties], they must be forced to carry out their obligations such as the five fundamental duties of Islam[22] and others like the delivering of trusts to their owners and the preserving of covenants in social relations.

6

Jihad and War Propaganda:

THE OTTOMAN JIHAD FATWA OF NOVEMBER 11TH, 1914

Introduction

When by the end of 1914 the Ottoman Empire joined the world war at the side of the Central Powers, a fatwa was issued by the Shaykh al-Islām, the highest religious authority and state mufti. It affirmed that the war under the given circumstances was legal according to the *Sharīʿa* and that jihad had become an individual duty on the strength of the general mobilization *(istinfār ʿāmm)* by the Ottoman Sultan. Its form is traditional Ottoman, consisting of questions in which all the details of the case are specified and to which a simple answer "yes" *(olur)* or "no" *(olmaz)* is given.

The interesting aspect of this fatwa is that it went beyond the justification of warfare for the Ottoman subjects. It also addressed the Muslims living under the rule of the enemies, the Allied Powers, such as the Muslims of India, Central Asia, North Africa and the Balkans, and stated unequivocally that they were obliged to come to the rescue of the Ottoman Empire and attack their non-Muslim rulers. Therefore, it can be regarded as an illustration of the Ottoman Pan-Islamic aspirations. In order to make it widely known among the peoples concerned, it was translated into Arabic, Persian, Urdu and Turkic. Within the Empire, several committees and organizations of *'ulamā'* as well as individual religious authorities issued proclamations in support of the fatwa. Abroad, the fatwa met with little active response.

In allied countries the fatwa aroused considerable indignation, which was not entirely free from hypocrisy. Since the word jihad evoked images of religious fanaticism and ruthless slaughter of infidels, Germany, which was suspected of having suggested the use of jihad propaganda to the Ottoman authorities, was reproached for resorting to mediaeval intellectual weapons. At the same time this indignation betrayed a certain anxiety as to the loyalty of the colonized Muslims. The colonial powers used to see everywhere the spectre of Pan-Islamism. They overrated its impact and therefore feared this open and undisguised appeal to religious loyalties. Illustrative is the discussion between the Dutch Orientalist Snouck Hurgronje and his German colleague Becker about this fatwa.[1]

The text of the fatwa has been published with a German translation in *Der Islam* 5 (1914), pp. 391–393. The present translation is reprinted from Rudolph Peters, *Islam and Colonialism: The Doctrine of Jihad in Modern History.* The Hague etc.: Mouton Publishers, 1979, pp. 90–91.

Question: When it occurs that enemies attack the Islamic world, when it has been established that they seize and pillage Islamic countries and capture Muslim persons and when His Majesty the Padishah of Islam thereupon orders the jihad in the form of a general mobilization, has jihad then, according to the illustrious Koranic verse: *'Go forth, light and heavy! Struggle in God's way with your possessions and yourselves; that is better for you, did you know'* (K 9:41), become incumbent upon all Muslims and has it become an individual duty for all Muslims in all parts of the world, be they young or old, on foot or mounted, to hasten to partake in the jihad with their goods and money?
Answer: Yes.

Question: Now that it has been established that Russia, England, France and the governments that support them and are allied to them, are hostile to the Islamic Caliphate, since their warships and armies attack the Seat of the Islamic Caliphate and the Imperial Dominions and strive (God forbid) for extinguishing and annihilating the exalted light of Islam [cf. K 9:32], is it, in this case,

also incumbent upon all Muslims that are being ruled by these governments, to proclaim jihad against them and to actually attack them?
Answer: Yes.

Question: If some Muslims, now that the attainment of the aim [viz. the protection of the Ottoman Empire] depends on the fact that all Muslims hasten to partake in the jihad, refrain from doing so (which God forbid), is this then, in this case, a great sin and do they deserve Divine wrath and punishment for their horrible sin?
Answer: Yes.

Question: If the states mentioned that are fighting against the Islamic government compel and force their Muslim population by [threatening them] to kill them and even to exterminate all members of their families, is it even in this case according to the *sharīʿah* absolutely forbidden for them to fight against the troops of the Islamic countries and do they [by transgressing this prohibition] deserve the hell-fire, having become murderers?
Answer: Yes.

Question: Is it in this case for the Muslims that are in the present war under the rule of England, France, Russia, Serbia, Montenegro and their allies, since it is detrimental to the Islamic Caliphate, a great sin to fight against Germany and Austria which are the allies of the Supreme Islamic Government and do they deserve [by acting so] a painful punishment [in the Here-after]?
Answers: Yes.

The court of Al-Azbar Mosque. Gatherings of scholars can be seen inside.

7

A Modernist Interpretation of Jihad:

MAḤMŪD SHALTŪT'S TREATISE *KORAN AND FIGHTING*

Introduction

Maḥmūd Shaltūt was born in 1923, in the small provincial town of Minyat Banī Manṣūr in Lower Egypt. After his traditional Islamic education in Alexandria and at al-Azhar University in Cairo, he became a teacher of Islamic law, first in Alexandria and from 1927 at al-Azhar University. In 1931 he was dismissed for being an advocate of reform of al-Azhar. In 1935, when the climate had changed and certain reforms had been introduced, he was allowed to return and was nominated vice-dean of the *Sharīʿa* faculty. The final years of his life, from 1958–1963, he served as Shaykh al-Azhar, Rector of the Azhar University, an office to which President Nasser had appointed him.

Shaltūt was a prolific author on Islamic topics, and especially on law and Koran exegesis. He belonged to the modernist school of Muḥammad ʿAbduh (d. 1905), whose influences are clearly discernible in his writings. A special interest of his in the field of Islamic law was the promotion of harmony between the different schools of law, and in particular between the Sunnites and the Shiʿites. His peaceful interpretation of the classical jihad doctrine is an elaboration of ʿAbduh's thoughts on the topic and is representative of the views of the Islamic establishment also in our days. They are founded on the recognition of national states in the Islamic world, belonging to an international order based on peaceful relations.

Shaltūt's first publication on jihad dates from 1933, when two of his lectures were published in a small book with the title *Al-daʿwa al-Muḥammadiyya wa-al-qitāl fī al-Islām* ("The Mohammedan

Mission and Fighting in Islam"), published by al-Maṭbaʿa al-Salafiyya in Cairo. Parts of it were included in the book *al-Qurʾān wa-al-qitāl* ("The Koran and Fighting"), which he wrote in 1940 and was published in 1948, and which is here presented in translation. For the translation I have made use both of the 1948 edition, published by Maṭbaʿat al-Naṣr and Maktab Ittiḥād al-Sharq and the edition published in 1951 by Dār al-Kitāb al-ʿArabī. The editions are identical. The present translation has appeared earlier in *Jihad in Mediaeval and Modern Islam: The Chapter on Jihad from Averroes' Legal Handbook 'Bidāyat al-Mudjtahid' and the Treatise 'Koran and Fighting' by the Late Shaykh al-Azhar, Maḥmūd Shaltūt.* Translated and annotated by Rudolph Peters. Leiden: E.J. Brill, 1977, pp. 26–79, 84–86.

Literature:

Kate Zebiri, *Maḥmūd Shaltūt and Islamic Modernism*. Oxford: Oxford University Press, 1993.

Wolf-Dieter Lemke, *Maḥmūd Shaltūt (1893–1963) und die Reform der Azhar*. Frankfurt: 1980.

The Koran and Fighting
by Maḥmūd Shaltūt

1. The Exemplary Method of Koran Interpretation
(Summary)

There are two methods of Koran interpretation. The first one consists in explaining the verses and chapters of the Koran, in their traditional order. This may be done from different points of views: grammatical, historical, stylistic, legal and philosophical. However, all these trends in interpretation obscure the Divine Guidance. Often verses are explained in ways completely opposed to their real meanings or purposes and sometimes they are even considered to have been abrogated. According to this traditional method, verses are interpreted on the basis of certain extra-Koranic assumptions or principles. One can see the result e.g. in the exegesis of the verses concerning fighting: about 70 verses are considered to have been abrogated, since they are incompatible with the legitimacy of fighting. Therefore this method of interpretation does scant justice to the fact that the Koran is the primary source of Islam. Moreover, the numerous different interpretations, which were the consequence of this method, created an intellectual anarchy and an aversion against the Koran and its interpreters.

The second method consists in collecting all the verses concerning a certain topic and analyzing them in their interrelation. Thus, the purpose of these verses and the rules that can be derived from them, become clear. There is no need to squeeze any verse into an unsuitable interpretation. Thus, justice is done to all the merits of the Divine Formulation. This second method is, in our view, the exemplary method of Koran-interpretation. It can promote the guidance of humanity as it shows that the Koranic topics are not merely theoretical, but that they also contain realistic examples that are directly relevant to everyday life. Nowadays the false notion is widespread that the Koran is just a spiritual book, only concerned with man's relation to God without any bearing on the practical exigencies of daily life. As a result many people, and among them even those who call themselves scholars, regard the Koran merely as a collection of texts for recitation in order to invoke God's protection or to seek recovery from illness. In this way, however, they undervalue the Koran and, in doing so, deprive themselves of an abundant source of knowledge, wisdom, legislation, politics, education and culture.

I applied this second method to the subject: *"The Koran and Women."* The topic I should like to discuss now is *"The Koran and Fighting."* This topic is of practical importance in our times, as wars are being fought all over the world, engaging everybody's attention. Moreover, it has a theoretical significance, as many adherents of other religions constantly take up this subject with a view to discredit Islam. Therefore, people would do well to learn the Koranic rules with regard to fighting, its causes and its ends, and so come to recognize the wisdom of the Koran in this respect: its desire for peace and its aversion against bloodshed and killing for the sake of the vanities of this world and out of sheer greediness and lust.

2. The Nature of the Islamic Mission *(daʿwa)*

A first requirement for the treatment of this topic is some knowledge of the nature of the Islamic Mission and an answer to the question whether this Mission needs to force people to conversion.

Sometimes when a man is invited to adopt a certain principle, he can readily do so and believe in it, peacefully and joyfully. However, other principles may be difficult to accept and repulsive to him. We see both phenomena around us and we know them in ourselves. What then is the reason?

The reason is clear. Whenever the truth one is invited to accept is a simple and easy one, not complicated or unnatural and not manifestly or secretly containing elements opposed to human nature, it is clear truth that speaks for itself and does not require any further means to enlist adherents. However, when the truth is contradictory, complicated and intricate, it is dim, obscure and repulsive to people. In order to make people accept such truths, special means are required—they have to be imposed on the people by force. If this is an established fact with regard to the human mind, let us now consider to which of these two categories the Islamic Mission belongs.

God sent Mohammed at an interval amongst the messengers, as a caller, a bringer of good tidings and as a warner [cf. K 5:19]. He revealed to him a book containing the principles of happiness for the community as well as for the individual: it commands to judge by reason, it attaches great importance to evidence, it propagates science and knowledge, it gives clear rules, it specifies crimes, it proclaims mercy, it urges to do good, it preaches peace, it puts an end to distress and strives for facility, it gives firm principles concerning politics and society, it fights injustice and corruption, it struggles against mental sluggishness, it disapproves of blind imitation of the ways of the forefathers, it shouts at people that another life more exalted than this life, is awaiting them and will offer them permanent bliss and eternal existence and that Man ends where he begins and that his life in the Hereafter will be determined by his life in this world.

Thus was the Mission of Mohammed, the messenger. Its foremost principle was the unity of the Creator and the worship only of him, and belief in him, free from defective and imperfect qualities or of any characteristics that can be compared with His creation [6:101–103]: *"The Creator of the heavens and the earth—how should He have a son, seeing that He has no consort, and he created all things, and He has knowledge of everything? That then is God your Lord; there is no God but He, the Creator of everything. So serve Him, for He is Guardian over everything. The eyes attain Him not, but He attains the eyes; He is the All-subtle, the All-aware."*

The Koran points out that thus it wants to honour Man and seeks to keep him from worshipping something that does not see nor hear and that is neither harmful nor beneficial. It announces that by this message the previous religions are confirmed, that it is not opposed to their original principles and that it does not discriminate between the different Messengers: they all proclaim the unity of God, they all require the worship of God, they all command to do what is good and forbid to do what is reprehensible and they all recommend virtue and preach against evil:

[2:136–137]: *"Say you: 'We believe in God, and in that which has been sent down on us and sent down on Abraham, Ishmael, Isaac and Jacob and the Tribes, and that which was given to Moses and Jesus and the Prophets, of their Lord; we make no division between any of them, and to Him we surrender.' And if they believe in the like of that you believe in, then they are truly guided; but if they turn away, then they are clearly in schism; God will suffice you for them; He is the All-hearing, the All-knowing."*

[3:64]: *"Say: 'People of the Book! Come now to a word common between us and you, that we serve none but God, and that we associate not aught with Him, and do some of us not take others as Lords, apart from God.' And if they turn their backs, say: 'Bear witness that we are Muslims.'"*

[29:46]: "Dispute not with the People of the Book save in the fairer

manner, except for those of them that do wrong; and say, 'We believe in what has been sent down to us, and what has been sent down to you; our God and your God is One, and to Him we have surrendered."

[42:13]: "He has laid down for you as religion that he charged Noah with, and that We have revealed to thee, and that We charged Abraham with, Moses and Jesus: 'Perform the religion, and scatter not regarding it.'"

As these and other verses with regard to the Islamic Mission show, this Mission is a clear and evident one, easy and uncomplicated, not obscure and abstruse, but digestible and intelligible for any mind. It is identical with the Mission of previous religions, the Mission of former Messengers. It is the call of natural reason and therefore not alien to human intellect [2:138]: *"The baptism [or: savour] of God; and who is there that baptizes fairer than God [or: who is better in savour];"* [30:30]: *"God's original (religion) upon which He originated mankind. There is no changing God's creation. That is the right religion."* Such is the Mission of Islam. Now, does such a Mission require force to make people believe in it? No, the use of force as a means of making people believe in this Mission, would be an insult to it, would make it revolting and would put obstacles in its way. If a man realizes that he is being compelled, or forced into something, this will prevent him from respecting and esteeming it and from reflecting upon it, let alone that he will be able to believe in it. Employing force as an instrument for conversion means wrapping this Mission in complexity, absurdity and obscurity and withholding it from the grasp of the human mind and heart. This, without doubt, would be a terrible injustice to this Mission as well as an insult and at the same time it would stand as an obstacle in its way. It would be incomprehensible for a Mission to pursue its aims while containing in itself elements conducive to its weakness and ultimate extinction or components that are harmful to it and distort its beauty. All this is clear and we could leave it at that, confident that people will respect it and take it as a guiding principle in their judgement concerning the relationship between Islam and fighting. However, we shall not content ourselves with this; we shall examine the texts referring to the Mission and investigate whether there are any texts that approve of coercion in matters of faith and whether there are any texts that express regard for faith based on compulsion. The answer should be evident, and from several points of view at that.

The Koran instructs us clearly that God did not wish people to become believers by way of force and compulsion, but only by way of study, reflection and contemplation. Moreover, the Koran teaches us that, had He wanted them to have such a kind of faith, He would have implanted it in their nature and made them like angels, unable to disobey His orders, performing what He orders them to do by nature and creation, powerless to rebel against Him or to escape from Him. However, He did not do so and He left Man free to choose between belief and unbelief, between guidance and going astray. Instead, He contented Himself with their pledges of the natural religion, making them confirm these pledges with regard to themselves and sending prophets to them to remind them and to summon them to think about the kingdom of heaven and earth, [4:165]: *"so that mankind might have no argument against God, after the Messengers"*; [5:19]: *"lest you should say, 'There has not come to us any bearer of good tidings, neither any warner.'"* Such is the custom of God as related in His Book [11:118]: *"Had thy Lord willed, He would have made mankind one nation; but they continue in their differences, excepting those on whom thy Lord has mercy. To that end He created them."* [10:99]: *"And if thy Lord had willed, whoever is in the earth would have believed, all of them, all together. Wouldst thou then constrain the people, until they are believers?"* [5:48] *"If God had willed, He would have made you one nation; but that he may try you in what has come to you. So be you forward in good works; unto God shall you return, all together; and He will tell you of that whereon you were at variance."* [6:35] *"And if their turning away is distressful for thee, why, if thou canst seek out a hole in the earth, or a ladder in heaven, to bring them some sign—but had God willed, He would have gathered them in the guidance; so be not thou one of the ignorant."*

Upon this principle of creation the Divine Revelations are founded: they demand profession of the unity of God and the sole worship of the Creator on the basis of investigation, demonstration, and free choice, proceeding on the principle that there is no power but reason and no coercion except force of argument. You will find that none of the Divine Revelations does impose convictions upon people by way of force and compulsion. Listen to what Nūḥ (Noah) said to his people [11:28]: *"He said, 'O my people, what think you? If I stand upon a clear sign from my Lord, and He has given me mercy from Him, and it has been obscured for you, shall we compel you to it while you are averse to it?"* Then listen to what the people of ʿĀd said to their prophet [11:53]: *"They said, 'Hood, thou hast not brought us a clear sign, and we will not leave our gods for what thou sayest; we do not believe thee.'"* Thereupon he answers [11:56]: *"Truly, I have put my trust in God, my Lord and your Lord; there is no creature that crawls, but He takes it by the forelock. Surely my Lord is upon a straight path."* Listen also to Ibrāhīm (Abraham) where he tries to convince his father in a friendly and gentle manner, by way of arguments and evidence, emotion and affection:

[19:43–47]: *"'Father, there has come to me knowledge such as came not to thee; so follow me and I will guide thee on a level path. Father, serve not Satan; surely Satan is a rebel against the All-merciful. Father, I fear that some chastisement from the All-merciful will smite thee, so that thou becomest a friend of Satan.' Said he, 'What, art thou shrinking from my Gods, Abraham? Surely, if thou givest not over I shall stone thee; so forsake me now for some while.' He said, 'Peace be upon thee! I will ask my Lord to forgive thee; surely he is ever gracious to me. Now I will go apart from you and what you call upon, apart from God. I will call upon my Lord, and haply I shall not be, in calling upon my Lord, unprosperous."* Listen finally to what God says to Mūsa (Moses) and Hārūn (Aaron) when he entrusted them with the task to spread His Mission [20:43]: *"Go to Pharaoh, for he has waxed insolent; yet speak gently to him, that haply he may be mindful."* Read all this very carefully, and then you will know that the only weapons God has given to his previous messengers in order to communicate His Mission to the people, were clear arguments and calling the attention to God's works. This is entirely in accordance with His custom concerning belief and unbelief, guidance and going astray.

All this God has told to His Prophet in His book. He explained to him how the messengers were propagating His Mission and He said to him [6:90]: *"Those are they whom God has guided; so follow their guidance."* Then He explained to him the methods of propagating the message in one unique and comprehensive verse

[16:125]: *"Call thou to the way of thy Lord with wisdom and good admonition and dispute with them in the better way."* This is the principle upon which Mohammad's Mission was founded [12:108]: *"Say: 'This is my way. I call to God with sure knowledge, I and whoever follows after me. To God be glory! And I am not among the idolaters."* The above-mentioned is characteristic for Mohammed's Mission as well as the Missions of his brethren who preceded him. However, there is one quality with which God exclusively endowed Mohammed's Revelation. In his Mission, He made him the prophet who was the least inclined to use compulsion and to employ special expedients for making people believe. The Mission of former prophets had frequently been accompanied by apparent miracles, inducing people to conversion, such as revivification of the dead, and healing of the blind and the leprous. But with regard to Mohammed's revelation God refused to conform to the desires of the heathens who demanded that he should give such tokens [17:90–93]: *"They say, 'We will not believe thee till thou makest a spring to gush forth from the earth for us, or till thou possessest a garden with palms and vines, and thou makest rivers to gush forth abundantly all amongst it or till thou makest heaven to fall, as thou assertest, on us in fragments, or thou bringest God and the angels as a surety or till thou possessest a house of gold ornament, or till thou goest up into heaven; and we will not believe thy going up till thou bringest down on us a book that we may read.' Say: 'Glory be to my Lord! Am I aught but a mortal, a Messenger?'"*

He explained that his only token was of the same kind as his clear Mission: based on rational demonstration that affects insight rather than eyesight and that takes hold of the heart before it takes hold of the outward senses [29:50–52]: *"They say, 'Why have signs not been sent down upon him from his Lord?' Say: 'The signs are only with God, and I am only a plain warner.' What, is it not sufficient for them that We have sent down upon thee the Book that is recited to them? Surely in that is a mercy, and a reminder to a people who believe. Say: 'God suffices as a witness between me and you.' He knows whatsoever is in the heavens and earth. Those who believe in vanity and disbelieve in God—those, they are the losers."* [26:4]: *"If We will, We shall send down on them out of heaven a sign, so their necks will stay humbled to it."*

With these and similar verses of which there are many to be found in the Koran, God explains that the Koran itself is sufficient to make people believe in Mohammed's Mission and that He does not want to force them by means of awe-inspiring tokens. On the other hand He explains that the task of the Messenger amongst them is no more than to communicate his Mission, to admonish and to announce good tidings, a task that God has laid down in the Meccan part of the Koran, dating from the period that the Muslims were few in number and without any power, as well as in the Medinan part, dating from the period that the Muslims had acquired considerable strength and fortitude. To the Meccan part belong the following verses: [81:27–28]: *"It is naught but a Reminder unto all beings, for whosoever of you would go straight."* [88:21–26]: *"Then remind them! Thou art only a reminder; thou art not charged to oversee them. But he who turns his back, and disbelieves, God shall chastise him with the greatest chastisement. Truly, to Us is their return; then upon Us shall rest their reckoning."*

To the Medinan part belongs this verse: [24:54]: *"Say: 'Obey God, and obey the Messenger; then, if you turn away, only upon him rests what is laid on him, and upon you rests what is laid on you. If you obey him, you will be guided. It is only for the Messenger to deliver the manifest Message.'"*

There are many similar verses confirming and supporting this, explaining the task of the Messenger and his function in propagating God's religion. How remote all this is from the smell of compulsion! How strong is its aversion from the use of force as a means of propagating the Mission. Moreover, the Koran states clearly and distinctly that faith produced by force is without value and that he who yields to force and changes his faith loses his honour. He replied to Firʿawn (Pharaoh) when he was on the point of drowning and said [10:90–91]: *"[. . .when the drowning overtook him, he said,] 'I believe that there is no God but He in whom the Children of Israel believe; I am of those that surrender.' 'Now? And before thou didst rebel, being of those that did corruption.'"* [40:84–85]: *"Then, when they saw Our might, they said, 'We believe in God alone, and we disbelieve in that we were associating with Him.' But their belief when they saw Our might did not profit them—the wont of God, as in the past, touching His servants; then the unbelievers shall be lost."*

In the same way the Koran states that repentance cannot be accepted if it has been aroused by coercion or by imminent chastisement. [4:18]: *"But God shall not turn towards to those who do evil deeds until, when one of them is visited by death, he says, 'Indeed now I repent.'"*

When the Koran asserts, as you see, the futility of faith and repentance aroused by coercion, not having freely and peacefully been accepted by the heart, how then could anyone infer that the Koran would require or enforce coercion in matters of religion, regardless of which religion is concerned? [2:256]: *"No compulsion is there in religion. Rectitude has become clear from error. So whosoever disbelieves in idols and believes in God, has laid hold of the most firm handle, unbreaking; God is All-hearing, All-knowing."*

The foregoing has proved that there is absolutely no justification for anybody, whoever it may be, to hold or profess that one of the ways in which the Mission of Islam has been propagated, has been conversion by means of the sword or by fighting. We can summarize this chapter in the following conclusions:

1. In the nature of the Islamic Mission there is no complexity, obscurity or unintellegibility that would require the use of manifest or secret compulsion.*
2. The Islamic legislation, on the strength of the Book of God, is not in conflict with God's principle of creation, which accounts for the fact that some people believe whereas others do not. This principle consists in leaving people free to choose for themselves on the basis of examination and conviction.
3. The Islamic Legislation, also on the strength of the Book of God, rejects, in plain and unambiguous words, the use of compulsion as a means to propagate religion, as do the previous legislations.
4. The Prophet of Islam was responsible towards his Lord only in so far as his missionary task was concerned. This task has been expounded in both the Meccan and the Medinan parts

*(Note by Shaltūt): By manifest compulsion is meant compulsion by physical force like iron or fire; by secret compulsion is meant compulsion produced by perceptible miracles to which one submits.

of the Koran. It consisted in communicating the Mission and admonition. He was not responsible for the conversion of people, which might have induced compulsion and the use of force.**

5. God's Book, the source of the Islamic Mission, does not respect faith brought about by compulsion, and it denies its having any consequence on the Day of Resurrection. How then can it enjoin compulsion or allow the use of it as a means to conversion?

One may find these conclusions in the Koran itself. Believing in them is part of believing in the Koran. This being established, one may now ask: Given these conclusions of which the Koran speaks, what then is the significance of the verses of fighting in the Koran?

This will be our second topic.

3. The Verses of Fighting

In this chapter we shall expound the Verses of Fighting in the Koran, in order to understand their meaning and purpose and to learn their relation to one another. After that we shall arrive at a conclusion which, together with the conclusions reached in the preceding chapter, will elucidate those verses that order fighting.

The Koran is concerned with two kinds of fighting: the fighting of Muslims against Muslims and the fighting of Muslims against non-Muslims.

The first kind belongs to the internal affairs of the Islamic state *(umma)* and concerns only this state with the exclusion of any other state. The Koran deals with the event of rebellion and breach of public order, either between two groups of subjects or between subjects and rulers. It gives certain provisions for this event with a view to preserve the unity of the Islamic state *(umma)* and the power of and the respect for the ruling class, and to

**(Note by Shaltūt:) This was different from his responsibility or that of the Caliphs in applying his legislation on his community.

protect the community against the evils of rebellion and mutual hostility. These provisions are to be found in *Sūrat al-Ḥudjurāt* [49:9–10]: *"If two parties of the believers fight, put things right between them; then, if one of them is insolent against the other, fight the insolent one till it reverts to God's commandment. If it reverts, set things right between them equitably, and be just. Surely, God loves the just. The believers indeed are brothers; set things right between your brothers, and fear God; haply so you will find mercy."*

This verse assumes a case of disagreement between two groups of believers that cannot be solved by peaceful means, so that both groups resort to the use of force and leave the final decision to the sword. In this case it prescribes, that the Islamic state *(umma)* represented by its government, investigate the causes of discord and endeavour to set things right between the parties. If this can be attained by means of negotiations, and both parties obtain what is due to them so that rebellion is warded off and safety and peace prevail, then God saves the believers the trouble of fighting. However, if one of the parties continues to oppress the other, refuses to return to the affair of God and attacks the authority of the believers, then they have become rebels against the legal power and public order. In that case the community of Muslims is obliged to fight them until they submit and return to what is right. Further, this verse points out the secret of success in solving discord arising between different groups. This secret is that the return of one of the parties to what is right, should not be used as a means to oppress them or to deprive them of their rights. Instead, justice must prevail and each party must have its due. Consider the end of the verse [49:9]: *"Surely, God loves the just."* Furthermore the second verse teaches that what these provisions aim at is to preserve the unity and undivisibility of the Islamic state and to safeguard the religious brotherhood which is one of the most important matters of faith, for it reads [49:10]: *"The believers indeed are brothers; set things right between your brothers, and fear God; haply so you will find mercy."*

These wise Koranic provisions were revealed by the mouth of the illiterate[1] Prophet, as instruments to secure peace and in order to exterminate rebellion and aggression, more than thirteen centuries before the human mind invented what is called the

"League of Nations" or the "Security Council" to serve as a means of preservation of peace, consolidation of liberties and enjoyment by all states of their rights.

Had the nations understood these wise provisions with true understanding, had they given them the attention they deserve and had they followed their purport, then these nations would never have gone astray from the path of wisdom and they would have been saved from the frequent disasters caused by rebellion and aggression on the one hand and disagreement and discord on the other.

These are the rules the Koran gives with regard to fighting between Muslims. It is evident that they bear no relation whatsoever to the principles of the Islamic Mission and faith.

The second kind of fighting, viz. fighting between Muslims and non-Muslims, has been dealt with comprehensively in many Koranic verses and chapters. The Koran goes into the causes which may lead to it, its aim, upon the attainment of which fighting must stop, the obligatory preparations for it by the Muslims and the necessary caution against an unexpected outbreak of it. It treats of many provisions and regulations and enters upon connected subjects like armistices or treaties. In the following we shall discuss the verses dealing with the cause of fighting, and with the aim of fighting, upon the attainment of which the fighting must stop and finally we shall go into the relation between the Verses of Forgiveness and the Verses of Fighting.

In Mecca, the Muslims suffered for several years under the worst kinds of punishment, oppressed in their religious freedom, persecuted for the sake of the creed in which they found reassurance and terrorized with regard to property and personal safety. For all these reasons they were compelled to emigrate. They left their dwellings and settled in Medina, patiently submitting to God's orders and gladly accepting His authority. Whenever they felt the urge to resist the oppression and to revenge themselves on the oppressors, the Prophet held them back, bidding them to be patient in expectation of a command from God. "I have not been ordered to fight" he used to say. This lasted so long that they were almost overcome by desperation, and consequently by doubts and misgivings. And just then God revealed the first verses of fighting [22:39–41]: *"Leave is given to those who are fought because they were wronged—surely God is able to help them—who were expelled from their habitations without right, except that they say 'Our Lord is God.'*[2] *Had God not driven back the people, some by the means of others, there had been destroyed cloisters and churches, oratories and mosques, wherein God's name is much mentioned. Assuredly God will help him who helps Him—surely God is all-strong, all-mighty—who, if We establish them in the land, perform the prayer, and pay the alms, and bid to honour, and forbid dishonour; and unto God belongs the issue of all affairs."* These verses deal with the permission to fight. This permission was motivated by the fact that the Muslims suffered injustice and were forced to emigrate and to leave their dwellings without justification.

They then explain that this permission corresponds with the customary practice that people ward each other off so that a certain equilibrium is attained, oppression is averted, and adherents of the different creeds and cults can perform their religious observances and keep believing in the pure doctrine of monotheism. Finally these verses point out that God only helps those who help and fear Him and therefore do not use war as an instrument for destruction and corruption, for subjecting the weak and satisfying their own desires and lust, but cultivate the land when it falls into their hands, obey God's orders and summon people to do what is good and reputable and not to do what is disreputable and wicked. God distinguishes between those who act destructively and those who act constructively [22:41]: *"And unto God belongs the issue of all affairs."* These verses are, as we have said, the first Verses of Fighting. They are very clear and do not contain even the slightest evidence of religious compulsion. On the contrary, they confirm that the practice that people ward each other off is one of God's principles of creation, inevitable for the preservation of order and for the continuation of righteousness and civilization. Were it not for this principle, the earth would have been ruined and all the different places of worship would have been destroyed. This would have happened if powerful tyrants would have held sway over religions, free to abuse them without restraint and to force people to conversion, without anyone to interfere. These verses are not only concerned with Muslims, but have clearly a general impact [22:40]: "*(. . .) there had been destroyed cloisters and churches, oratories and mosques (. . .)*"

Let us now have a look at the Verses of Fighting that are to be found in *Sūrat al-Baqara* [2:190–194]: "*And fight in the way of God with those who fight you, but aggress not: God loves not the aggressors. And slay them wherever you come upon them, and expel them from where they expelled you; persecution is more grievous than slaying. But fight them not by the Holy Mosque until they should fight you there; then, if they fight you, slay them—such is the recompense of unbelievers—but if they give over, surely God is All-forgiving, All-compassionate. Fight them, till there is no persecution and the religion is God's; then if they give over, there shall be no enmity save for the evildoers. The holy month for the holy month; holy things demand retaliation. Whoso commits aggression against you, do you commit aggression against him like as he has committed against you; and fear you God, and know that God is with the godfearing.*"

These verses order the Muslims to fight in the way of God[3] those who fight them, to pursue them wherever they find them and to scatter them just as they had once scattered the Muslims. They prohibit the provocation of hostility and this prohibition is reinforced by God's repugnance to aggression and by his dislike of those who provoke hostility. Then they point out that expelling people from their homes, frightening them while they are safe and preventing them from living peacefully without fear for their lives or possessions is persecution worse than persecution by means of murder and bloodshed. Therefore those who practise or provoke these things must be fought just like those who actually fight. These verses also prohibit fighting in holy places or in holy periods, unless the Muslims are under attack. For if their sacred protection is violated and fighting becomes lawful for them, they are allowed to meet the hostility by the same means by way of retaliation. These points having been explained, the verses finally define the aim upon the attainment of which the war must end. This aim is accomplished when there is no more persecution in matters of religion, and religion is God's [cf. K 2:193 and 8:39], so that people obtain religious freedom and are not oppressed or tortured, because of their religion. As soon as this aim has been accomplished and people feel safe, fighting must cease.

In these verses and the principle they contain with regard to the reason and the aim of fighting, there is not a single trace to be found of any idea of conversion by force. On the contrary, these verses, like the previous ones, say in plain and distinct words that the reason for which the Muslims have been ordered to fight is the aggression directed against them, expulsion from their dwellings, violation of God's sacred institutions and attempts to persecute people for what they believe. At the same time they say that the aim upon the attainment of which Muslims must cease fighting is the termination of the aggression and the establishment of religious liberty devoted to God and free from any pressure or force.

The principles expounded in these verses can be found, in the same or similar words, in many other verses of fighting, e.g., in *Sūrat al-Nisāʾ*, *Sūrat al-Anfāl* and *Sūrat al-Tawba* [4:75]:

"How is it with you, that you do not fight in the way of God, and for the men, women, and children who, being abased, say, 'Our Lord, bring us forth from this city whose people are evildoers, and appoint to us a protector from Thee, and appoint to us from Thee a helper.'" [4:84]: *"So do thou fight in the way of God; thou art charged only with thyself. And urge on the believers; haply God will restrain the unbelievers' might; God is stronger in might, more terrible in punishing."* [4:90–91]: *"If they withdraw from you, and do not fight you, and offer you peace, then God assigns not any way to you against them (. . .). If they withdraw not from you, and offer you peace, and restrain their hands, take them, and slay them wherever you come on them."*

Read these verses and have a closer look at the following phrases: *"(. . .) haply God will restrain the unbelievers' might (. . .)"* and *"If they withdraw not from you, (. . .),"* then you will realize the spirit of persecution that the people harboured against the Muslims and on account of which the Muslims were ordered to fight. This is exactly the same principle as that which has been expounded in *Sūrat al-Baqara*, as we have seen, and we will find this principle also in *Sūrat al-Anfāl* [8:39]: *"Fight them until there is no persecution and the religion is God's entirely; then, if they give over, surely God sees the things they do,"* and in *Sūrat al-Tawba* [9:12–13]:

"But if they break their oaths after their covenant and thrust at your religion, then fight the leaders of unbelief; they have no sacred oaths; haply they will give over. Will you not fight a people who broke their oaths and purposed to expel the Messenger, beginning the first time against you? Are you afraid of them? You would do better to be afraid of God, if you are believers." And [9:36]: *"And fight the unbelievers totally even as they fight you totally; and know that God is with the godfearing."* Read these verses and consider firstly the phrase: *"But if they break their oaths after their covenant and thrust at your religion . . .",* then the phrase: *". . . beginning the first time against you . . ."* and finally the phrase: *". . . as they fight you totally . . ."* then you will realize that these verses were revealed with regard to people recalcitrantly practising persecution, amongst whom the elements of depravation were so deeply rooted that they did not respect pledges anymore and that virtue became meaningless to them. There is no doubt that to fight these people, to purify the earth from them and to put an end to their persecution, is to serve the commonweal and a benefaction to mankind as a whole.

After the aforementioned verses, we find in *Sūrat al-Tawba* two verses which, at first sight, seem to contain prescriptions contradicting the just mentioned principles concerning fighting. We shall quote them here and reveal their true meaning in the light of the previous verses which, because of their frequency and unequivocalness, must be considered fundamental with regard to the legality of fighting and the reasons for it. Therefore, other verses should be compared with the principles they contain and interpreted accordingly.

The first verse reads [9:29]: *"Fight those who believe not in God and the Last Day and do not forbid what God and His Messenger have forbidden—such men as practice not the religion of truth, being of those who have been given the Book—until they pay the tribute out of hand and have been humbled."* The second one goes [9:123]: *"O believers, fight the unbelievers who are near to you and let them find in you a harshness; and know that God is with the godfearing."* The first verse commands the Muslims to fight a certain group which is characterized by the fact that *"they do not believe in God etc."*. Previously they had broken their pledges and hindered and assailed the propagation of the Islamic Mission [cf. K 9:7–16]. These acts constitute for the Muslims reasons for fighting them. Therefore this verse does not say that the quality of being an unbeliever etc. constitutes a sufficient reason for fighting, but mentions the characteristics peculiar to them in order to give a factual description and as a further incitement to attack them once their aggression will have materialized. They modified the religion of God and took their scholars and monks for Lords apart from Him [cf. K 9:30], while making things allowed and forbidden according to their whims, since they did not accept that only God can do so. There was nothing to hold them back from breaking pledges, and violating rights, and they were not inclined to desist from aggression and tyranny.

These are the people which, according to this verse, must be fought continuously until, by being thoroughly subjected, they can do no more harm and will desist from the persecution they used to practise. The Koran introduced a special token for this submission, viz. the payment of poll-tax *(jizya)*, which means that they actually participate in carrying the burdens of the state and providing the means for the commonweal, both for Muslims and non-Muslims.*

Two phrases in this verse indicate the reason for fighting which we have already pointed out. These phrases are: *"and have been humbled"* and *"out of hand"*. They determine the state wherein they will come when poll-tax *(jizya)* is collected from them, viz. a state of submission to the authority of the Muslims and subjec-

*(Note by Shaltūt:) Poll-tax *(jizya)* is not, as some people think, a sum paid in return for the right to refuse conversion to Islam or in return for their lives. It is, as we have said, a symbol for their submission and for their desistance from fighting and impeding the Islamic Mission, and a token of their participation in the affairs of the state, which grants them protection of their lives and property. Abū Yūsuf[4] mentioned in his *Kitāb al-Kharāj*, p. 35: "After Abū ʿUbaydah[5] had concluded a peace treaty with the people of Syria and had collected poll-tax *(jizya)* and land-tax *(kharāj)* from them, he was informed that the Byzantines were raising troups against him and that the situation had become critical for him and the Muslims. He then wrote to the governors of those cities with which a treaty had been concluded that they must return the poll-tax *(jizya)* and the land-tax *(kharāj)* they had collected and say to them: "We return to you your property since we have been informed that troops are being raised against us. You have stipulated that we should protect you, whereas now we are not able to do so. We now return what we have taken from you, but we will abide by the stipulation and what has been written down, if God grants us victory over them."

tion to their laws. There is no doubt that this implies that previously they had been recalcitrant and that there had been reasons for the Muslims to fight them. This is how this verse is to be understood. This interpretation is supported by the context and brings this verse in agreement with the other verses. For if this verse had meant that they must be fought because of their unbelief and that unbelief had been the reason why they should be fought, then it would have been laid down that the aim of fighting then consisted in their conversion to Islam. Collecting poll-tax *(jizya)* from them would not have been allowed in that case and they would not have been allowed abide by their own religion.

The second verse: *"fight the unbelievers that are near to you"* is not to be compared with the previous verses because those verses indicate the reason and motive for fighting, whereas this verse has been revealed as a directive for a practical war plan, to be followed when legitimate fighting actually breaks out. Thus it informs the Muslims that, when the enemies are manifold, it is imperative to fight the nearest first of all, then the nearest but one and so on, in order to clear the road from enemies and to facilitate the victory.*

This principle, formulated by the Koran, is still being followed today by belligerent states, for attacking states do not advance unless they have cleared the roads before them and are sure that there are no more obstacles in their way. Thus it is clear that these two verses have no link with the reason for fighting, as formulated by the other verses.

---

*(Note by Shaltūt:) Some people who were bent on disparaging Islam did not go beyond the ostensible interpretation of ". . .*fight the unbelievers that are near to you* . . ." and pretended that the Islamic religion ordered to fight the unbelievers in general, regardless of whether they had committed aggression or not, until they had been converted to Islam. They said that this rule was founded on this verse. However, the meaning of the word "unbelievers" in this and similar verses is: "those hostile polytheists who fight the Muslims, commit aggression against them, expel them from their homes and their property and practise persecution for the sake of religion." The morals of these polytheists have been discussed in the opening verses of *Sūrat al-Tawba*. The word "people" in the tradition: *"I have been ordered to fight the people"*[6] should be understood in the same manner. For according to the Consensus *(ijmāʿ)*, fighting must only cease at what is mentioned in this tradition if the enemies are Arab polytheists.[7] As for other enemies, the war against them must cease on the condition that they *"pay the tribute out of hand and have been humbled."* If this interpretation is accepted, the different verses are in agreement, there is no contradiction left between the Koran and the Tradition and the aforementioned false allegation has been disposed of.

From the preceding words one may infer:

1. That there is not a single verse in the Koran which could support the opinion that the aim of fighting in Islam is conversion;

2. That, as explained by the verses mentioned above, there are only three reasons for fighting, viz. to stop aggression, to protect the Mission of Islam and to defend religious freedom;

3. That in giving its prescriptions for fighting, the Koran did not admit of avidity, selfishness and humiliation of the poor as motives for it, but intended it as an instrument for peace and tranquillity and for a life founded on justice and equality.

4. That poll-tax (*jizya*) is not a financial compensation for the granting of one's life or preservation of one's own religion, but a symbol of submission and desistance from harmful acts and a contribution in carrying the burdens of the state.

After this exposé nobody can vilify Islam anymore or misinterpret the Koranic verses and maintain as some ignoramuses have done, that Islam has taken up fighting as a means of propagating its Mission and as an instrument for conversion, and that its Mission and creed were founded on and propagated by suppression and the use of force.

Here we shall cite a verse from *Sūrat al-Mumtaḥina* which may be considered as an Islamic charter concerning the relations between Muslims and non-Muslims [60:8]: *"God forbids you not, as regards those who have not fought you in religion's cause, nor expelled you from your habitations, that you should be kindly to them, and act justly towards them; surely God loves the just."*

Read this charter and then turn your attention to *Sūrat al-Māʾida,* one of the parts of the Koran that were revealed most recently. There you may read the following with regard to the relations between Muslims and non-Muslims [5:5]: *"Today the good things are permitted to you, and the food of those who were given the Book is permitted to you, and permitted to them is your food. Likewise believing women in wedlock, and in wedlock women of them who were given the Book before you if you give them their wages, in wedlock and not in license. Whoso disbelieves in the faith, his work has failed, and in the world to come he shall be among the losers."*

Read all this and you will know the lofty spirit of righteousness, equity, co-operation and affinity that Islam cherishes with regard to its relations with non-Muslims. It is a kind of relationship so magnificent that, compared with it the most modern principle known to the human mind in international relations wanes into insignificance.

4. The Connection Between the Verses of Forgiveness and the Verses of Fighting

In this treatise we cannot pass over a problem that has occupied the minds of many people while examining the Koran and comparing its verses. These people fall into two categories:

A group of adversaries of the Religion, who look for arguments against it in the Koran itself.

A group of Koran-interpreters whom religious zeal has driven to harmonize between supposed inconsistencies within the Koran and who are inclined to consider some verses as having abrogated other verses. Some of them let themselves be carried away to such an extent that they seem to have prepared the road, unintentionally, for attacks by adversaries of the Religion. As for the adversaries, they have examined the relations between the different Verses of Fighting and between the Verses of Fighting as a whole and the Verses of Pardon and Forgiveness. They then said: Whereas you see that some verses of fighting only allow fighting, there are others that make it incumbent to urge on to it. And whereas you see that some of these verses order to fight aggressors and forbid to commit aggression, there are other verses that order to fight them all without mercy and clemency and without distinguishing between aggressors and others. And whereas you see that these verses as a whole order to fight and regulate fighting, there are many other verses to be found in all chapters of the Koran, instructing to be forgiving, to counter evil with good and to summon to God with wisdom [cf. K 16:125]. All these, allegedly, are inconsistencies incompatible with the fact that the Koran of Mohammed is a divine revelation, disclosed to him by God. As for the Koran-interpreters, they hold that the Verses of

Fighting have abrogated the Verses of Forgiveness and Pardon, even verses like [41:34]: *"Not equal are the good deed and the evil deed. Repel with that which is fairer."* and [16:125]: *"Call thou to the way of thy Lord with wisdom and good admonition and dispute with them in the better way."*

They claim that verse 36 of *Sūrat al-Tawba* (chapter 9): *"And fight the unbelievers totally even as they fight you totally"* has abrogated the preceding Verses of Forgiveness. One of their most peculiar opinions is that the phrase *"And slay them wherever you come upon them"* in the end of verse 191 of *Sūrat al-Baqara* (chapter 2) abrogates the immediately preceding one: *"And fight in the way of God with those who fight you"* and also that verse 193 of the same chapter: *"Fight them, till there is no persecution"* abrogates the following words of verse 191: *"But fight them not by the Holy Mosque until they should fight you there"*.

This pericope, occurring in *Sūrat al-Baqara* and consisting of four verses, thus becomes a pericope containing two abrogating and two abrogated verses: the second has abrogated the first and the fourth the third. Al-Rāzī[8] has said in his exegesis on the Koran, commenting on this view: "It is improbable that the Wise One brings some verses together in pairs of which one verse abrogates the other." It is not improbable that this interpretation has paved the way for the opinion of the adversaries of the Religion, namely that the Koran is inconsistent. They do not accept the notions of abrogation as claimed by the commentators and how can they accept it from us while even some of our own scholars do not. After this exposé you will probably realize that there is no contradiction or incompatibility between the different verses of fighting and no room for opinions that some of them have been abrogated by others, since abrogation may only be applied when there is a contradiction. These verses are therefore fixed and unassailable. They all amount to the same thing and establish one and the same rule, one and the same reason and one and the same end.

As for the Verses of Forgiveness and Pardon, they are meant to shape morality. They are valid within their own range as long as they do not infringe on pride and honour. As there is a separate legislation for every situation, these verses are also fixed and unassailable.

Legislation based upon consideration for different situations, and for the different conditions of individuals and groups, a legislation that requires of people that they follow in every situation that which is most suitable, cannot be accused of being an inconsistent legislation or of being a legislation of which one part abrogates the other. People with common sense will consider it as a wise and extremely precise legislation that promotes the interest of those who fall under its authority and that will realize its ultimate aim viz. happiness of the individual and the community.

5. The Verses Concerning the Organisation of Fighting

One of the conclusions arrived at in the first part was that there are only three reasons for fighting, viz. repelling aggression, protecting the Mission of Islam and defending religious freedom. Only in these cases has God made fighting lawful and urged on to it. He revealed many prescriptions and rules that guarantee victory. In this chapter we will expound the verses that deal from this angle with fighting.

If one studies these verses of God's Book, one will discover that they lay down general principles for the Muslims, constituting a handbook for warfare ranking very high among similar institutions of modern civilization.

A handbook for warfare for a nation that wants to acquire pride and honor, must be based upon three elementary considerations:

1. Strengthening the morale of the nation;
2. Preparation of material force;
3. The practical aspects of warfare.

In outlining how people can live a good life, the Koran also deals with these three elementary considerations. This is done in a manner which comprises everything that human skill has produced in different ages and varying cultures; it is not restricted to one age but leaves room for new institutions and instruments. Powerful and extensive as this method is, it dominates the hearts of the people, fills them with notions of mercy and compassion and provides them with the spirit of loyalty and a desire for God's approval in purifying the earth from corruption and clearing it from tyranny and aggression. You will find that these notions are represented in all of these three elements.

The first element, viz. strengthening the morale of the nation.

The Koran says [4:74–76]: *"So let them fight in the way of God who sell the present life for the world to come; and whosoever fights in the way of God and is slain, or conquers, We shall bring him a mighty wage. How is it with you, that you do not fight in the way of God, and for the men, women, and children who, being abased, say, 'Our Lord, bring us forth from this city whose people are evildoers, and appoint to us a protector from Thee, and appoint to us from Thee a helper. The believers fight in the way of God, and the unbelievers fight in the idols' way. Fight you therefore against the friends of Satan; surely the guile of Satan is ever feeble."* These words mobilize the fighting spirit by saying that it is fighting in the way of God, who doubles the reward of the human beings and the reward for those who struggle *(mujāhidūn)*; that it is fighting for the sake of the weak, for the sake of righteousness towards one's fellowmen, for the sake of resistance against tyranny and despotism; and that it is fighting to suppress evil and corruption.

The Koran also says [9:19–21]: *"Do you reckon the giving of water to pilgrims and the inhabiting of the Holy Mosque as the same as one who believes in God and the Last Day and struggles in the way of God? Not equal are they in God's sight; and God guides not the people of the evildoers. Those who believe, and have emigrated, and have struggled in the way of God with their possessions and their selves are mightier in rank with God; and those—they are the triumphant; their Lord gives them good tidings of mercy from Him and good pleasure; for them await gardens wherein is lasting bliss, therein to dwell forever and ever; surely with God is a mighty wage."* Read this verse and repeat it a few times for yourself. Turn your attention to the words: *"Surely with God is a mighty wage."* Then you will know that for those who struggle in person or with their money in the way of God the reward is unlimited, and cannot be comprehended but by the Great Exalted One who knows all things, visible and unvisible.

The Koran also says [9:111]: "*God has bought from the believers their selves and their possessions against the gift of Paradise; they fight in the way of God; they kill and are killed; that is a promise binding upon God in the Torah, the Gospel, and the Koran; and who fulfills the covenant truer than God? So rejoice in the bargain you have made with Him; that is the mighty triumph.*"

With these words it reminds them of the Divine Promise that He has taken upon Him on behalf of those who struggle on His way. This Promise He has announced in all His Books. Now He presents it in the form of a contract between buyer and seller that implies obligations for both parties. It assures them that in complying with the obligations of this Promise and in sacrifices made in order to keep it, there is ultimate bliss.

Another verse goes [9:24]: "*Say: 'If your fathers, your sons, your brothers, your wives, your clan, your possessions that you have gained, commerce you fear may slacken, dwellings you love—if these are dearer to you than God and His Messenger, and to struggle in His way, then wait till God brings His command; God guides not the people of the ungodly.*"

This verse comprises all factors that may lead to cowardice and weakness and it demands that all believers sacrifice themselves on the way of God and Truth, for the sake of welfare and happiness. For neither fathers, sons, brethren, wives or clan, nor the properties, which have been paid for with comfort and happiness, nor the trade that he fears to decline or the dwellings that are dear to him, nothing of all this may come between the believer and the sacrifices and struggle that the love for God and His Messenger demands of him [49:15]: "*The believers are those who believe in God and His Messenger, then have not doubted, and have struggled with their possessions and their selves in the way of God; those—they are the truthful ones.*" Therefore, the true creed consists of believing in God and His Messenger with a faith that is above all doubts and uncertainty and requires the sacrifice of one's life and property in the struggle on the way of God. In this powerful manner, which often occurs in the Koran, God fights the factors of weakness and the attitudes of fear and inspires the souls of the Community with sentiments of courage, sacrifice and contempt for the vanities of this world, in order to attain Truth and its victory.

Just as the Koran, in general, seeks to inspire the souls of the Community with these sentiments, and thus tries to create men that are strong in spirit and heart, it strives especially to inspire with these feelings the souls of the strugglers themselves. Speaking of those strugglers that have attained victory and success in the past, it says [2:249–51]: *"How often a little company has overcome a numerous company, by God's leave! And God is with the patient. So when they went forth against Goliath and his hosts, they said, 'O Lord, pour out upon us patience, and make firm our feet, and give us aid against the people of the unbelievers. And they routed them, by the leave of God, and David slew Goliath; and God gave him the kingship and wisdom, and He taught him such as He willed."*

And addressing the Prophet and reminding him of his role in encouraging the strugglers, in exhorting them to be audacious and firm, and in assuring them of the existence of God in such a way that they could be confident, it says [3:124–26]: *"When thou saidst to the believers, 'Is it not enough for you that your Lord should reinforce you with three thousand angels sent down upon you? Yea; if you are patient and godfearing, and the foe comes against you instantly, your Lord will reinforce you with five thousand swooping angels.' God wrought this not, save as good tiding to you, and that your hearts might be at rest; help comes only from God the All-mighty, the All-wise."* And also [3:139–42]: *"Faint not, neither sorrow; you shall be the upper ones, if you are believers. If a wound touches you, a like wound already has touched the heathen; such days We deal out in turn among men, and that God may know who are the believers, and that He may take witnesses from among you; and God loves not the evildoers; and that God may prove the believers, and blot out the unbelievers. Or did you suppose you should enter Paradise without God know[ing] who of you have struggled and who are patient?"*

It belittles what may befall them in the way of God and instructs them that faith gives an unbending power and an unweakening resolution, that God's practice consists in giving alternately success to both parties, but that the ultimate victory belongs to those who are patient [4:104]: *"Faint not in seeking the heathen; if you are suffering, they are also suffering as you are suffering, and you are hoping from God for that which they cannot hope; God is All-knowing, All-wise."*

These are but few of the many things that can be said regarding the strengthening influence of the Koran on the morale of the Community in general and the strugglers in particular.

The second element, viz. preparation of material power.

The Koran says: [8:60]: *"Make ready for them whatever force and strings of horses you can, to terrify thereby the enemy of God and your enemy." and* [4:102]: *"The unbelievers wish you should be heedless of your weapons and your baggage, then they would wheel on you all at once."* The first verse points out two things that are very important in the life of nations, force and *"ribāṭ."* Force depends on number and equipment. The word force can be used for all implements of war and transportation and for all kinds of supply. The word *"ribāṭ"* can be used for anything that reinforces frontier posts. This verse also explains how peace and stability are promoted by preparation, because by that the enemy is so frightened that he will not get the idea of taking advantage of some weak spot. As for the second verse, it points out that one has to be on one's guard and take precautions lest the enemy unexpectedly start a surprise attack on them.

Instructions of the Koran Concerning the Benefit to be Derived From Iron and Factories

In this connection we ought not to miss the opportunity of quoting the following unique and significant verse, which draws attention to the force that can be derived from iron, a force that strengthens the power of the believers, necessary for keeping and preparing their rights. This verse goes [57:25]: *"Indeed, We sent Our Messengers with the clear signs, and We sent down with them the Book and the Balance so that men might uphold justice. And We sent down iron, wherein is great might, and many uses for men, and so that God might know who helps Him, and His Messengers in the Unseen. Surely, God is All-strong, All-mighty."*

Look how He linked together the Book, the Balance and Iron by the fact that they had all been revealed and how to Iron, by means of which the Balance can stand up and justice can be maintained, he ascribed these two characteristics: violent force and great utility. Think of this and then have a look at what the implements for war at sea, on land and in the air are made of. Is there not iron in all these implements? Then consider the words that follow: *". . .and so that God might know who helps Him, and His Messengers in the Unseen"* and you will know that the assistance of God is granted to those who have subjected the Iron and who have won power and strength from it.

If the Muslims recognize the value of God's favour in providing them and all mankind with iron, which He revealed, they should also recognize the favour he bestowed upon Dā'ūd (David) in disclosing to him the ways of using this material. God has told us this story in His Book in order that we may derive lessons from it. Read these words in *Sūrat Saba'* [34:10–11]: *"And We gave David bounty from Us: 'O you mountains, echo God's praises with him and you birds!' And We softened for him iron: 'Fashion wide coats of mail, and measure well the links.'"* And *"And do ye righteousness, for surely I see the things you do."* Read then how God bestowed favour upon Sulaymān (Solomon), in the verses 12 and 13 of the same chapter [34:12–13]: *"And to Solomon the wind; its morning course was a month's journey, and its evening course was a month's journey. And We made the Fount of Molten Brass to flow for him. And of the jinn, some worked before him by the leave of his Lord; and such of them as swerved away from Our commandment, We would let them taste the chastisement of the Blaze; fashioning for him, whatsoever he would—places of worship, statues, porringers like water-troughs, and anchored cooking pots. 'Labour, O House of David, in thankfulness, for few indeed are those that are thankful among My servants.'"**

Here we should quote the words of al-Rāzī in his exegesis of verses 30–33 of *Sūrat Sād* [38:30–33]: *"And We gave unto David*

*(Note by Shaltūt:) This verse informs us that Sulaymān's (Solomon) factories produced palaces and their utensils like bowls and pots, and that they produced images. The word "images" has found many explanations. One of them is that they made them like animals, underneath the throne and that they moved mechanically at the ascent (of the throne). Al-Alūsi[9] has said: "Human skills have attained this amount of strangeness."

Solomon; how excellent a servant he was! He was a penitent. When in the evening were presented to him the standing steeds, he said, 'Lo, I have loved the love of good things better than the remembrance of my Lord, until the sun was hidden behind the veil. Return them to me!' And he began to stroke their shanks and necks.", so that you will know that the use of cavalry *(ribāṭ)* is very ancient and was customary in the oldest civilizations, those with the best equipment and the strongest ideas. Al-Rāzī says: "The use of cavalry *(ribāṭ al-khayl)* had been recommended in their religions, just as it is in the religion of Mohammed. Once Sulaymān (Solomon) had to go on a raid. He ordered horses to be brought and put into a gallop. Then he observed that he did not like it because of wordly things or personal profit, but that he liked it because God ordered him to do so in order to strengthen his religion. That is the meaning of the words: *"than the remembrance of my Lord"*. Then Sulaymān (Solomon) ordered to put them into a gallop and make them run until they would disappear behind the curtain, i.e. pass out of sight. He then ordered the trainers to lead those horses back to him. When they had returned he began to stroke their legs and their necks. The purpose of this stroking was as follows: 1. to honour the horses and to show how high their rank was, as they belong to the most important helpers in repelling the enemy; 2. to show that in governing and pursuing his policy he humbled himself to such a degree that he himself carried out even the lowest duties; 3. to demonstrate that he was the greatest expert concerning horses, their diseases and their defects, for he was examining them and touching their legs and necks in order to investigate whether there were symptoms of some disease. . . ." Another verse regarding crafts and their usefulness to nations is to be found in the story about God's prophet Nūḥ (Noah) [11:37]: *"Make thou the Ark under Our eyes and at Our suggestion."* These are life-boats. Just as nations need life-boats, they are also in want of ships for defence and attack, ships for the transportation of merchandise and all other purposes required by the exigencies of progress of the nations. God has said [16:14]: *"It is He who subjected to you the sea, that you may eat of it fresh flesh, and bring forth out of it ornaments for you to wear; and thou mayest see the ships cleaving through it; and that you may seek of His bounty, and so haply* *you will be thankful."* As long as the Muslims do not occupy themselves with the teachings of their religion and the instruction of their Book, in order to understand and to observe them, they will continue to live a contemptible life full of hardship, deficient in power and strength.*

The third element, viz. the practical aspects of warfare.

The Koran deals with the general principles of this topic from numerous angles.

1. Regarding the reasons for exemption from military service the Koran says [9:91]: *"There is no fault in the weak and the sick and those who find nothing to expend, if they are true to God and His Messenger. There is no way against the good-doers—God is All-forgiving, All-compassionate—."* Thus it restricts the reasons of exemption to frailty, which may be caused by incapacity or old age, to sickness and to the inability to contribute. The Koran does not include among them the fact that one is a university graduate or student or that one has learnt the Koran by heart, that one has paid a financial compensation, nor that one is the son of a man of authority, be it great or small. All these things have become customary in our days of weakness and decay, contrary to the practice in the days of the Prophet and in the following era. The idea of compiling the Koran had been born by fear lest the knowledge of the Koran should vanish with the extinction of the reciters *(qurrāʾ),* for they were the most audacious and intrepid fighters in the war of al-Yamāma[10] and because of their boldness and courage in storming the ranks of the enemy many of them were killed.

2. Regarding declaration of war, the Koran gives warning against attacking the enemy unawares and gives the following rule [8:58]: *"And if thou fearest treachery any way at the hands of a people, dissolve it with them equally; surely God loves not the treacherous."* This verse orders to denounce treaties when wickedness is

*(Note by Shaltūt:) As the preparation of force depends on money, many verses insist on spending money in the path of God. E.g. [8:60]: *"And whatsoever you expend in the way of God shall be repaid to you in full; you will not be wronged"*. This means that it will be repaid in full by means of concentration of your force in your country and conquest of the country of your enemies. Another verse says [2:195]: *"And expend in the way of God; and cast not yourselves by your own hands into destruction."* where destruction means destruction by thrift and avarice regarding national defence.

feared from the enemy and prescribes that this denunciation should be clear and explicit lest the Muslims commit treachery, of which God disapproves and which He does not accept.

3. As regards the call to jihad, it warns against tardiness and sluggishness [9:38–39]: *"O believers, what is amiss with you, that when it is said to you, 'Go forth in the way of God,' you sink down heavily to the ground? Are you so content with this present life, rather than the world to come? Yet the enjoyment of this present life, compared with the world to come, is a little thing. If you go not forth, He will chastise you with a painful chastisement, and instead of you He will substitute another people; and you will not hurt Him anything, for God is powerful over everything."* It admonishes them that if they are sluggish in answering the call to jihad they will suffer a painful punishment, a punishment that consists in humiliation and subjugation and in the transfer of power and authority to another people.

4. As regards the purging of the army from dissenting and dissatisfied elements it says [9:47–50]: *"Had they gone forth among you, they would only have increased you in trouble, and run to and fro in your midst, seeking to stir up sedition between you; and some of you would listen to them; and God knows the evildoers. They sought to stir up sedition already before, and turned things upside down for thee, until the truth came, and God's command appeared, though they were averse. Some of them there are that say, 'Give me leave and do not tempt me.' Have not such men fallen into temptation? And surely Gehenna encompasses the unbelievers. If good fortune befalls thee, it vexes them; but if thou art visited by an affliction, they say, 'We took our dispositions before,' and turn away rejoicing."* And also [9:57]: *"If they could find a shelter, or some caverns, or any place to creep into, they would turn about and bolt away to it."* [9:83]: *"So, if God returns thee to a party of them and they ask leave of thee to go forth, say: 'You shall not go forth with me ever, and you shall not fight with me any enemy. You were well-pleased to tarry the first time, so now tarry with those behind.'"* And finally [9:96]: *"They will swear to you by God, that you may be well-pleased with them; but if you are well-pleased with them, God will surely not be well-pleased with the people of the ungodly."* If you study the verses revealed in connection with the Tabūk-campaign[11] in *Sūrat al-Tawba* (chapter 9), you will discover the bad

characteristics that are evidence of an abominable army and you will find things that deserve special attention during a period of mobilization and preparation of strength in order to obtain victory. Read then in *Sūrat al-Aḥzāb* (chapter 33), verse 12 to 20, from [33:12]: *"And when the hypocrites, and those in whose hearts is sickness, said. . . ."* until [33:20]: *"If they were among you, they would fight but little."*[12] in order to know more about the peculiarities of deserters.

5. As regards organizing the mobilization, the Koran points out that mobilization should be in proportion to the needs. If necessity calls for the participation of everybody, then everybody must set out. If partial participation will do, then it is sufficient for only a part to set out, whereas the rest may continue their normal domestic activities and serve as reserve troops for the army. This principle is to be found in the verse [9:123]: *"It is not for the believers to go forth totally; but why should not a party of every section of them go forth, to become learned in religion, and to warn their people when they return to them, that haply they may beware."*[13] and in: [4:71]: *"O believers, take your precautions; then move forward in companies, or move forward all together."*

6. As regards the organization of the army and the distribution of its unities over the positions of defence, look at what the prophet did, as it has been related in the verse [3:121]: *"When thou wentest forth at dawn from thy people to lodge the believers in their pitches for the battle"* and consider next [61:4]: *"God loves those who fight in His way in ranks, as though they were a building well-compacted."*

7. As regards the obedience to the supreme command, the observance of battle-order, the avoidance of factors leading to failure and the safeguarding of a strong faith, the Koran says [8:45–46]: *"O believers, whensoever you encounter a host, then stand firm, and remember God frequently; haply you will proper. And obey God, and His Messenger, and do not quarrel together, and so lose heart, and your power depart; and be patient; surely God is with the patient."**

---

*(Note by Shaltūt:) If, in order to unify the nation and to guard it from failure, the imam deems it appropriate to suspend normal public law and to lay down special rules for this situation, it is compulsory for him to do, since, in this case, it is a means of attaining something that is obligatory. In our times this principle is known as the proclamation of martial law.

8. As regards flight from the battle order, the Koran warns against it and foretells the evil outcome [8:15–16]: *"O believers, when you encounter the unbelievers marching to battle, turn not your backs to them. Whosoever turns his back that day to them, unless withdrawing to fight again or removing to join another host, he is laden with the burden of God's anger, and his refuge is Gehenna—an evil homecoming!"*

9. As regards the order of attack when there are numerous enemies, the Koran requires that the nearest be first attacked, then the next nearest and so forth, in order to clear the road for the army from any hostile obstacle [9:123]: *"O believers, fight the unbelievers who are near to you and let them find in you a harshness; and know that God is with the godfearing."*

10. As regard military secrets, the Koran warns against divulging them, because it considers this as one of the characteristics of the Hypocrites *(al-munāfiqūn).* It prescribes that secrets must be kept by the supreme command and that believers, if they hear any news, must verify it before they rely on it and act on the strength of it. It says [33:60]: *"Now, if the hypocrites do not give over, and those in whose hearts there is sickness and they that make commotion in the city, We shall assuredly urge thee against them and then they will be thy neighbors there only a little"*; [8:27]: *"O believers, betray not God and the Messenger, and betray not your trusts and that wittingly"*; [4:83]: *"When there comes to them a matter, be it of security or fear, they broadcast it; if they had referred it to the messenger and to those in authority among them, those whose task it is to investigate would have known the matter. And but for the bounty of God to you, and his mercy, you would surely have followed Satan, except a few"*; and finally [49:6]: *"O believers, if an ungodly man comes to you with a tiding, make clear."*

11. As regards truce and peace treaties, the Koran orders to respond to a call for peace and termination of war if the enemy is inclined to it and if they show signs of sincerity and fidelity [8:61–62]: *"And if they incline to peace, do thou incline to it; and put thy trust in God; He is the All-bearing, the All-knowing. And if they desire to trick thee, God is sufficient for thee; He has confirmed thee with His help, and with the believers."*

12. As regards captivity and the treatment of prisoners of

war, the Koran says [8:67]: *"It is not for any Prophet to have prisoners until he make wide slaughter in the land."*

When the Imam has caused havoc in the land and when the taking of captives has been allowed to him, he may choose between liberating them out of kindness without any ransom or compensation and taking ransom from them, which may consist of property or men. The choice must be made on the basis of what he sees as the common interest. [47:4]: *"When you meet the unbelievers, smite their necks, then, when you have made wide slaughter among them, tie fast the bonds; then set them free, either by grace or ransom."*

13. As regards treaties and the observance of them, the Koran gives special attention to the observance of treaties, prescribing to pay heed to them and forbidding treason and violation of them. It teaches that the aim of treaties is to replace disorder and war by safety and peace and it warns against using them as an artful means to deprive the other party of its rights or to oppress the weak. Consider the words of the Exalted in *Sūrat al-Naḥl* [16:91–92]: *"Fulfil God's covenant, when you make covenant, and break not the oaths after they have been confirmed, and you have made God your surety; surely God knows the things you do. And be not like a woman who breaks her thread, after it is firmly spun into fibres, by taking your oaths as mere mutual deceit, one nation being more numerous than another nation. God only tries you thereby; and certainly He will make clear to you upon the Day of Resurrection that whereon you were at variance."**

14. When the Imam realizes that the Muslims will come to harm on account of treaties and that this harm will exceed the advantages to be gained by observing them, he is obliged to denounce them. This denunciation must be openly declared. Read

---

*(Note by Shaltūt:) This verse warns against breach of treaties or the conclusion of them in such a way that not all the parties concerned feel safe; for then these parties will remain dependent on force and force is ignorant of peace or justice. It also warns against using them as an artful means to plunder the weak, who are compelled by circumstances to consent to them. History teaches that these treaties are immoral and ill-fated. [16:94]: *"Take not your oaths as mere mutual deceit, lest any foot should slip after it has stood firm, and you should taste evil, for that you barred from the way of God, and lest there should await you a mighty chastisement."* Compare then the teachings of this verse with the treaties concluded by modern civilized nations, which are sources of calamities to the world. May those endowed with insight take this to heart (cf. K 59:2).

the words of the Exalted at the beginning of *Sūrat al-Tawba* [9:3]: *"A proclamation, from God and His Messenger, unto mankind on the day of the Greater Pilgrimage: 'God is quit, and His Messenger, of the idolaters.'"*

These are the principles concerning the practical aspects of warfare which we were able, in our time, to derive from the verses of the Holy Koran. However, as the treasures of the Holy Koran are never exhausted, Man, whenever he will investigate its significations and examine its meanings, will arrive at something new. The best aid for the understanding of the Holy Koran are current events and historical facts, for they are the best interpreters and the clearest road to comprehension of its purposes and its principles. If one studies the military activities of the Prophet contained in it, one will grasp many of these purposes and principles. This will strengthen the believers in their conviction that the Koran is nothing but a revelation, revealed by the Creator of all powers who is cognizant of the intentions of the souls.

6. The Practical Application of the Koranic Prescriptions Concerning Fighting

In this epilogue we shall present the practical application of the principles expounded by the Koran, during the epoch of the Prophet and his two Successors, Abū Bakr and ʿUmar. Later the Muslims were afflicted by internal and external events that prevented them from observing God's prescriptions and laws and compelled them, especially where fighting was concerned, to adopt a practice of a much wider range than that which God had prescribed for the jihad in His way.

The stages in the lives of the Prophet and the believers who were with him, are the following:

1. The secret Mission, which a small group of people believed in. They were associated with the Prophet by close ties of family relationship or friendship, which revealed to them the sublime spirit and the excellent character of the Prophet.

2. The public Mission directed to his clan and then to all mankind.

3. The period of negotiations during which the Meccans tried to tempt the Prophet to desist from propagating his Message in exchange for as much property, power and sovereignty as he wished.

4. The period of violence and oppression. History has recorded bloodcurdling instances of torture.

5. The period of Emigration to Ethiopia in order to save the Religion and to rescue lives.

6. The period of artful tricks and plots and conspirations against the Prophet, the Muslims and even against all Banū ʿAbd Manāf[14] in order to prompt the latter to deliver the Messenger and his companions, and not to protect them from the aggression of the Polytheists. One of these actions was the boycott of the people of Abū Ṭālib,[15] which had grave consequences for the Muslims and which—were it not for the affair of God—nearly broke their spirit of resistance.

7. The period of seeking refuge in al-Ṭāʾif, where Thaqīf[16] was asked for help, who then met the Prophet and his company with mockery and derision and drove them back to where they came from.

8. The period of the Emigration *(Hijra)* to Medina. This had been prepared for by delegations that had visited the Prophet and by the pains taken by him to explain the Mission to the tribes. Both factors propagated the Mission with its inherent loftiness and splendour so that it won partisans amongst the Medinan youth who promised the Messenger that they would propagate and protect the Mission until death. One of the consequences of this Emigration was that the fury and rancour of the polytheists increased as the opportunity to assassinate Mohammed escaped them, because they had gone to great efforts to attain it.

9. The period of enmity between the Muslims and the Jews in Medina. No sooner had the Messenger settled down there or it appeared that the Jews, whom he thought to be in favour of his Mission because they were People of the Book *(Ahl al-Kitāb)* and because they had previously asked his assistance in their wars against the Polytheists, denied his Mission and hatched

plots against him and his companions. This induced him to extend his hand to them in order to prevent civil strife. He concluded a pact with them to the effect that he would leave them and their religion alone. By this treaty he felt to some extent safer. He then directed his concern and efforts to his original enemies who, after his Emigration, were pouring out their venom on his brothers who were prevented to emigrate because of their material circumstances, and who kept waiting for opportunities to oppose this mission and to scatter its adherents.

10. The period of provocation. The Prophet foresaw that unless he would take pains to propagate his Mission in Medina, which in fact was the task entrusted to him by his Lord, the Meccans would inevitably find a way to penetrate his new town and attack him by surprise, especially since the Jews with whom he had concluded a treaty were not so sincere that he could trust them to keep their pledge. It was not improbable that they would open up opportunities in Medina for the enemy outside and that they would subsequently join forces in order to expel the believers from Medina, as they had previously been expelled from Mecca.

For all these reasons the Messenger and his companions prepared themselves for resistance of those who opposed him and his Mission, the people of Mecca. He engaged in skirmishes with them and showed them his strength and his determination to continue with his Mission, to strive for its propagation and protection and to take pains to rescue [47:5]: *"the men, women, and children who, being abased, say, "Our Lord, bring us forth from this city whose people are evildoers, and appoint to us a protector from Thee, and appoint to us from Thee a helper."* This was the spirit wherein actual fighting between the believers and the polytheists began. Battles between both parties took place, some of which have been related in the Glorious Koran. Finally God crowned all these with the Conquest and Clear Victory.

11. The Jews break their pledge. The Jews had not been able to purify their hearts from the filth of rancour and envy. God's continuous favours to His Prophet and his faithful companions kindled the fire of antagonism in their hearts, which induced them to break the pledges they had concluded with the Messenger. This was done by Banū Qaynuqāʾ, Banū al-Naḍīr and Banū

Qurayẓa.[17] They all insulted the Messenger and defied the believers at a time when he had to keep the number of his adversaries as small as possible and to restrict the domain of fighting.

This is how God tried the faithful. They could not but denounce the pledge they had with them [i.e. the Jews] and enter a new stage in their relations, the stage of hostility and war after the stage of alliance.

These were the stages the Messenger went through, before and after the Emigration. It is obvious that the Polytheists of Mecca had been fighting the Prophet right from the start of his Mission, and that they were the first to commit aggression: time and again they chased the believers from their dwellings, they tyrannized the oppressed, subjecting them to all kinds of maltreatment and torture. It is also apparent that the Jews of Medina were only attacked by the Messenger after they had broken their pledge and had begun to offer resistance, just as the polytheists had done before.

From all these events it appears clearly that the Messenger only fought those who fought him, and that his fighting had no other aims than repelling oppression, warding off rebellion and aggression and putting an end to persecution for the sake of religion. And this is exactly what the verses regarding the reason for fighting prescribe, as we have seen before.

The wars that, after the death of the Messenger, were conducted by Abū Bakr and ʿUmar were a completion of the building for which the Byzantines *(al-Rūm)* and the Persians *(al-Furs)* had laid the foundations with their own hands during the Prophet's lifetime. These two caliphs had no other choice than to repel evil, to give the people opportunities to hear the Message and to give security to the Muslims with regard to their religion and their countries.

On the strength of being a prophet, the Prophet sent his Mission to the kings of the Byzantines and the Persians. To the King of the Byzantines he dispatched his famous letter wherein he summoned him to be converted to Islam and held him, in case he refused, answerable for the sins of his people. When the letter had been translated for him, he assembled his patriarchs and high officials, submitted the letter to them and asked for their advice as to whether he should accept the summons or not. They then turned stubbornly away like donkeys and roared like lions, showing their disgust for his attitude with regard to the summons. However, he remained friendly with them, saying: "I have spoken these words to test your firmness concerning religion and kingship." Thus he abandoned his original intentions, preferring kingship over Islam. Then the officials and patriarchs began to sow the venomous seeds of hatred against the Mission and the Messenger in the hearts of commanders and subordinates. One of the consequences was that when Shuraḥbīl al-Ghassānī met the envoy of God's Messenger to the Prince of Buṣrā—at the time of the Muʾta-affair[18]—and learnt what he came for and that he was an envoy of Mohammad, he gave orders to behead him. They surmised that the tolerance of the believers would not go so far as to condone such an attack on their honour. Therefore they intensified their alertness and assembled a force of Byzantines and Christian Arabs in order to liquidate Mohammed's case. When the Messenger heard this, he equipped an army to weaken the impetuosity of those who were aroused against him and mocked his Mission. As soon as this army reached the place where the envoy had been killed, they found the Byzantine troops in a state of alertness. The two armies clashed and fought fiercely. Three Muslim heroes were killed and had it not been for a stratagem that God disclosed to Khālid ibn al-Wālid, not a single soldier of the army would have escaped. After that there were continuous reports that the Byzantines were assembling troops against the Muslims, determined to attack them. Then the Prophet prepared himself and set out with an army before they could attack him in his own territory. When he arrived at Tabūk, he found out that they had abandoned their idea. The Prophet remained a few days, during which some princes concluded peace treaties with him. He then returned to Medina, thinking about those who missed the victory because of Khālid ibn al-Walīd's stratagem and assuming that they definitely would return. Therefore, he equipped an army under the command of Usāma ibn Zayd. Immediately after this army had set out, Mohammed died. After this, Abū Bakr al-Ṣiddīq took over the command over the Muslims. He was of the opinion that firmness, loyalty and wisdom required that he dispatched the army the Messenger had prepared to counter the danger of these aggressors. After that, wars between the Muslims and the Byzantines followed in rapid succession until the Muslims conquered their lands and enabled the people to come to the Religion of God.

Just as thus the spirit of hostility of the Byzantines came to light, it manifested itself also among Persians. The Persians, however, were more arrogant and powerful than the Byzantines. All this became clear when the Messenger sent his letter to Kisrā.[19] The latter tore it to pieces and cast it on the floor out of haughtiness and arrogance. His presumption was to such an extent that he sent word to his governor in Yemen to send two strong men to Mohammed to take him with them. They actually came to the Messenger and informed him of the task they had to perform. Then the Messenger said: "This day Kisrā will be killed." Once the two men had learned that the words of the Messenger had come true, they became Muslims. Their conversion was the reason that the governor of Yemen was also converted. Afterwards al-Baḥrayn and ʿUmān, countries that were also under Persian protection, were joined to Yemen. The Persians thought that the victory of the Muslims over the Byzantines was due only to the weakness of the Byzantine armies. They began to attack the neighbouring Arab tribes, employing thereby the kings of al-Ḥīra, who applied themselves devotedly to aggression on the Muslims. Then the army of the Muslims set out against them and war broke out between them until the proxy of the Persian had to flee to al-Madāʾin. So the kings of al-Ḥira surrendered to the Muslims. This fostered the hatred of the Persians against the Muslims. They became again conscious of their enormous power and equipped an army to expel the Muslims from their country. Fighting broke out and in the end the Muslims advanced to the lands of the Persians. So Kisrā's throne fell and all the Persian lands yielded to the helpers of God.

From this succinct exposé it will be clear that, in the first period, the Muslims only attacked people when they showed a spirit of hostility, opposition and resistance against the Mission and contempt for it. It also shows that when such a hostile spirit became manifest to them and they were convinced of its danger to themselves and to the Mission, they hastened to put it out of the way before its evil would grow beyond control. They did not wait for the enemy to attack them in their own country. This is in accordance with a natural sociological law: "Only contemptible people are fought in their own house." Nevertheless, one of their prescriptions was that, when they arrived in the land of an enemy whose hostility to them was evident, they let him choose one out of three things: conversion to Islam, poll-tax *(jizya)* or fighting, in the hope that he would come to himself and that in his heart wisdom would get the upperhand over the spirit of enmity and antagonism. Read if you like some of the instructions of the Prophet to his army commanders: *"If you meet your heathen enemy, summon him to one of three things,"*[20] then you will know that the [enemy's] spirit of hostility preceded the dispatchment of the [Muslim] army and that leaving the choice was only prompted by the hope for peace and abandonment of the spirit of hostility.

It also appears that the wars the Muslims conducted in the first period did not aim at forcing the people to the Religion, nor at subjugating or humiliating them, and that they were not prompted by greed for money or greater power.

In one's relations with the *dhimmīs,* who are no adherents of Islam, one should resort to the legislation of the Koran and also read how the Rightly Guided Caliphs[21] and the righteous army commanders dealt with those who were no adherents of Islam in order to know—on the basis of reason and evidence, not on the basis of supposition and conjecture—the extent of the tolerance of Islam in its treatment of its non-Muslim subjects and its love for universal peace and human solidarity. Then, one will also know how exalted its universal human laws are that attract people of their own free will and under the protection of which non-Muslims have lived continuously for centuries, without complaining about injustice and without offence to their rights.

I hope that after this exposé, the reader will not entertain doubts any longer as to the fact that the Koran and the Deeds of the Prophet together establish a theory concerning fighting, as I have described in this treatise. May God prepare us for the task, the Religion requires of us—of making known His laws and guidance, which guarantees the Muslims their power and honour. He is hearing and responsive.

8

The Doctrine of Jihad in Modern Islam

Introduction

Writings on jihad vary a great deal in character and genre. Essentially, however, they are meant to serve two aims: the mobilization of Muslims for a specific occasion such as a revolt or a war, or the instruction of Muslims as to the 'real' or 'true' doctrine of jihad. However, this is an analytical distinction and if we analyze modern writings on jihad with the help of these motives, we find that they form some sort of continuum with, on the one extreme, writings with a purely mobilizing character, on the other, writings with a merely instructive character and in between the bulk of modern jihad literature, combining both motives in all shades of intensity.

The publication of writings with a purely mobilizing character is generally occasioned by a specific, well-defined political situation or occurrence. It is a genre as old as Islamic history itself. In fact, one is justified in considering the Koran as the first instance of this type, as it contains scores of verses with a clearly mobilizing character, such as [61:10–12]: *"O believers, shall I direct you to a commerce that shall deliver you from a painful chastisement? You shall believe in God and His Messenger, and struggle in the way of God with your possessions and your selves. That is better for you, did you but know. He will forgive you your sins and admit you into gardens underneath which rivers flow, and to dwelling places goodly in Gardens of Eden; that is the mighty triumph"* and [9:38–39]: *"O believers, what is amiss with you, that when it is said to you, 'Go forth in the way of*

From R. Peters, *Islam and Colonialism: The Doctrine of Jihad in Modern History.* The Hague etc.: Mouton, 1979, pp. 105–150, 190–200

God,' you sink down heavily to the ground? Are you so content with this present life, rather than the world to come? Yet the enjoyment of this present life, compared with the world to come, is a little thing. If you go not forth, He will chastise you with a painful chastisement, and instead of you He will substitute another people; and you will not hurt Him anything, for God is powerful over everything." The second century H. saw the appearance of collections of Traditions, exclusively devoted to the theme of jihad. The first one was compiled by ʿAbd Allāh al-Mubārak, who died in 181 H.[1] Later on works were written that generally included mobilizing Koranic verses and traditions, chapters on the virtues of jihad and the rewards of the martyr in the Hereafter and short stories on the heroism of early Muslim personalities.[2] On the other hand, many *fatwās* were published, elucidating specific points of the law with regard to jihad.

If we look at the modern writings with a purely mobilizing character, we see that both types are still extant. We find treatises, published on the occasion of a war or revolt, extolling the virtues of jihad and the bliss of the martyrs in the Hereafter and quoting the relevant Koranic verses and Traditions. A typical example is a booklet, published by the Azhar University on the occasion of the June war of 1967 under the title *'Jihad in Islam'* [3] which consists of the following chapters: *Jihad in the Holy Koran,* an enumeration of Koranic verses with regard to jihad, to the reward of the martyrs and to the Jews, being 'the worst enemies of humanity,' *Jihad in the texts of the Sunnah,* a collection of Traditions on about the same topics, and a last chapter with the title: *Marvellous Islamic images of sacrifice,* dealing with feats of Muslim heroism and contempt of death from Mohammed's time up to the Palestine war of 1948.

Fatwās concerning jihad have been published in great numbers in recent times. Generally they were to the effect that jihad had become an individual obligation *(farḍ ʿayn),* because the enemy had invaded Islamic territory. Illustrative of this type of *fatwās* is the one issued in April 1948 by the *mufti* of Egypt *(muftī al-diyār al-Miṣriyyah)* Ḥasanayn Muḥammad Makhlūf. He was asked to expound the position of Islam concerning personally volunteering for, or financially contributing to the struggle in Palestine. His response was:

> The answer is that jihad in person, or by means of financial contributions in order to rescue Palestine is legally obligatory upon those inhabitants that are able to do so, as well as upon the inhabitants of the Islamic states, since Jewish zionists attempt by force of arms to establish a Jewish state in one of the most honourable Arabic and Islamic countries, to wit Palestine, and this not only in order to take possession of Palestine, but also to dominate all Islamic states and to eliminate their Arabic character and their Islamic culture. . . . However, as today the methods of war have become complex, it is obligatory for anyone personally participating in jihad to submit to the rules that the states of the Arab League lay down for participation in jihad, in order that the expected victory be realized.[4]

It is obvious that the content of these *fatwās* is to a large extent political, as the application of the *sharīʿa* in a given situation, depends on the political evaluation of that situation and may give rise to different answers. In this *fatwā* the political element pops up in the last sentence, which is directed against the bands of Egyptian Muslim Brethren operating in Palestine without the approval of the Arab governments. One has to bear in mind that this *fatwā* was issued in April 1948, a month before the official military involvement of the Arab states in the Palestine war. Another illustration of the political character of these *fatwās* is the declaration issued by the Congress of the Academy of Islamic Research *(Majmaʿ al-Buḥūth al-Islāmiyya)* held in Cairo in November 1977. Whereas on previous occasions this congress, in which Islamic scholars from all over the Islamic world participate, had declared that, in view of the prevailing circumstances, jihad against Israel had become an individual duty of all Muslims with the aim of realizing the aims of the Palestinian people,[5] which can only mean the destruction of the zionist State of Israel and the establishment of a Palestinian State on the territory of mandatory Palestine, it now issued a statement to the effect that the aim of the jihad against Israel was the liberation of the territories occupied in 1967, the establishment of an independent Palestinian state therein and the return to Jerusalem. Thus the Congress conformed to the new policy of Egypt and most other Arab states with regard to Israel.[6] Besides these *fatwās* declaring that jihad in the given circumstances, has become an individual duty, many *fatwās* are issued, establishing that a certain struggle or revolt is to be considered as jihad so that the combatants are exempt from the obligation of fasting during the month of *Ramaḍān*.[7] Finally there are *fatwās* that deal with all kinds of legal aspects of war, e.g. the question whether those who collaborate with the (non-Muslim) enemy are to be considered apostates, or whether the conclusion of a peace-treaty is allowed in the given circumstances, or whether emigration from a country occupied by a non-Muslim power is obligatory.[8] Since, as we have seen, the content of *fatwās* on jihad is largely determined by political motives, they can be used as instruments of psychological warfare. Indeed, the jihad doctrine is so flexible in its application that during the colonial period both the British and the French managed to obtain *fatwās* to the effect that they were the legal rulers and that rebellion against them was not allowed.[9]

We now come to literature with a dual character, written with the aim of both instructing and mobilizing people. At first, the mobilizing aspect will be treated. In general one can say that in works with this dual character, the intended mobilization is not occasioned by a concrete and specific political occurrence, but that it more or less fits in a more general framework of struggle against colonialism, imperialism, zionism or communism. The subjugation of the Islamic countries to colonial powers, the impotence of the Arab world *vis-à-vis* the establishment of the state of Israel and the economic backwardness—for all these phenomena, there is, in the view of their authors, one fundamental thing to blame: the fact that the Muslims have abandoned the prescriptions of Islam, and thus have cut off themselves from their principal source of strength. The remedy is self-evident:

> If the Muslims want to get out of the situation they are in, what they must do is join forces, believe sincerely in God (He is exalted), act in accordance with God's Book and the teachings of His Messenger (may God bless him and grant him salvation),

> take their matters firmly in hand as a preparation for fighting, mobilize themselves for struggle and offer themselves as a sacrifice for their religion and their land.[10]

Or from a more military view, as formulated by the Iraqi general Maḥmūd Shīt Khaṭṭāb:

> The human factor is still the decisive factor in war; it is still the most important force for any weapon or any equipment. However, man without creed is like foam, the foam of a torrent. The Arabs have a heavenly creed that has led them to victory, for their victories were no doubt victories produced by creed. When the Arabs became weak, their creed protected them against disintegration and collapse. . . . The return to Islam will entail the proclamation of Islamic jihad. In that case, there will be 75 million Muslim fighters on the battlefields facing Israel. They will be able to eliminate Israel, even without weapons. . . . The way to return to Islam is to revise the education of the young generation and to lay down new programs for educating them, based on the teaching of the true religion, and to act according to the teachings of Islam, to the letter and to the spirit.[11]

In this connexion, some authors have pointed out that the Israeli military successes were due to the religious inspiration of the Israelis, and especially the Israeli army.[12] Whereas this kind of mobilization is directed against an outside enemy, there is also another form that emphasizes the need to spread Islam, to establish a truly Islamic government and to struggle against tyranny and oppression. These calls for jihad came from fundamentalist movements like the *Jamāʿat-i Islāmī* in India and Pakistan and from the *Society of Muslim Brethren* in the Middle East and were in the first place directed against the local governments, that were not really Islamic governments:

> What I want to clarify in connexion with the topic we are discussing now, is that Islam is not only a set of theological dogmata and a collection of ceremonies and rites, as nowadays the word religion seems to be understood. In fact, it is an all-

> embracing order that wants to eliminate and to eradicate the other orders which are false and unjust, so as to replace them by a good order and a moderate program that is considered to be better for humanity than the other orders and to contain rescue from the illnesses of evil and tyranny, happiness and prosperity for the human race, both in this world and in the Hereafter. The call of Islam for this cause . . . does not concern only one nation with the exclusion of others, or one group with the exclusion of others, for Islam calls all people to its Word. . . . Whosoever believes in this call and accepts it in a proper way, becomes a member of the *'Islamic party'*. . . . As soon as this party has been established, it starts with jihad for the aim for which it has been founded. For by the nature of its existence, it will spare no efforts to eliminate and eradicate the regimes that are not founded on the bases of Islam and to replace them by a moderate cultural and social order.[13]

In works with a predominantly mobilizing character, the instructive aspect generally derives from their main function: the people that are to be rallied for the jihad should first be informed as to their rights and duties. When, however, the instructive aspect gets the upper hand, we can generally observe that the major aim of these writings is to defend Islam against the ideological attacks of the West. As the Western powers often justified their colonial expansion by the idea of a *mission civilisatrice,* it served their interests if Muslim society was depicted as backward and Islam as a religion of bloodthirsty, lecherous fanatics. Therefore, the unfavourable mediaeval image of Islam was revived. The writings on jihad with an instructive character, generally represent an ideological defence against the *'scimitar-syndrome'* in the West: the idea that Islam is a violent and fanatical creed, spread by savage warriors, carrying the Koran in one hand and a scimitar in the other. They are apologetical in that they try to refute false ideas on Islamic jihad and to demonstrate that the Islamic prescriptions of warfare are morally and practically superior to those of the Christian West. The accusations against which the authors feel obliged to defend Islam are the following:

> Firstly, that [Islam] is based on subjugation and conquest with the aim of imposing itself by power and strength on God's creatures of all races and religions;

> Secondly, that it denies Man freedom of opinion and creed;
> Thirdly, that Islam, in propagating its message, has declared war against all peoples and races of different religious communities and sects;
> Fourthly, that war is the fundamental relationship between Islam and all other nations and states and that peace can only exist for a fixed time in view of a temporary necessity;
> Fifthly, they claim that Islam does not heed pledges, does not keep obligations and does not respect treaties and pacts;
> Sixthly, some authors on international law went as far as to include the Muslims among the barbaric peoples to whom the honour of belonging to the international community must be denied.[14]

At first, as in the case of the Indian modernists of the latter half of the nineteenth century, the defence against the unfavourable image of Islam was only timidly voiced. Convinced of the superiority of the West and Western culture as they were, they tried to show that Islam was a 'respectable' religion that fostered the same values as Christendom and Western civilization in general. Later, many Muslim thinkers came to see these accusations as a functional part of the European colonial policy towards the Islamic world. Since Islam, in their view, was the ideological stronghold against Western penetration they regarded these Western accusations as attempts to weaken Islam so as to be able to subject the entire Islamic world. Thus their tone in refuting these Western allegations against Islam became bolder and more aggressive. They pointed at the political implications and violently denounced the evil designs and cunning methods of the Western powers. The Western accusations with regard to the doctrine of jihad were, in their view, to be placed in this political context:

> Many of them [=the Western orientalists] have written on certain aspects of it [=jihad], on the basis of what their fanaticism, their whims and their repulsion have dictated to them, with the aim of attacking Islam in its scientific and intellectual origin. For this is the very reason why orientalism came into being and why orientalists began launching their attacks against the Islamic East by assailing its nationalism, its language and its reli-

> gion. Their main interest was jihad, as this is the principle that forms the foremost rank for protecting Islam. Therefore, they made it the object of a large-scale attack, in order to weaken the morale of the Muslims and to make them feel that *they* are the oppressors of other peoples. They still depict the Muslims as ferocious animals, lying in wait to hurl themselves upon the world in order to destroy all traces of civilization and culture. This will make people averse to accepting Islam in this form and will diminish the alleged danger of the Muslims for the Christians. However, it is well known that the opposite is true, for orientalism was resuscitated in order to pave the way for colonial domination by spreading scepticism about the fundamental values of the Arabs and Muslims and in order to turn the attention to Western civilization by means of articles and books that the authors try to disguise as scientific research, but that in fact are only meant to have a venomous influence and to serve evil purposes.[15]

A typical feature of these apologetical writings, and a feature that one can also observe in other branches of this literature, is the comparison between Western and Christian practice on the one hand and Islamic ideals on the other. It is not difficult to guess to whose advantage this comparison always turns out. Thus the excesses of warfare by Western powers are fully emphasized and opposed to the Islamic rules of war-conduct. In order to put an end to the problem of atrocities in warfare, a general application of the Islamic rules is proposed.[16]

A specific type of apologetic literature on jihad, which is entirely instructive in character and lacks any mobilizing aspects, are those writings that expound the theory of jihad as a form of international law. Their apologetical character lies in the emphasis on the basically peaceful character of the relationship between the Islamic and the other states and in the demonstration that Islam has been capable of constructing a detailed, just and merciful system of international law. Generally this system is depicted as being by far superior to positive international law, of Western origin, and being more capable of promoting world peace and security. This type of literature will be dealt with on pp. 130ff.

Modern and Classical Jihad Literature Compared

In this section classical and modern literature on jihad will be compared as to style and as to the topics that are dealt with. In general, it is evident that differences between these two derive from differences in function. Thus we see that the works whose main function is mobilization, treatises as well as *fatwās*, hardly differ from each other in both periods. On the other hand there is a clear difference with regard to writings with an instructive character, which can be explained by the fact that the classical *fiqh*-texts on jihad had no aim other than expounding the sacred law on a specific subject. As the authority of the *Sharīʿa* had not been challenged, there was no need to justify the rules with general moral or rational concepts. This situation, however, underwent a marked change in the latter half of the nineteenth century because of the accelerated European expansion. As the economic and social changes required the introduction of western codes, the supremacy of the *Sharīʿa* was no longer self-evident. Consequently, the authors on legal subjects were forced back into the defensive and had to exert themselves in finding justifications for applying the *Sharīʿa*. This accounts for a very clear alteration in style. Modern writings on jihad are less legalistic and do not indulge in the casuistic quibbles and legal niceties, that were the result of the classical lawyers' desire to give solutions for all thinkable cases. At the same time, these writings do not show any differentiation as to *madhhab*. The authors do not feel themselves bound to a specific School. In presenting the topic, they emphasize more the moral justifications and the underlying ethical values of the rules, than the detailed elaboration of those rules. This also explains a certain shift in the importance of certain topics. Whereas in modern jihad literature topics of a merely technical character do not get any attention, there are also many topics in modern literature, that are hardly or not dealt with in classical literature. The most important of these topics are:

The definition of jihad. As we shall see on pp. 112ff., this definition generally includes all kinds of moral and spiritual jihad, that are hardly touched upon in classical *fiqh*-literature.

The principle of peaceful relations between the Islamic and the other states. The classical doctrine of jihad considered all wars against unbelievers as legal wars, sanctioned by the *Sharīʿa.* In fact, the *Sharīʿa* required that the head of state organize once a year a military raid into enemy territory. Since the second half of the nineteenth century, however, modernist authors have asserted that the relationship between the Islamic and the other states had essentially a peaceful character. They argue that this principle is firmly rooted in the Koran and cite the following verses [4:90]: *"If they withdraw from you, and do not fight you, and offer you peace, then God assigns not any way to you against them."* [4:94]: *". . . Do not say to him who offers you a greeting* [salām, *which also means peace*], *'Thou art not a believer,' seeking the chance goods of the present life."* and [8:61]: *"And if they incline to peace, do thou incline to it; and put thy trust in God."*[17] The classical interpretation that the fundamental relation between the Islamic and the other states is war, is, according to modernist authors, due to the situation prevalent during the first centuries of Islam, as the Islamic state was then surrounded by bitter enemies. A logical complement of this modernist exegetical *volte-face* was the development of a set of rules for determining *when* war is allowed. This is closely related to the next topic.

The legal aims of jihad. Defining the legal aims of jihad is indispensable for answering the question when jihad is allowed. Therefore this theme receives a great deal of attention in modern literature, whereas, in classical literature, the question of the aim of jihad, is only perfunctorily treated by using very general and abstract formulae like: *'voiding the earth of unbelief'* or *'making God's word the highest.'* From this, one could infer that this question did not arouse much interest in the classical period. To this topic pp. 116 will be devoted.

A survey of early Islamic military history. Surveys of the military *faits et gestes* of Mohammed and the first Muslims differ to some extent according to their function. The most common purpose of these surveys is to explain that Mohammed's intentions were basically peaceful, but that the obstinacy and enmity displayed by the unbelievers *vis-à-vis* the Islamic mission, made recourse to arms inevitable:

> These were the stages the Messenger went through, before and after the emigration. It is obvious that the polytheists of Mecca had been fighting the Prophet right from the start of his Mission, and that they were the first to commit aggression: time and again they chased the believers from their dwellings, they tyrannized the oppressed, subjecting them to all kinds of maltreatment and torture. It is also apparent that the Jews of Medina were not attacked by the Messenger until they had broken their pledge and had begun to offer resistance, just as the polytheists had done before. From all these events it appears clearly that the Messenger only fought those who fought him, and that his fighting had no other aims than repelling oppression, warding off rebellion and aggression and putting an end to persecution for the sake of religion.[18]

Another purpose of these surveys is to inspire the reader with combativeness and fervour, to be derived from the example of the Prophet. There are even special books that entirely serve this purpose.[19]

Women and jihad. Many books on jihad contain sections on the participation of women in fighting. The treatment of this topic certainly serves some apologetical aims, as thus the authors try to prove that women have played an important role in early Islamic society and that they belonged to its enthusiastic supporters:

> If the Westerners are proud of their high national feelings and of their alert national consciousness, and adduce as an example that their women always hasten to spend their property for the sake of the defence of their countries, then the women of the Muslims have preceded them in this virtue.[20]

At the same time it served the purpose of demonstrating that women occupied a position (nearly) equal to men in early Islam:

> Islamic history has established that Muslim women marched out just like men marched out, and participated in jihad side by

> side with them. . . . Of course, women did not carry weapons to fight with, since their nature differs from the nature of men and since their capacities in this field are limited. Therefore, they performed those tasks that were suitable to them, provisioning. These tasks are important and valuable for the fighters, for an army in combat needs an uninterrupted stream of food, water and weapons.[21]

These sections generally consist of an enumeration of Traditions demonstrating that women accompanied the armies and that they provided the fighters with drinks, cooked the meals, nursed the wounded and raised the morale of the combatants.[22]

The strategical and tactical lessons of the Koran. Many authors devote part of their books on jihad to the strategical and tactical prescriptions of the Koran. This subject shows great similarity to a modern genre of Koran exegesis, known as scientific exegesis *(tafsīr ʿilmī)*[23] as they both proceed from the basic assumption that the Koran mentions or hints at the essential elements of all modern sciences, arts and crafts.

> If one studies these verses [i.e. verses connected with the practical side of warfare] of God's Book, one will discover that they lay down general prescriptions for the Muslims, constituting a handbook for warfare ranking very high among similar institutions of modern civilization.[24]

In the first place, the Koran deals with the spiritual side, i.e. with the morale of the combatants. Many verses speak of the reward that awaits those who struggle in the way of God, e.g., K 4:74–76, K 9:19–22, 111. Other verses warn the believers against factors that may lead to cowardice and weakness [9:24]: *"Say, 'If your fathers, your sons, your brothers, your wives, your clan, your possessions that you have gained, commerce you fear may slacken, dwellings you love—if these are dearer to you than God and His Messenger, and to struggle in His way, then wait till God brings His command; God guides not the people of the ungodly."* Many verses inspire the believers with hope by reminding them that God is on their side and will aid them [3:124–126]: *"When thou saidst to the believers, 'Is it not enough for you that your Lord should reinforce you with three thousand angels sent down upon you? Yea; if you are patient and godfearing, and the foe comes against you instantly, your Lord will reinforce you with five thousand swooping angels.' God wrought this not, save as good tiding to you, and that your hearts might be at rest; help comes only from God the All-mighty, the All-wise."* As war is a costly enterprise, the believers must continuously be exhorted to partake in jihad with their wealth by financially contributing to the war-efforts. The Koran abounds in verses to this effect. As regards the practical aspects of warfare, K 8:60 is often quoted: *"Make ready for them whatever force and strings of horses you can, to terrify thereby the enemy of God and your enemy."* This verse contains many useful lessons for the Muslims. It orders them to prepare their power according to their capabilities and possibilities. Thus, the Muslims must themselves produce military equipment such as guns, rifles, tanks, aeroplanes and battleships, so that they are not at the mercy of those who produce ammunition and war equipment.[25] It also orders them to deploy their armies at the frontiers of countries since there the enemies are likely to attack. Further it points out that the preparation of strength depends on the possibilities available, so that it differs according to time and place. The aim of this preparation is to deter the enemy and to maintain a situation which in modern military usage is called armed peaces.[26] Another verse quoted in this connexion is [9:123]: *"O believers, fight the unbelievers who are near to you and let them find in you a harshness; and know that God is with the godfearing."* In modern literature, this verse is usually interpreted as a tactical instruction concerning the order of attack: the Muslims must first attack the nearest enemy, then the next-nearest and so on, in order to clear the road of any hostile obstacle for the army. By means of this interpretation, modernist authors dissociate themselves from the classical, mainly Hanafite, opinion, that this is one of the verses that order the Muslims to fight all unbelievers.[27]

The Definition of Jihad

In general, literature on jihad is for the greater part devoted to jihad in the sense of struggle, of fighting. However, almost all of these writings lay stress on the fact that the word jihad has a much wider semantic content. They point out that it is derived from the verb *jāhada,* exerting oneself or striving, and thus has a friendlier connotation than the word *qitāl* (fighting). The latter notion necessarily entails killing and bloodshed, whereas jihad, meaning exerting oneself for some praiseworthy aim, does not.[28] Therefore, the translation of jihad by *'Holy War'* is considered to be incorrect and resented.[29] This wider meaning of jihad includes those notions that developed in classical Islam as a consequence of the 'internalizing' *(intérioration)* of the jihad-doctrine.[30] Like the classical authors modern authors also mention *jihād al-nafs,* the struggle against oneself and *djihād al-shayṭān,* the struggle against the devil. Both notions imply the struggle against one's bad inclinations and against seduction and enticement by nearby pleasures. This form of jihad is usually called the *'Greater Jihad,'* on account of a saying of the Prophet. Once, when he came home from a raiding party, he said: *'We have now returned from the Smaller Jihad to the Greater Jihad.'* When asked what he meant by Greater Jihad, he answered: 'The jihad against oneself.' Although this Tradition is quite famous and frequently quoted, it is not included in one of the authoritative compilations.

Another notion of jihad is the struggle for the good of Muslim society and against corruption and decadence. In fact, it is coextensive with the concept of *al-amr bi-l-maʿrūf wa-l-nahy ʿan al-munkar* (commanding what is good and forbidding what is abominable). All Muslims must partake in this struggle and 'work with all their intellectual and material abilities for the realization of justice and equality between the people and for the spreading of security and human understanding, both among individuals and groups.'[31] Inasmuch as this notion of jihad implies the realization of the Islamic values in Muslim society, education is very crucial. Therefore, some authors speak of *jihād al-tarbiya* (educational jihad).[32] In Tunisia, this notion of jihad was applied to the field of economy, when President Bourguiba called the struggle to overcome economic backwardness jihad:

> Tunisia, which is an Islamic country, suffers from a certain degree of decline and backwardness, that brings disgrace upon us

> in the eyes of the world. The only possibility to free ourselves from this shame is continuous and assiduous work and fruitful and useful labor. Escaping from this backwardness is jihad-obligation, ruled by the same prescriptions as jihad by means of the sword.[33]

This interpretation was brought forward as an argument in a discussion on the fasting of *Ramaḍān*. As during this month production stagnates, Bourguiba was looking for arguments to prove that fasting was not religiously obligatory for workers. Since the participants in jihad are excused from the duty to fast during *Ramaḍān*, he claimed that the struggle against economic underdevelopment could be put on a par with jihad with the sword.[34] This new interpretation was later accepted by the *ᶜulamāʾ*.[35]

Related to the notion of *jihād al-tarbiya* (educational jihad), which means the spreading of the Islamic values in Muslim society and may be compared with the idea of *home mission*, is the notion of *jihād al-daᶜwa*, spreading Islam amongst the unbelievers by peaceful means, such as argumentation and demonstration,[36] and thus equivalent to *external mission*. This notion is sometimes termed *jihād al-lisān* or *jihād al-qalam* (jihad of the tongue or jihad of the pen). It is founded on [16:125]: *"Call thou to the way of thy Lord with wisdom and good admonition and dispute with them in the better way."* Some modern authors hold that this is nowadays the most important form of jihad. As during the first period of Islam means of communication were lacking, conquest was the only method for spreading the message of Islam. Nowadays, intensive communication is possible without having recourse to military expeditions. Therefore, fighting as a means of propagation of Islam, has become obsolete and must now be replaced by the concept of *jihād al-daᶜwa*.[37] Some authors fear lest the emphasis on the peaceful side of the jihad-concept, may divert the Muslims from the necessary struggle. Therefore, they try to connect these peaceful forms of jihad with the idea of fighting. They interpret these forms of spiritual and moral jihad as a prerequisite for fighting in the way of God:

> Jihad begins with jihad against oneself by purifying one's soul from [bad] inclinations and passions and with its orientation

> towards God, [for one ought] not [to struggle] out of love for fame, or desire for pleasure or in hope of worldly matters. Whoever fights to show his courage and to acquire fame and money, cannot be regarded a *mujāhid*, for a *mujāhid* fights only to please God, to obtain what He has in store for him, to raise the truth and to make God's word the highest.[38]

The same motive, the fear that the Muslims would be distracted from fighting, played a role in the frontal attack by the fundamentalists against these notions of moral and spiritual jihad. They hold that there is no justification whatsoever for calling spiritual and moral jihad the *'Greater Jihad,'* as the Tradition: *'We have now returned from the Smaller Jihad to the Greater Jihad'* cannot be regarded as authentic. They believe that this idea has been spread on purpose to weaken Muslim combativeness.[39] Consequently, they stress the militant aspects of jihad, the notion of *al-jihād bi-l-nafs* (partaking in jihad by putting one's life at stake, i.e. fighting) or *al-jihād bi-l-sayf* (jihad with the sword). This is in fact the most important notion in nearly all writings on jihad and therefore receives most attention. Jihad in the sense of fighting, however, is restricted by the phrase *fī sabīl Allāh,* in the way of God. This implies that jihad is not just plain, ordinary war, but must be somehow connected with religion and the interest of the believers:

> The way of God is the road that leads to His gratification, by means of which His religion is protected and the situation of His worshippers thrives.[40]
>
> Fighting in the way of God is fighting in order to raise God's word, to safeguard His religion, to spread His mission and to defend His party, so that they will not be robbed of their rights and not prevented to bring their affair [=religion] to the open. Therefore, it comprises more than fighting for the sake of religion, because it includes defence of the religion and protection of its mission, but also the defence of territory when an aggressor covetously plans to take possession of our countries and to enjoy the riches of our land.[41]

The implications of these restrictions, i.e. the legal aims of jihad, will be dealt with in the next chapter. Jihad, however, is not only the act of fighting itself, but also everything that is conducive to victory, like contributing money to provide for military equipment *(al-jihād bi-l-māl):*

> Any activity that strengthens the military front and supports the jihad is also jihad in the way of God, like e.g. stepping up productivity, strengthening the internal front, financially contributing to war-efforts and looking after the fighters' families. The Prophet has said: *'Whoever supplies a warrior in the way of God with equipment, is also a warrior and whoever takes the place of a warrior in his family by means of* [*his*] *wealth, is also a warrior.'*[42]

In peacetime Muslims must fulfil their collective jihad-duty by military training and material preparation for warfare.[43]

The Legal Aims of Jihad

As it appears from the works on *fiqh,* there was no great concern about the justification of fighting against unbelievers in classical Islam. If mentioned at all, the subject was only briefly touched upon and summarily formulated as 'strengthening Islam,' 'protecting the believers' of 'annihilating unbelief.' Apparently this topic was not of great importance as fighting against unbelievers was justified in itself. When modern authors accepted the principle of peaceful relations between the Islamic state and the rest of the world, a theory was required for deciding what wars against non-Muslims were legal and could be called jihad, and what wars were not. Thus the idea of jihad as *bellum justum* won through. Some modern authors,[44] however, hold that the idea of *bellum justum* did already exist in classical Islam. They quote in this connexion the famous Arab historian Ibn Khaldūn (d. 1406), who distinguishes between 'wars of jihad and justice' *(ḥurūb jihād wa-ᶜadl)* and 'wars of sedition and persecution' *(ḥurūb baghy wa-fitna).* The first kind he defines as punitive wars against rebels and wars out of zeal for God and His religion, 'what in the *Sharīᶜa* is called jihad.' The other form of warfare consists, according to Ibn Khaldūn, in wars conducted by tribes and barbaric nations that live on spoils and booty.[45] It is, however, doubtful whether Ibn Khaldūn's statement may be regarded as a legal distinction between just and unjust wars in the modern sense. Probably it amounts to no more than a distinction between wars fought by the Islamic state on the one hand, and all other wars, like those between non-Islamic states, outside attacks on the Islamic states, internal rebellion against Islamic legal authority and intertribal warfare on the other. Nevertheless, it is not wholly unjustified to speak of jihad as *bellum justum* in classical Islam, for there was some embryonic development of *jus ad bellum* (the rules with regard to the beginning of wars, as opposed to *jus in bello,* the rules that must be observed during actual warfare). According to the classical doctrine, a formal declaration of war was obligatory under certain circumstances, and truce imposed certain restrictions as to when warfare could be resumed. Moreover, there was a rule, although never explicitly formulated as it ran counter to the conception of the Islamic state as a whole, that an Islamic state could not wage war upon another Islamic state, unless it were established that the other state was to be regarded as a rebellious force against which punitive action was allowed. In practice, however, these prescriptions had only some importance inasfar as they necessitated Islamic rulers to have their military actions justified by *fatwās,* issued by the state-*muftī.*

The theory of jihad as *bellum justum* that developed in modern Islam, concentrates upon the causes of warfare waged by the Muslims. This cause must be 'in the way of God *(fī sabīl Allāh),* which excludes fighting for territorial expansion, for booty, for vengeance and for other worldly aims.[46] Modern authors usually limitatively enumerate the causes for which war may be waged. These causes fall into two categories: those connected with the *propagation of Islam* and those connected with the idea of *defence.* Of the first kind are the following causes:

1. Strengthening monotheism and destroying polytheism and false gods. This is based on the nearly identical verses K 2:193 and K 8:39 *('Fight them until there is no persecution and the religion is God's [entirely]').*

2. Protecting the Islamic mission against those who stand in its way. This is also called protecting freedom of religion.[47] This

freedom of religion is to be realized by removing all obstacles that block free missionary activities. All men must be free to hear the call of Islam and to embrace Islam without any hindrance, oppression or persecution on the part of the authorities or on the part of their fellow-men. This cause is also scripturally founded on K 2:193 and K 8:39 ('. . . *until there is no persecution* . . . .').

As for the causes connected with the idea of defence, these are:

1. Repelling aggression on Muslim lives and property in case of an actual or expected attack by enemy forces. This is founded on [2:190]: *"And fight in the way of God with those who fight you, but aggress not."*

2. Preventing oppression and persecution of Muslims outside the Territory of Islam. This is closely linked up with the idea of protecting freedom of religion. It is based upon [4:75]: *"How is it with you, that you do not fight in the way of God, and for the men, women, and children who, being abased, say, 'Our Lord, bring us forth from this city whose people are evildoers, and appoint to us a protector from Thee, and appoint to us from Thee a helper.'"*

3. Retaliating a breach of pledge by the enemy. This is supported by [9:12]: *"But if they break their oaths after their covenant and thrust at your religion, then fight the leaders of unbelief; they have no sacred oaths; haply they will give over."*

Without any exception, all authors emphatically state that fighting may never serve the aim of compelling people to conversion. Their main scriptural arguments are [2:256]: *"No compulsion is there in religion. Rectitude has become clear from error. So whosoever disbelieves in idols and believes in God, has laid hold of the most firm handle, unbreaking; God is All-hearing, All-knowing."*[48] and [10:99]: *"And if thy Lord had willed, whoever is in the earth would have believed, all of them, all together. Wouldst thou then constrain the people, until they are believers?"* As additional arguments they adduce the Traditions that forbid to kill women, children and aged people, although they are unbelievers. Had jihad served the aim of forcing unbelievers to conversion, it would have been allowed to kill all unbelievers. Finally, it is pointed out that Islam is a logical religion based upon natural reason:

> Now, does such a Mission require force to make people believe in it? No, the use of force as a means of making people believe in this Mission, would be an insult to it, would be a discouragement to it and would put obstacles in its way. If a man realizes that he is being coerced, or forced into something, this will prevent him from respecting and esteeming it and reflecting upon it, let alone that he will be able to believe in it. Employing force as an instrument for conversion means wrapping this Mission in complexity, absurdity and obscurity and witholding it from the grasp of the human mind and heart.[49]

Generally, modern authors do not mention the prescriptions with regard to the unbelievers that are not qualified to become *dhimmīs* (i.e. the pagan Arabs or, according to others, all unbelievers except Jews and Christians), who only have the choice between Islam and the sword. Admittedly, this problem is of small practical importance nowadays, which may explain why it is passed over in silence. Those authors, however, who do deal with this subject, adduce that these pagan Arabs had committed aggression against the Muslims, so that fighting against them was justified for that reason.[50] Others, however, fully admit that these groups are to be excepted from the principle of freedom of religion and that they cannot be accorded the right to abide by their religion as polytheism and idolatry cannot be tolerated on Islamic territory:

> Islam has excluded the pagan Arabs from this principle and has allowed jihad in order to compel them to become Muslims, and that for very wise reasons, which are evident for those endowed with insight. The most important of these is that the souls of that magnificent nation must be purified from the evils of idolatry and that ignorance and barbarism must be eradicated from the Arab peninsula, which lies exactly between the realms of the East and those of the West.[51]

Surveying the field of modern literature on jihad, we see that modernist authors underline the defensive aspect of jihad, and hold that jihad outside Islamic territory is only permitted when the peaceful propagation of Islam is being hindered or when Muslims living amongst unbelievers are oppressed. Fundamentalist writers on the other hand do not depart to a great extent from the classical doctrine and emphasize the expansionist aspect.[52] The modernist, defensive tendency originated in India in the latter half of the nineteenth century. One of the first spokesmen of this current of thought was Sayyid Aḥmad Khān, who wrote in 1871, referring to the situation in India:

> First, what is *jihad*? It is war in defence of the faith *'fi sabílillàh'*. But it has its conditions, and, except under these, it is unlawful. It must be against those who are not only *Kafirs* [unbelievers, RP], but also 'obstruct the exercise of the faith' (K 47:1). The doctors of the law in all ages, not merely the Moulvies, Meccan or of Northern India, whom Mr. Hunter quotes, have laid down that to constitute the essential conditions for *jihad* on the part of the protected Musalmans as against a Christian power protecting them, there must be *positive* oppression or obstruction to the Moslems in the exercise of their faith; not merely want of countenance, negative withholding of support, or absence of profession of the faith; and further, this obstruction and oppression which justifies *jihad* must be, not in civil, but in religious matters; it must impair the foundation of some of the 'pillars of Islam,' and not merely touch the existence of Kazees, the maintenance of tombs of saints (a practice declared by the stricter Moslems to be heretical), or the administration of the country through Moslem officials. These are merely negative abstentions from the faith *(kufr)*, not that positive oppression *(zulm)* and obstruction to the exercise of the faith *(sadd)* which alone can justify *jihad.*[53]

Aḥmad Khān was not the only one to express these views. They were shared by many of his contemporaries.[54] By arguing in this fashion, Aḥmad Khān and the Indian modernists drastically restricted the scope of the jihad duty. Not only did they assert that jihad was essentially defensive, but they also limited this to defence against religious oppression impairing the pillars of Islam, i.e. the five ritual obligations of the Muslims (the profession of faith, prayer, ritual taxes, fasting and pilgrimage), thereby excluding from it all other kinds of political oppression. Thus they introduced a separation between the religious and political spheres, an obvious innovation with regard to a religion that claims to dominate all domains of human activity. This irenic interpretation of the jihad doctrine was prompted by the fact that the British regarded the Indian Muslims as the main instigators of the 1857 revolt. Hence they distrusted them and discriminated against them in favour of the Hindus with regard to government employment and army commissions. Since these were precisely the professions upon which the livelihood of the upper and middle class Muslims depended, the latter wanted to show that Islam was a respectable religion and that the doctrine of jihad was no obstacle for the loyal service of the British Empire. With their publications on jihad they tried to achieve two aims:

> My first object is that the Mohammedans ignorant of the texts bearing on Jihad and the conditions of Islam may become acquainted with them, and that they may not labour under the misapprehension that it is their religious duty to wage war against another people solely because that people is opposed to Islam. Thus they, by ascertaining the fixed conditions and texts, may be saved for ever from rebellion. . . . My second object is that non-Mohammedans and the Government under whose protection the Mohammedans live, may not suspect Mohammedans of thinking that it is lawful for us to fight against non-Mohammedans or that it is our duty to interfere with the lives and property of others, or that we are bound to convert others forcibly to Mohammedanism, or to spread Islam by means of the sword. The result of these two aims will, I hope, be that the bonds of concord will be drawn closer between the rulers and the ruled, and between British subjects generally and Mohammedans, so that peace and security may be established for ever in this country.[55]

By the end of the nineteenth century the idea that jihad is defensive warfare became current in the Middle East, and especially in Egypt, through the works of Muḥammad ʿAbduh and Muḥammad Rashid Riḍā.[56] They, however, did not follow the narrow interpretation of the Indian modernists and emphatically asserted that the jihad duty also applied in case a foreign aggressor invaded Islamic territory for political and economic reasons. Hence they could appeal to the doctrine of jihad in order to resist colonial conquest. At the present, most authors on jihad follow this defensive tendency, although recently, there seems to take place a certain radicalization towards a more fundamentalist approach. Nevertheless, the text books for religious instruction used in Egypt all describe jihad as a defensive war.[57]

The point of departure of the modernists is that jihad is only to be waged as a reaction against outside aggression. Muḥammad Rashīd Riḍā formulated this as follows: 'Everything that is mentioned in the Koran with regard to the rules of fighting, is intended [to be understood] as defence against enemies that fight the Moslems because of their religion.'[58] They envisage various forms of aggression against which jihad is lawful, such as a direct attack on the territory of Islam or the suspicion thereof, and also the oppression of Muslims residing outside the frontiers of the Islamic state. Assistance to these and securing the missionary activities are both viewed as defence against an assault on the freedom of religion. The scriptural arguments they adduce are mainly derived from the Koran. The Koran abounds with verses that have a bearing on the relationship with the unbelievers. These verses range from prescriptions to preach Islam peacefully to unconditional commands to fight them. In classical Islam, this contradiction was solved by means of abrogation. Departing from the gradual evolution in the relationship between Mohammed and the unbelievers, which was reflected in the Koran, it was assumed that the unconditional command to fight the unbelievers, to be found in those verses that were revealed in the latest stage of Mohammed's life, had abrogated all other prescriptions. The modernists, however, have rejected this method of interpretation. They have taken the verses that explicitly mention the causes for fighting, and in general belong to the last stage but one, the period in which God permitted the believers to offer resistance against the attacks of the unbelievers, as the verses determining the causes of warfare against non-Muslims. The most important of these are [2:190]: *"And fight in the way of God with those who fight you, but aggress not: God loves not the aggressors."* [2:192]: *"But if they give over, surely God is All-forgiving, All-compassionate."* [2:194]: *"The holy month for the holy month; holy things demand retaliation. Whoso commits aggression against you, do you commit aggression against him like as he has committed against you; and fear you God, and know that God is with the godfearing."* [4:75]: *"How is it with you, that you do not fight in the way of God, and for the men, women, and children who, being abased, say, 'Our Lord, bring us forth from this city whose people are evildoers, and appoint to us a protector from Thee, and appoint to us from Thee a helper.'"* [4:90–1]: *"If they withdraw from you, and do not fight you, and offer you peace, then God assigns not any way to you against them (. . .). If they withdraw not from you, and offer you peace, and restrain their hands, take them, and slay them wherever you come on them."* [9:12–13]: *"But if they break their oaths after their covenant and thrust at your religion, then fight the leaders of unbelief; they have no sacred oaths; haply they will give over."* [14]: *"Will you not fight a people who broke their oaths and purposed to expel the Messenger, beginning the first time against you? Are you afraid of them? You would do better to be afraid of God, if you are believers."* [8:61]: *"And if they incline to peace, do thou incline to it; and put thy trust in God; He is the All-hearing, the All-knowing."* [60:8]: *"God forbids you not, as regards those who have not fought you in religion's cause, nor expelled you from your habitations, that you should be kindly to them, and act justly towards them; surely God loves the just."* Having quoted these and similar verses, one of the modernist authors exclaims:

> Read those verses . . ., then you will realize that they were revealed with regard to people recalcitrantly practising persecution, amongst whom the elements of depravation were so deeply rooted that they did not respect pledges anymore and that virtue became meaningless to them. There is no doubt that to fight these people, to purify the earth from them and to put an end to their persecution is a service to the commonweal and a benefaction to mankind as a whole.[59]

Taking the aforementioned verses as the decisive ones in the relationship with unbelievers, modernists were obliged to reinterpret the verses that were traditionally understood as giving an unconditional command to fight them. They accomplished this task by means of contextual exegesis. Thus, [9:5]: *"Then, when the sacred months are drawn away, slay the idolaters wherever you find them, and take them, and confine them, and lie in wait for them at every place of ambush."* which is traditionally taken as the sword-verse, must, according to the modernists, be read in the context of the first part of *sūra* 9 *(sūrat al-tawba),* directed against the Meccans that had broken their treaty-obligations with the Muslims. This must be regarded as the immediate cause for the command to fight in K 9:5, although it is not expressly mentioned in this verse. In the same way [9:29]: *"Fight those who believe not in God and the Last Day and do not forbid what God and His Messenger have forbidden—such men as practice not the religion of truth, being of those who have been given the Book—until they pay the tribute out of hand and have been humbled"* is re-interpreted. The modernists deny that this verse contains an unconditional command to fight all People of the Book (Jews and Christians) until they pay poll-tax *(jizya),* but infer from the context that only those Jews and Christians were meant that had violated their pledges and assailed the propagation of the Islamic mission. An additional argument for this interpretation is to be found in the phrase *"have been humbled"* which implies, according to modernist authors, that previously, they were recalcitrant and that there had been reasons for the Muslims to fight them. This verse also shows, that unbelief is not the reason for fighting the People of the Book, for, if this were the case, fighting ought to be continued until conversion and not to cease when they agree to pay poll-tax. As for [9:123]: *"O believers, fight the believers who are near to you and let them find in you a harshness; and know that God is with the godfearing."*, we have seen before that this verse is to be taken as a tactical instruction, not as a general command to fight the unbelievers. Finally the modernists had to cope with the Tradition according to which Abū Bakr has said: *'I have been ordered to fight the people until they profess that there is no god but God and that Mohammed is the messenger of God, perform the ṣalāh and pay the zakāh. If they do so, their lives and property are inviolable to me, unless [when] the [law of] Islam permits them [to be taken].'* This was done by interpreting the word *'people'* in the restricted sense of *'polytheist Arabs,'* who had committed aggression against the Muslims.

The fundamentalists[60] also hold that jihad aims at defending Islam. They repudiate, however, the view that this is the sole aim and emphasize, on the contrary, the function of jihad in propagating Islam. The most important objects of jihad are, in their view, to bring about: an end to the domination of man over man and of man-made laws, the recognition of God's sovereignty alone, and the acceptance of the *Sharīʿa* as the only law. Jihad, in trying to realize these objectives, is a permanent revolutionary struggle for the sake of the whole of mankind:

> For Islam is not concerned with the interest of one nation to the exclusion of others and does not intend to advance one people to the exclusion of others. It is not at all interested in what state rules and dominates the earth, but only in the happiness and welfare of humanity. Islam has a concept and a practical program, especially chosen for the happiness and progress of human society. Therefore, Islam resists any government that is based on a different concept and program, in order to liquidate it completely. . . . Its aim is to make this concept victorious, to introduce this program universally, to set up governments that are firmly rooted in this concept and this program, irrespective of who carries the banner of truth and justice, or whose flag of aggression and corruption is thereby toppled. Islam wants the whole earth and does not content itself with only a part thereof. It wants and requires the entire inhabited world. It does not want this in order that one nation dominates the earth and monopolizes its sources of wealth, after having taken them away from one or more other nations. No, Islam wants and requires the earth in order that the human race altogether can enjoy the concept and practical program of human happiness, by means of which God has honoured Islam and put it above the other religions and laws. In order to realize this lofty desire, Islam wants to employ all forces and means that can be employed for bringing about a universal all-embracing revolution. It will spare no efforts for the achievement of this supreme objective. This far-reaching struggle that continuously exhausts all forces and this employment of all possible means are called jihad.[61]

This concept and this program aim at establishing an Islamic order of society, where the *Sharīʿa* is the leading principle:

> Islam proclaims the liberation of man on earth from the subjection to something that is not God. Therefore, Islam has to march out in order to put an end to the actual situation that conflicts with this universal proclamation, by means of both elucidation and action. It has to deliver blows at the political forces that make men the slaves of something that is not God, i.e. that do not rule them according to the *Sharīʿa* and the authority of God, those forces that prevent them from hearing the elucidation and from freely embracing the Creed, without being hindered by any authority. [It has to destroy those forces] in order to establish a social, economic and political order that allows this liberation movement to proceed effectively, after having put an end to the dominating power, regardless of whether this is purely political, or obscured by racialism or by the ideology of class-supremacy within one race. However, Islam does not seek to force people to embrace the Creed. . . . In the first place it aims at putting an end to these regimes and governments that are based on the principle that human beings rule human beings and on the subjection of men to other men. Thereupon it actually sets the individual free to choose the creed according to his own free will, after having liberated him from political pressure and after having given him elucidation that illuminates his soul and intellect.[62]

These quotations from the works of the fundamentalists are illustrative of their style and way of presentation. In fact, this is the sole feature that distinguishes fundamentalist from classical texts on jihaḍ, since both views on the relationship with unbelievers are essentially identical. The fundamentalists have wrapped up these old ideas in a modern packing, by using phrases like 'permanent revolution,' 'liberation of man,' and 'practical program,' that are all borrowed from modern political usage. This style shows striking resemblances with that of the tracts of the various Jesus-movements in Western Europe and the U.S.A., that by using similar catch-phrases with a politically progressive connotation, try to disguise their conservative message.

In contrast with the modernists, the fundamentalists adhere to the classical doctrine of *marḥaliyya,* the gradual evolution in the relationship between Mohammed and the unbelievers, culminating in the unconditional command to fight them.[63] Illustrative of the controversy between both groups, are their interpretations of [2:193 and 8:39] *"Fight them until there is no persecution and the religion is God's (entirely)."* The modernists emphasize the first part of this verse and point out that, in this case, fighting is lawful as a defence against persecution,[64] whereas the fundamentalists stress the second part and read this verse as a command to fight against the unbelievers with the aim of establishing a universal Islamic order, ruled by God's law.[65] Because of their defensive stand, the modernists are under serious attack by the fundamentalists, who accuse them of *'defeatism'* for having yielded to the ideological assaults of orientalists. For that is the reason why they have transformed the classical doctrine of jihad into a doctrine of defensive war, by interpreting the relevant Koranic verses separately and not in their historical order and by trying to demonstrate that all wars the Prophet has fought, were defensive wars:

> We shall now have a look at the impact of the malicious attacks by the orientalists on Muslim scholars, and at how the latter responded to it and defended jihad. In this connexion I am interested in the response to those scholars that have spiritually and intellectually capitulated to the attacks of the orientalists, under the pressure that at present is exerted upon the Muslims, the scholars that tried to rid their religion of these insinuations, without, however, realizing the serious consequences of what they were writing. They began to cast about for excuses for jihad, to interpret clear Koranic verses and to falsify historical facts in order to be able to say to those orientalists: 'We have nothing to do with the jihad and the sword. Jihad has been made obligatory because of certain incidental and temporary circumstances. Now, it is not obligatory anymore, since the cause has disappeared. We hold that jihad has no other aim than defence of our lives and of the country we live in.'[66]

The fundamentalists are of the opinion that one cannot apply the categories *'offensive'* or *'defensive'* to jihad, because, in their view, jihad is universal revolutionary struggle. Looking for moral justifications for jihad, as the modernists do, is senseless, since Koranic prescriptions do not require any justification. If one really wants to apply the categories *'offensive'* and *'defensive'* to jihad, one will see that there are offensive as well as defensive aspects. The offensive aspect is that all states and governments will be resisted as long as they are based on principles contradictory to Islam, especially if they are founded on the principle of the sovereignty of Man. The defensive aspects are, firstly, the self-evident fact that the present territory of Islam must be protected as a basis for expansion and, secondly, the fact that the Islamic movement protects Man against all factors that hinder his freedom and emancipation, regardless of whether these factors consist in religious convictions and ideas, social structures, or political regimes. So, if one wants to call Islam peaceful, one has to bear in mind that:

> When Islam strives for peace, it does not want a cheap peace, a peace that does not mean more than that one is safe in that particular territory where people embrace the Islamic faith. No, it wants a peace wherein all religion belongs to God, which means that all people worship God alone and that they do not take each other as objects of worship to the exclusion of God.[67]

These last words bring another difference between the modernists and the fundamentalists to light. The latter lay stress upon the Koranic words [9:7]: *"How shall the idolaters have a covenant with God and His Messenger?"* and hold that a peace treaty with polytheists is not allowed.[68]

They only accept peace when it is the result of the final victory of Islam. The modernists on the other hand, accept the principle of peaceful coexistence between the Islamic state and the rest of the world. On the authority of [8:61]: *"And if they incline to peace, do thou incline to it; and put thy trust in God; He is the All-hearing, the All-knowing."*[69] they consider it obligatory for the Muslims to respond positively if the enemy asks for a peace treaty, even, according to some, if they harbour suspicions that this request has been made perfidiously and treacherously, or that the enemy wishes to benefit from the cessation of fighting in order to prepare a new war.[70]

The divergence between the modernist and the fundamentalist view on the doctrine of jihad goes back to an essential difference in political outlook. The modernists accept to a great extent the situation they live in. Consciously or unconsciously they have adopted the Western liberal values that became current in the Islamic world as a result of economic and political penetration. Their attempts to reform Islam aimed at incorporating these values in their religion. They seem to have acquiesced in the division of the Islamic world in national states and Islamic unity is for them some vague ideal that can be invoked for the sake of certain political issues connected with religion. The Indian modernists of the latter half of the nineteenth century even condoned colonial rule and limited the scope of the jihad obligation to such an extent that resistance against colonialism was excluded. Later modernists did not go that far. They were opposed to colonial domination but accepted the fact that the struggle against foreign rule was waged within the framework of a secular nationalist ideology and that religion played but a secondary role. Hence they often referred to jihad as being a struggle 'for the sake of the fatherland and the defence of religion' *(fí sabīl al-waṭan wa-l-difāʿ ʿan al-dīn).*[71] Although this notion of jihad is in complete conformance with the classical doctrine that makes jihad an individual duty whenever an outside enemy attacks the territory of Islam, the novelty lies in the wording and the use of the word fatherland *(waṭan).*[72] For many modernists the concept of jihad has now become coextensive with that of a national war conducted by an Islamic state against a non-Islamic state, and hence they apply it to the wars between the Arab states and Israel. This identification went so far that during the October war of 1973, the Rector of the Azhar-University, ʿAbd al-Ḥalīm Maḥmūd, stripped the concept of jihad of its exclusively Islamic character by declaring that:

> Jihad is an obligation for all, without distinction between Muslims and Christians. It is the first duty of all who live under the sky of Egypt, the fatherland of all. . . . Being killed *(istishhād)* for the sake of the fatherland gives access to Paradise. This is confirmed by all divine laws *(sharāʾiʿ samāwiyya)* that have been revealed to the People of the Book.[73]

The fundamentalists, on the other hand, do not acquiesce in the present situation. Their ideal is the establishment of a truly Islamic state founded upon the prescriptions of the *Sharīʿa*. Jihad is for them the means of achieving this ideal. They wage their struggle against all who stand in the way of realizing this ideal and hence against those regimes in the Islamic world that do not apply the *Sharīʿa*, against the Western powers and against communism and zionism. In fact they carry on the struggle of the early jihad movements, which were also motivated by the ideal of invigorating the Islamic world by returning to the fundamental principles of Islam. Only their language has been modernized and brought up to date. They do not admit of a separation between religion and politics. Religion is to dominate all their activities and they reject therefore secular ideologies such as nationalism.

In fact the modernist and the fundamentalist tendency represent two different reactions to Western penetration. The modernists have reacted in a defensive manner, by adopting Western values and reforming their religion in the light of these newly imported ideas. They have transformed Islam into a religion that is well suited for the Westernized elite. The fundamentalists, on the other hand, have reacted in a self-assertive manner, by rejecting everything Western and emphasizing the real Islamic values. Both reactions are clearly reflected in their views on the doctrine of jihad.

A New Interpretation of the Jihad Doctrine: Islamic International Law

As has been shown in the preceding section, modernist authors have argued that the doctrine of jihad offers a theory of *bellum justum*. Some of them have elaborated this point and have interpreted this doctrine as *Islamic international law* or as *Islamic law of nations.*[74] This conception, however, was not really a new one. We can find it already in the works of some nineteenth-century European authors.[75] For a scholar like Pütter, who wrote in the first half of the nineteenth century, it was only logical to hold the view that there existed a separate Islamic international law, as a really general international law did not exist in his time. The law that dominated the domain of international relations between European states, was called Christian international law and was confined to the Christian states. This situation came to an end in 1856, when the Ottoman Empire was admitted to the advantages of the 'Public Law and Concert of Europe.' As a consequence, international law gradually lost its exclusively Christian character. Until quite recently, however, it was not a really universal law, as its application was restricted to civilized nations only. Thus, nearly all Asian and African nations remained outside the pale of international law. In view of this exclusive character of Western international law, the notion of Islamic international law could easily come into being. There is, however, a fundamental difference between both concepts. Christian as well as modern international law are founded on the fact that they are regarded as binding by all states concerned. On that basis they give prescriptions for international intercourse, which, in the case of Christian international law, is confined to the Christian nations. Islamic law, on the other hand, is not interested in the relations between the Islamic states as, ideally, there is but one. Its object is to provide Muslims with a code of behaviour in their relations with non-Muslims. Thus, its prescriptions are only binding for Muslims, be it individuals or the head of the state *(Imām)*. It is not concerned with the question whether non-Muslims do also consider its rules as binding. Because of the Islamic claim to universality, it does not recognize non-Muslims and non-Muslim states as legal subjects equal to Muslims and the Islamic state. Thus, the Islamic rules are completely internal and unilateral. An enlightening illustration of this can be found in the rules concerning prisoners of war. On the one hand they prescribe how Muslims must treat enemy prisoners. On the other hand they decree how Muslims must act when they happen to fall into enemy hands. Whether the enemy regards these rules as equally binding or not, is of no concern to Islamic international law. With the exception of treaty obligations, non-Muslims, insofar as they are not protected by *amān* or *dhimma*, cannot, in general, claim any right under Islamic international law.[76] In view of the divergence between Islamic doctrine and what is nowadays understood by international law[77] contemporary European authors deny the character of international law to the Islamic doctrine of jihad[78] or call it at the most 'resembling international law' (*völkerrechtsähnlich*).[79]

In the following I shall deal with two topics. The first is how modern Muslim authors view the relation between Islamic and positive international law and the viability of the Islamic system. Secondly I shall give a succinct exposé of how these authors now describe the practical rules of Islamic international law.

Although most of these authors profess Islamic international law to be a universal system, they actually adhere to the classical doctrine, as they define it as an internal law for Muslims in their relations with non-Muslims, irrespective of whether these last accept its obligatory character or not. Thus we find the following definitions of Islamic international law:

> L'ensemble des règles dont l'usage est imposé exclusivement aux musulmans pour régler leurs rapports de guerre et de paix avec les non-musulmans, individus ou états, dans le pays de l'Islam ou en dehors de ce pays;[80]
>
> That part of the law and custom of the land and treaty obligations which a Muslim de facto or de jure State observes with its dealings with other de facto and de jure States. . . . It depends wholly and solely upon the will of the Muslim State;[81]
>
> The sum total of rules and practices which Islam ordains or tolerates in international relations.[82]

Although other authors do not give express definitions, it is evident from their writings that they subscribe to this classical doctrine. Only two authors explicitly envisage the applicability of Islamic international law between separate Islamic states. Although this runs counter to the classical theory that recognizes but one single Islamic state, they argue that the Koran has admitted of the division of the Islamic world into separate political entities, where it says in [49:9]: "*If two parties of the believers fight, put things right between them; then, if one of them is insolent against the other, fight the insolent one till it reverts to God's commandment. If it reverts, set things right between them equitably, and be just. Surely, God loves the just."*[83]

Most authors do not expressly discuss the problem raised by the conflicting claims to universality of both Islamic and modern international law. They pass it over in silence or, at best, touch upon it in a vague and contradictory manner. The following quotations from one and the same book—in which the italics are mine—offer an illustrative example of their ambiguous attitude:

> Obviously, it is not necessary that there should be only one set of rules, or one system of international law, at a time, for the conduct of all the States of the world. And several systems of international law *could* and in fact *did* exist in different parts of the globe.[84]
>
> We can see now that the relevant portions of the Qur'an and Sunnah *form permanent positive law* of the Muslims in their international dealings.[85]
>
> Modern international law, *in use practically all over the world,* is in fact the law originated in Western Europe.[86]
>
> The international contentions on law of air are now *part of Muslim law,* in so far as they have been adhered to by independent Muslim states.[87]

The authors evade the problem by presenting their writings as historical or comparative studies, by means of which they want to demonstrate that the standard of Islamic international law, in view of its adaptability to modern conditions and of its humane rules, is equal or even superior to that of positive international law.[88] Some authors, however, see possibilities for future application of Islamic law in the domain of international relations:

> It must be recalled that Article 30 of the International Court of Justice mentions the writings of the highly qualified publicists of other nations as the subsidiary source of law.[89] So far only the treatises of European jurists have been referred to as evidence of law. It is hoped that with increasing cooperation among the Muslim States and their insistence on the adoption of Islamic laws and judicial system will call for occasional reference to or reliance on the works of Islamic jurisprudence [*sic*]. A recogni-

> tion of the merits of Islamic law becomes all the more imperative, now that the Western Powers no longer enjoy paramountcy in most Muslim countries, who, now freed from alien domination, are rediscovering their cultural heritage.[90]

Another author justifies his new interpretation of the classical doctrine with the contention that there is an increasing trend in the Muslim world towards the revival of Islam and the implementation of its concepts. As the rigid classical doctrine, in his view, is likely to cause a breach between the Islamic and non-Islamic states, 'it is about time to introduce an adequate interpretation to be of service to the cause of world peace and security. Apart from many details of considerable interest, Islamic legal theory presents an advance on modern thought as regards the fundamental problems of international law.'[91] Finally it has been proposed to use the principles of Islamic international law as a regional form of international law to be applied in the projected Arab Court of Justice.[92]

An important characteristic of the writings on Islamic international law is that in nearly all of them the point is stressed that Islamic international law, at least in its principles, is superior to positive international law.[93] The argument that one meets most frequently is that Islamic international law can boast of a venerable age of thirteen centuries, whereas the present system of international law was created only four hundred years ago. The illustrious and humane principles of Islamic international law were formulated and applied at a time when, in the rest of the world, international relations were still dominated by barbaric anarchy and the savage law of the jungle. Muḥammad al-Shaybāni, the first Muslim author to compose a major work devoted exclusively to *siyar,* the Islamic law dealing with relations with non-Muslims, is often called the Hugo Grotius of Islam. In addition to this, there exists a thesis that has become popular and found many supporters amongst Muslim authors, to the effect that European international law has been strongly influenced by the *Sharīʿa* via intercultural contracts during the Crusades and in Spain. E. Nys[94] and Baron Michel de Taube[95] were the first to assume a certain influence of Islamic law on Western international law. Muslim authors have run away with this thesis and usually present it in a much exaggerated form.[96] This idea, it be noted in passing, finds its parallel in the contention that European civil law is to a great extent indebted to the *Sharīʿa*.[97]

Further evidence for the superiority of Islamic international law is, according to Muslim writers, to be found in the remarkable fact that Islamic international law has, since its inception, thirteen centuries ago, stood for principles that were only recently recognized in modern international law. The foremost of these is the principle of equality and reciprocality which, in modern international law, was formally accepted only with the creation of the United Nations. Previously, there existed a distinction between Christian and heathen nations, a distinction that was gradually replaced by one between civilized and uncivilized or savage nations. To these last full international personality was denied. Muslim authors enlarge upon this inequality and oppose it to the principle of equality and reciprocality as guaranteed in Koranic verses like [2:213]: *"The people were one nation; then God sent forth the Prophets, good tidings to bear and warning, and He sent down with them the Book with the truth, that He might decide between the people touching their differences."*; [60:8]: *"God forbids you not, as regards those who have not fought you in religion's cause, nor expelled you from your habitations, that you should be kindly to them, and act justly towards them; surely God loves the just."*; [2:194]: *"The holy month for the holy month; holy things demand retaliation. Whoso commits aggression against you, do you commit aggression against him like as he has committed against you; and fear you God, and know that God is with the godfearing."*[98] Actually, these sweeping assertions about Islam recognizing the equality of all mankind and the reciprocality in interstate relations, amount to no more than gratuitous and noncommittal slogans. When they come down to the details of the relations between Muslims and non-Muslims, they hardly depart from the classical doctrine and maintain the legal distinction between Muslims and non-Muslims and between the Islamic and the other states. Only one author attempts to give a more or less concrete and elaborate form to the notion of a community of equal states in Islamic international law. This community, however, does not embrace all states, as its membership is subject to certain restrictions. The author founds his theory on [3:64]: *"Say: 'People of the Book! Come now to a word common between us and you, that we serve none but God, and that we associate not aught with Him, and do some of us not take others as Lords, apart from God.'"* By *'a word common between you and me'* (Ar.: *kalimat sawāʾ*) the author understands 'a word on the basis of equality, an agreement.' His interpretation then goes on:

> The Arabic text, thus, connotes that the agreement to which the Scriptuaries [i.e. the People of the Book, RP] are called is based on the principle of legal equality since the only condition is to admit the oneness of God, not to become Muslims. From the Islamic point of view the acknowledgement of the oneness of God is the preliminary prerequisite for establishing peaceful relations among the Muslims and the non-Muslims. In other words, the Islamic state could not tolerate being bound with another state by common interests unless the latter's civilization is based on the idea of unity of Deity. A state under Muslim international law is not entitled to claim the right of legal equality unless it attains a certain degree of civilization, that is to say when its civilization is moulded with the idea of the unity of God.[99]

The author compares this restriction to the conditions of membership of the United Nations, as mentioned in Article 4 of the Charter of the U.N.: 'Membership of the United Nations is open to all other peace-loving states which accept the obligations contained in the present charter and, in the judgement of the organization, are able and willing to carry out these obligations.'[100] The author doubts whether communist countries, 'with their dialectical materialism' could be admitted to the pale of international law.[101]

An argument of equal importance for establishing the superiority of Islamic international law is, according to modern authors, its peaceful character. From its beginning, thirteen centuries ago, it has recognized peace as the fundamental relationship between the Islamic and the other states. Moreover, it has developed clearcut definitions of the notions of *bellum justum* and of aggression, something which, if we may believe these authors, positive international law has, until now, not achieved. For more details and for the scriptural arguments for this opinion I refer to the previous sections.

Treatises on Islamic international law can roughly be divided into two categories. Some authors take modern works on international law as a starting point and compare the various topics with the Islamic prescriptions. If they cannot find corresponding prescriptions, which occurs frequently, they develop them themselves by interpreting the Koran and the *Sunna*. Thus, they pay much attention to theoretical topics like sources of Islamic international law, the nature of its rules, international legal personality, sovereignty, treaties and the like.[102] Other authors do not go deeply into the theories and notions of positive international law. They depart from the classical doctrine of the *Sharīʿa,* which they reinterpret and rearrange so as to cast it in the mould of a more or less Western inspired system.[103] In the following I shall first deal with two points of a more theoretical character as expounded by authors of the first category, viz. the notion of international legal personality and the problem of the obligatory character of international law. Then I shall proceed with a succinct survey of the more concrete rules of Islamic international law.

International personality is still a hotly debated issue in international law. For a long time, modern international law has recognized as legal subjects only sovereign states. Exceptionally, as in the case of crimes against humanity, international legal norms are directly addressed to individuals, but in general, this takes place via municipal legislation codifying international legal rules. Only recently are voices heard advocating the extension of international personality to individuals and to colonized peoples, but prevailing opinion hesitates and is reluctant in conferring it to subjects other than states. This is connected with the doctrine that there exist two separate and distinct realms of law: that of international law and that of municipal law. Modern authors on Islamic international law assert that international personality does not offer any problem at all in Islamic law, precisely because it does not admit of a division between international and municipal law. The *Sharīʿa* addresses its rules to individuals as well as collectivities. Although classical doctrine did not develop any theory on the corporate personality of collectivities, modern authors claim that the foundations of such a theory can be found in the following Koranic verses [49:13]: *"O mankind, We have created you male and female, and appointed you races and tribes, that you may know one another. Surely the noblest among you in the sight of God is the most godfearing of you. God is All-knowing, All-aware."*; [3:104]: *"Let there be one nation of you, calling to good, and bidding to honour; those are the prosperers."*; [17:16]: *"And when we desire to destroy a city, We command its men who live at ease, and they commit ungodliness therein, then the Word is realized against it, and We destroy it utterly."*[105] One author elaborates on the theory of corporate personality in Islamic international law and contends that the *Sharīʿa* offers better criteria for deciding whether international personality should be conferred to a given territorial community than positive international law does, viz.: territory, population and a sovereign government. Islam, according to this author, establishes the following criteria: (1) socio-cultural unity (which in classical Islam was called unity of religion); (2) representative political leadership (as, in classical Islam, the caliph should be public choice); and (3) unity of legal system (which in classical Islam was called unity of the *Sharīʿa*). In his view, these three criteria can remedy the present situation in positive international law, whereby international personality is denied to colonized peoples and certain international organizations.[106]

In contemporary theory of international law, there is no unanimity as to the source of its obligatory character. This theoretical problem has, until now, not been solved in a satisfactory manner. Some hold that its source is to be found in the subjective will of the individual states. However, accepting this implies that states can shirk the obligations imposed by international law by merely withdrawing their consent. As law characteristically emanates from an authority of a higher order than that of its legal subjects, some have looked upon the collective will *(Vereinbarung)* of all states, as the source of the obligatory character of international law, as this must be of a higher authority than the will of the individual state. However, the weakness of this theory lies in the fact that it presupposes a unity of separate wills. As conflict of interests between states is rather the rule than the exception, it is hard to postulate the existence of this unified will. Other theories have turned away from these subjective principles. One of these derives the obligatory character of international law from the fact that every community presupposes the observance of certain rules to ensure mutual solidarity, for, if it fails to do so, this community would cease to exist. Thus, the basis of international law is to be found in the social fact *(fait social)* that the existence of a community depends on the observance of certain restrictions by its members. These restrictions develop into binding legal norms when the members of the community become conscious of them. This theory, however, can account for the existence of law, but it cannot explain what precisely is the basis of its binding character. Finally, there is a school of thought that holds that the validity of any legal rule must be derived from another rule that governs its creation. This presupposes the existence of one supreme fundamental norm from which the validity of all inferior rules is derived. However, the existence of such a rule is axiomatic and cannot be verified, which certainly weakens its explanatory force. *Vis-à-vis* these controversies and conflicting theories, Islam offers, according to modern Muslim authors, a clear and simple solution: the obligatory character of Islamic international law derives from divine revelation. Since the rules of the *Sharīʿa* are God's commands, they are sanctioned by religion. Thus, legal rules in Islam have a moral dimension, which according to Muslim authors, is lacking in Western laws, and, especially, in positive international law. The enforcement of Islamic prescriptions is therefore enhanced by this religious or moral sanction. In the Koran, one repeatedly finds exhortations to fulfil pledges, like: [16:91]: *"Fulfil God's covenant, when you make covenant, and break not the oaths after they have been confirmed, and you have made God your surety; surely God knows the things you do."*; [17:36]: *"And fulfil the covenant; surely the covenant shall be questioned of"*; [9:4]: *"Excepting those of the idolaters with whom you made a covenant; then they failed you naught neither lent support to any man against you. With them fulfil your covenant till their term; surely God loves the godfearing."* This means that the principle of *pacta sunt servanda* is a religiously sanctioned norm in Islam. On the strength of K 9:4, this norm applies also in the domain of international relations. This, precisely, constitutes the superiority of Islamic to positive international law.[107] This same argument is also brought up by advocates of reintroduction of the *Sharīʿa* in the field of civil and penal law.[108]

I shall now give a survey of the more concrete rules of Islamic international law as expounded by Muslim authors on the subject. Many of these topics have also been dealt with by other authors in their reinterpretation of the classical doctrine of jihad. In this exposé, I shall globally adhere to the systematic arrangement of the authors on Islamic international law. Generally, they group the subject-matter under two headings: international relations in peace-time and international relations in war-time. The topics that fall under the first heading are: the principle of peaceful relations between the Islamic and the other states, diplomacy and treaties. Because of its doctrinal pedigree, which goes back to truce and armistice, some authors discuss this last topic under the second heading. This heading, international relations in war-time, includes the following topics: lawful and unlawful wars, ultimatum and declaration of war, treatment of enemy persons and property, prisoners of war, safeconduct and quarter, and the conclusion of war.

As the principle of peaceful relations has been discussed before I shall not go into it here. That diplomacy is dealt with as a peacetime institution is significant as it shows the desire of modern authors to emphasize the peaceful character of the doctrine of jihad. For the only classical rule with regard to envoys is that they are automatically granted safeconduct *(amān)*. Now, this only makes sense in case of hostile relations. Modern authors, however, put this automatically granted safeconduct on a par with the modern institution of diplomatic immunity. As the status of diplomats is hardly touched upon in the classical *fiqh*-books, most modern authors amplify this topic with historical instances of diplomacy between the Islamic and other states.[109]

As a consequence of the classical Islamic doctrine, that does not admit of permanent peaceful relations between the Islamic and the other states, the classical works on *fiqh* discuss only three kinds of treaties: collective *amān* or quarter, temporary armistice or truce and the permanent treaty of *dhimma* whereby a population is brought under the sway of the Islamic state. In the last case, the non-Muslim population is allowed to abide by their own religion, but has to pay a special tax, *jizya*. Modern authors, however, who hold that the relations between the Islamic and the other states are essentially peaceful, assert that all kinds of treaties are allowed in Islamic international law. In peace time, the Islamic state may conclude permanent commercial treaties, pacts of friendship and the like. They found their opinion on the general Koranic commands to fulfil pledges and on Mohammed's example, as tradition has it that he has concluded a treaty with the Jews of Medina.[110] In order to develop a general theory on permanent treatises, modern authors had to do away with the restrictions that the *Sharīʿa* imposes on armistices and truces, for most schools hold that armistices can only be concluded for a limited period. The Hanafites did allow treatises with unlimited duration, but they stipulated that the *Imām* has the right to rescind treaties whenever this is in the interest of the Muslims.[111] According to modern authors, this last implicit condition, viz. that a treaty will remain valid as long as it is in the interests of the Muslims, closely resembles the doctrine of the *clausula rebus sic stantibus* in positive international law. Therefore, Hanafite opinion would be acceptable, were it not that it is contrary to the general Koranic injunctions to fulfil pledges and with [8:58]: *"And if thou fearest treachery any way at the hands of a people, dissolve it with them equally."*, which requires that there be objective indications of treachery.[112] These same general Koranic injunctions and Mohammed's example in concluding a pact with the Jews of Medina, serve as arguments against the classical doctrine that only admits of temporary treaties.[113] Few authors mention the general conditions for the validity of treaties. They do not depart very far from the classical doctrine and enumerate the following requirements: Treaties must be concluded by the *Imām* or his proxy. In the latter case the treaty is subject to ratification by the *Imām* in order to ascertain that the proxy has not exceeded the limits of his mandate. The stipulations of treaties may not be contrary to the fundamental laws of Islam. This is founded on the Tradition: *'Every stipulation that is not to be found in the book, is void.'*[114] Treaties concluded under duress are null and void as they must be based upon mutual consent. Finally, the stipulations of treaties must be specific, so that the rights and obligations of the parties are well defined and do not admit of different interpretations. The Koran warns against treaties with obscure stipulations in [16:94]: *"Take not your oaths as mere mutual deceit, lest any foot should slip after it has stood firm, and you should taste evil, for that you barred from the way of God, and lest there should await you a mighty chastisement."*[115]

Under the heading international relations in wartime, we find, after a general discussion on lawful and unlawful wars, that we have dealt with before, the rules concerning declaration of war or ultimatum. This is the modern version of the summons to Islam (*daʿwa*), which according to the classical doctrine, must in some cases precede fighting.[116] Contrary to the classical rules, modern authors assert that previous notification of an attack accompanied by a summons to Islam or to the acceptance of *jizya* is obligatory in all cases. Its aim is not only to warn the civil population in enemy territory of the coming hostilities, but also to inform the enemy that Islam fights for a religious cause and not for conquest or worldly gain. Proudly, the authors conclude that the Islamic injunctions concerning declaration of war are thirteen centuries older than modern international codification in this domain as embodied in the *Hague Convention on the Opening of Hostilities* of 1907. These rules, however, our authors hasten to add, are hardly observed in the West, as surprise attacks have rather become the rule than the exception. They ascribe this phenomenon to the fundamental weakness of positive international law, which lacks a religious or moral sanction, contrary to Islamic law.[117]

The law of warfare is the pet subject of modernist authors. Usually they give a selective anthology of the most humane regulations to be found in the classical works on *fiqh*[118] and compare them with modern international conventions on warfare. Characteristic is the subsequent quotation that follows an enumeration of the acts forbidden by modern conventions:

> As we have already said, Islam forbids all this and even more. It forbids to kill and to fight the wounded, it forbids to fight those who have shed their weapons, it forbids to kill monks and religious dignitaries and to destroy their cells and churches. Islam forbids sabotage, whereas modern international law

> allows the destruction of highways, bridges and anything that can be of use to the enemy.[119]

In general, they adopt the terminology of the modern regulations on warfare. Thus, the prohibition of killing women, infants and decrepit old men, is put on a par with the modern prohibition to attack the civilian population. Only occasionally is attention paid to the modern technological development of warfare. One author goes into the question whether Islam allows the use of the atomic bomb. On the strength of [8:60]: *"Make ready for them whatever force and strings of horses you can, to terrify thereby the enemy of God and your enemy."*) he concludes that its production is permitted. Its use, however, is restricted to retaliation or defence in case of a nuclear attack by the enemy, because of [2:194]: *"Whoso commits aggression against you, do you commit aggression against him like as he has committed against you."*[120] One other author touches upon modern methods of warfare. But as he is carried away by his enthusiasm over alleged early Muslim inventions of poisonous gas and the use of gliders in battles, he hardly goes into the legal implications, except that he holds that modern conventions on warfare, insofar as they have been adhered to by Muslim states, form part of Islamic international law.[121] Finally, some authors mention that Islam prohibits attacks upon ambulances, medical orderlies and stretcher bearers.[122]

According to classical doctrine, the *Imām* has the choice between four policies with regard to prisoners of war; he may kill them, enslave them, exchange them against a ransom or he may liberate them without any condition.[123] Modern authors, however, argue on the strength of [47:4]: *"When you meet the unbelievers, smite their necks, then, when you have made wide slaughter among them, tie fast the bonds* [i.e. take prisoners]; *then set them free, either by grace or ransom* [i.e. liberate them out of kindness or in return for ransom], *till the war lays down its loads."*, that the *Imām*'s choice is restricted to liberating them with or without ransom. Killing of prisoners of war is forbidden according to these authors, who also adduce the opinion of some early lawyers in support of their theory. Individual prisoners, however, may be killed if there is some specific reason for it. Thus they explain the historical instances of killing of prisoners during Mohammed's lifetime. As to enslavement, they hold that in early days this was permitted, since the enemy acted likewise with Muslim prisoners of war. They found this opinion on [16:126]: *"And if you chastise, chastise even as you have been chastised."* Many authors remark that, just as the Geneva convention of 1929 prescribes, Islam considers prisoners of war as prisoners of the state and not as prisoners of the individuals or military units that have captured them. Prisoners of war must be treated well, fed and clothed. This prescription derives from [76:8]: *"They give food for the love of Him, to the needy, the orphan, the captive."*[124]

As the treatment of *amān* by modern authors remains within the traditional framework and does not offer striking examples of modernist interpretation, I shall not go into it, but proceed with the rules concerning the conclusion of war. The following possibilities are envisaged for wars to end: (1) mere cessation of hostilities; (2) victory of the Muslim army; (3) surrender of the enemy, i.e. conversion to Islam; and (4) treaty of peace or armistice.[125] Most authors, however, only discuss the last possibility, the termination of war by means of a treaty of peace or armistice. The crucial question in this connexion is whether the Muslims may conclude a permanent treaty of peace with unbelievers, since the classical doctrine only admits armistices with a limited duration or with a unilaterally revocable character.[126] As we have seen, most authors are of the opinion that in peace time all kinds of permanent treaties are allowed. Although they also profess that Muslims may conclude permanent peace treaties with their enemies in order to put an end to the war between them, they differ when it comes to details. For some assert that the only permanent treaty of peace that Islam allows is the pact of *dhimma*. As this implies that the non-Muslims must recognize the suzerainty of the Islamic state and pay a special tax, the *jizya*, one cannot really call it a treaty of peace. It rather has the character of surrender. Besides the pact of *dhimma*, they only admit of temporary armistices. Thus they remain within the scope of the classical doctrine.[127] Other authors, however, hold that permanent treaties of peace other than the pact of *dhimma* are possible, provided that the propagation of Islam is secured and is not subject to any hindrance on the part of the other state.[128]

It is evident that the writings I have discussed in this chapter have a highly apologetic character. The classical doctrine of jihad has been stripped of its militancy and is represented as an adequate legal system for maintaining peace in the domain of international relations. Emphasis is laid upon the ethical values underlying this system. Islamic international law, according to our Muslim Panglosses, is the best of all possible systems. It surpasses positive international law in peacefulness, tolerance, respect for human dignity, denunciation of colonialism and exploitation, fidelity to pledges and humanity. To enhance these exalted principles, they contrast them with the wicked practices of contemporary international intercourse, rife with dishonesty, atrocities and outrages against humanity. Moreover, many authors extol the legal genius of Islam, as it has been able to develop a theory of international law, long before modern international law came into being. This theory, they argue, is adaptable to satisfy present-day conditions and offers solutions to problems that modern international law has until yet not been able to cope with. Its superiority is a consequence of its religious character that bestows a moral sanction on it. As a result, its enforcement is achieved in a better way than in positive international law. The writings on Islamic international law are typically part of the mainstream of apologetic writings that defend Islam against an unfavourable image that used to be prevalent in the West. Apart from jihad, this defence is concerned with the position of women, slavery, penal law, human rights and the like. In all these fields, it is claimed that the Islamic rules can easily stand comparison with Western institutions.

9

The Relevance of the Jihad Doctrine in Sadat's Egypt[1]

Since the beginning of the 1970s the doctrine of jihad has made a comeback in the Islamic world. While in previous decades it appeared to have faded to a mere theory—mainly a topic for academic discussion—occasionally it was allowed to play a marginal role in politics when Islamic dignitaries invoked it to spur on the fighting spirit of Muslim soldiers in the Arab–Israeli wars. However, since the beginning of the 1970s this has changed, and Islamic symbols and idioms have become more central to political discourse as Islamic movements have reappeared on the political scene. As a consequence, the doctrine of jihad has returned to favour.

The following paper deals with the political role of the jihad in Egypt under Anwar Sadat (1970–81). The word jihad has many meanings, usually connected with an effort towards a commendable aim, which is as a rule religious (such as the struggle against Satan or one's own evil inclinations) but need not be so. Ten years ago for instance, jihad for cleanliness of public places and the removal of garbage from the streets was proclaimed by the authorities in Cairo. The term will be discussed here, however, in its sense of fighting and armed struggle, which is its principal meaning in traditional Islamic law. Indeed, it seems appropriate to use the term in this way here, as the period under consideration was terminated by a violent act that was justified by the doctrine of jihad.

When is violence permissible and against whom? These prac-

From Rudolph Peters, "The Political Relevance of Jihad Doctrine in Sadat's Egypt," in *National and International Politics in the Middle East. Essays in Honour of Elie Kedourie.* Edited E. Ingram. London: Frank Cass, 1986, pp. 252–271.

tical and concrete questions regarding the application of jihad doctrine are the central ones in this paper. The abstract and theoretical aspects of jihad are of minor importance, as hardly any novel points of view have been put forward on the subject during our period. The traditionalists copy the phrases of the classical works on *fiqh;* the modernists emphasize the defensive aspect of jihad, regarding it as tantamount to *bellum justum* in modern international law; and the fundamentalists view it as a struggle for the expansion of Islam and the realization of Islamic ideals.[2]

After a survey of the growth of Islamic movements in Egypt,[3] two discussions of jihad doctrine will be analyzed here. The first is a debate on the application of the rules of jihad to the Camp David Agreement between Egypt and Israel. The other revolves around the question of whether jihad against the Egyptian government is allowable under the present circumstances.

The Arab–Israeli war of 1967 is usually regarded as having been crucial to Islamic revival in the Middle East. It marked not only the defeat of Israel's Arab neighbours, but also that of two radical Arab nationalist regimes, the result of which was to discredit the secular nationalist and socialist ideologies they espoused. One response was the rise of leftist radicalism, claiming that the defeated regimes had not been radical enough and represented by groups of intellectuals and university students, and by the various Palestinian nationalist organizations. Between 1967 and the October War of 1973 both were repressed: the leftist groups of intellectuals and students were dealt with locally, while King Hussein of Jordan acted as the proxy of the other Arab states in the region in subduing the Palestinian National Movement in 1970 and 1971.

The containment of the left was a corollary of the realignment of forces in the Middle East, another more lasting result of the 1967 defeat. If only for financial reasons, Egypt and Syria had to come to terms with the conservative Arab oil-producing countries, by abandoning their radical stance and bringing their policies more in line with the wishes of their patrons. As a result, a certain Islamization of political vocabulary and symbolism in political discourse took place, particularly evident in the October

War of 1973 ('Operation Badr'), when religious images and concepts were much more frequently used than they had been in 1967.

Perhaps an even more important aspect of the new state of affairs in the region was the *rapprochement* between the erstwhile radical regimes and the United States. President Nasser's acceptance of William Rogers's plan for a settlement in the Middle East in 1970 anticipated Sadat's pro-Western policy, which—via the expulsion of the Soviet military advisers, the removal of the pro-Soviet faction in the state-apparatus, and the crack-down on Communist and Nasserist students—ultimately led to the Camp David Agreement in March 1979.

Connected with the establishment of American hegemony in the Middle East was the economic integration of the Arab states, especially Egypt, into the capitalist world market. After 1967, in order to gain the support of the middle and upper classes who had been alienated from the regime by its socialist economic policies, Nasser had inaugurated a policy of producing and importing more consumer goods. Sadat not only continued this policy, but gave it more prominence by announcing his Open Door Policy in 1975. The effect of all this was the rise of a section of the bourgeoisie that profited from the increased import trade of luxury consumer goods and, above all, from the increased economic links with other countries. This group delighted in the ostentatious display of its rapidly-acquired wealth, while the overwhelming majority of Egyptians was obliged to live off extremely meagre public sector salaries, or eke out a scanty livelihood as agricultural wage labourers. Such conspicuous consumption by the newly rich sharpened the social and economic contradictions in society.

Heightened social and economic tensions provide a fertile soil for radical movements militating against the established order for a just society. Such tensions are emphasized in the idioms in which radical movements express themselves, whether they derive from secular ideologies like socialism, anarchism, or fascism, or from religious thought. The ideology to which a specific movement subscribes is therefore contingent on the prevailing cultural and political conditions, and it is to these we must look for an explanation of why most of the Egyptian radical movements in the 1970s were inspired by Islam.

One important cause was the tension that existed in Egyptian culture. In the wake of reorientation towards the West, Western consumer goods and living styles had invaded certain sections of Egyptian society, via the mass media. In short, Western popular culture was much more in evidence in 1975 than in the preceding quarter of a century, and posed a threat to many people, especially those who lacked the financial means to join in, and thus felt themselves excluded. At the same time, the introduction of Islamic norms and ideals into politics and public life was stimulated by the government, which hoped to use Islam as a weapon against the left and simultaneously to curry favour with the Arab oil states. This contradiction between Western culture and the Islamization of public life and political discourse, in addition to the disparagement of leftist ideas in the wake of the 1967 defeat, and the government's persistent attack on the evils of 'atheist ideologies,' created the conditions for the rise of Islamic movements, which sought to reform society in the direction of the Islamic norm.

The first movement of this kind consisted of the *Jamāʿāt Islāmiyya* (Islamic Groups) at the Egyptian universities. They were founded around 1972 with active support from the government, in the hope of their countering the Communist and Nasserist student organizations then dominating political life at the universities and since 1968 the source of frequently staged protest meetings, demonstrations, and sit-ins against the government. However, though they were backed by the regime, the *Jamāʿāt Islāmiyya* were not mere instruments with no will of their own. They had their own ideas and objectives, as is evidenced by their falling-out with the government over Sadat's journey to Jerusalem in 1977.

By then they had acquired a large following among students, as a result of assiduous work and clever organizing which, together with discreet government backing, had enabled them to take over the student unions in 1976–7. Part of their popularity was due to their ability to provide Islamic solutions to common problems such as transportation for women students, who were being harassed in the overcrowded buses of the Cairo public transport system. The condition in this case, however, was that women must thereafter wear Islamic dress. As an alternative to the expensive private lessons necessary to pass examinations, study groups were organized in mosques. Cheap copies of textbooks were distributed, and efforts made to improve student housing. At the same time the *Jamāᶜāt Islāmiyya* militated at the universities for the application of Islamic norms such as the separation of the sexes in lecture halls, the banning of film shows and singing, and the establishment of prayer rooms. As a demonstration of their popularity, they organized mass prayer meetings in large squares or in stadiums. Like all Islamic movements, the *Jamāᶜāt Islāmiyya* wanted to create a truly religious society. They tried to mainly by peaceful means, which is to say by preaching, by creating a large following, and by themselves attaining influential positions in society.

The year 1977 was a turning-point for the *Jamāᶜāt Islāmiyya.* Because of their critical stance towards Egypt's new policy *vis-à-vis* Israel, the government withdrew its support and began to work against them. It withheld subsidies from the student unions they dominated and tried to rig the unions' elections. Finally, in 1979, all student unions were banned, which deprived the *Jamāᶜāt Islāmiyya* of their legal cover, their organization, and their funds. Many of their militants became more radical and in 1979 and 1981 were implicated in sectarian violence in Upper Egypt and Cairo. Their activities came to an end when many of their active members were arrested during Sadat's crack-down on religious groups in September 1981.

A second tendency within the Egyptian Islamic movement is represented by the group supporting the old magazine of the Muslim Brotherhood, *al-Daᶜwa,* which was allowed to resume publication in 1976. This group considers itself as the rightful heir of the Muslim Brotherhood of the 1930s and 1940s, and Hasan al-Banna's portrait is prominently featured on the magazine's pages. The social background of its following, however, is totally different. Whereas the membership of the Muslim Brotherhood of old was drawn chiefly from the lower and middle classes, the *al-Daᶜwa* group represents the interests of the section of the bourgeoisie that has profited from the Open Door Policy and has close economic ties with the Arab oil countries. This group wants Egypt to forge tighter political and economic links with oil countries, and is therefore against any *rapprochement* between Egypt and Israel.

It also wants to realize the ideal of the Islamic state by the introduction of Islamic Law, the *Sharīʿa,* not by the overthrow of the state, but rather by means of press campaigns and lobbying, by legal means, and adherence to the established political conventions. A number of the group were arrested in September 1981 and their organ was banned. However, the group remained in existence and came to an agreement with the opposition Wafd party to join its election platform, with the result that the *al-Daʿwa* group is now represented in the People's Assembly.

Both the *al-Daʿwa* group and the *Jamāʿāt Islāmiyya* operated legally. As they were committed to the Islamization of state and society by peaceful means, they represented the reformist trend in the Islamic movement. The revolutionary trend consisted of a number of radical organizations that did not eschew the use of violence as a means of realizing their aims. They justified this by the doctrine of *takfīr,* the view that in spite of all appearances, the rulers or even society as a whole is godless *(kāfir),* an idea whose origins can be traced back to heretical sects in the early centuries of Islam and has recently been revived among the Muslim Brothers detained in the Egyptian prisons and detention camps.[4] The members of these organizations were mainly students and young university graduates with rural backgrounds. Entangled in the contradictions between their conservative background and university life in the big cities, they would frequent mosques and religious gatherings, where they could easily be recruited by the leaders and older members of these organizations.

There have been, and probably still are, several of these groups. But as they work clandestinely it is difficult to keep track of and get information about them. However, three of them have attained notoriety, being implicated in bloody incidents, after which their membership and leaders were tried and sentenced. In April 1974, a group led by Ṣāliḥ Sirriyya, a young Palestinian with a doctorate in science, carried out an attack on the Military

Academy in Heliopolis, as the first stage in a planned *coup d'état.* The organization, named *Munaẓẓamat al-Taḥrīr al-Islāmī,* but later commonly referred to as the Military Academy Organization *(Munaẓẓamat al-Fanniyya al-ʿAskariyya),* was started in 1971 when Sirriyya came to Egypt. The plan—an act of violence—*ghaḍba lillāh* (an outcry for the sake of God)—was to topple the government and establish a true Islamic state. The attempt was foiled, however, and the members of the group arrested and brought to trial.

Three years later, in July 1977, the members of another group, calling itself 'The Association of Muslims' *(Jamāʿat al-Muslimīn),* but better known as *Jamāʿat al-Takfīr wa-l-Hijra,* were arrested for having kidnapped and assassinated the minister of *Awqāf,* Muḥammad Ḥusayn al-Dhahabī. This organization was also established around 1971. Its leader, Muṣṭafā Shukrī, an agricultural engineer, had recruited members both in Upper Egypt and in Cairo and Alexandria. There is a curious contradiction between the basic tenets of the movement and the violent acts that marked its end. As had many other groups, it considered all outsiders as unbelievers *(takfīr).* However, as it realized it did not yet have the strength to fight the prevailing unbelief, it saw its duty as separation from society *(hijra)* and building a genuine Islamic community. After the growth of this community and the attainment of a position of strength, it would wage the struggle against the rest of society with the object of establishing a totally Islamic society and state. It was a typical long-term strategy. However, when in the beginning of 1977 a number of the organization's members were arrested, many others pressed for immediate action to free their imprisoned brethren. They kidnapped al-Dhahabi—in their view a prominent representative of the corrupt establishment of official ulema—and demanded that the government set their comrades free, publish their statements widely in the media, and pay them a large sum of money. When these demands were not met, they killed their hostage.

The last of these three groups is the Jihad Organization *(Tanẓīm al-Jihād),* which was responsible for President Sadat's assassination. This group only recently established itself in Upper Egypt and Cairo and was not fully organized before 1980. It prepared for a *coup d'état,* which in its opinion would almost automatically be followed by a popular revolt. There were some soldiers among the organization's members and one of them, Khālid al-Islāmbūlī, was directly responsible for the murder of Sadat in October 1981.

In many countries of the Islamic world it is common practice for governments to seek endorsement of important or controversial policies by the official ulema, in order to show that these policies conform to or, at least, do not run counter to the prescriptions of Islam. This is exactly what Sadat did when he prevailed upon the Al-Azhar University and the religious institutions connected with it to issue statements on the legality according to the *Sharīʿa* of the Camp David Agreement of March 1979. Apparently, it took some time to convince them to endorse this new policy—in the past they had often issued declarations to the effect that war against Israel was obligatory and that the conclusion of a peace treaty forbidden[5]—for the *fatwā* was not drafted before 9 May 1979. For reasons unknown, this *fatwā* seems not to have been published.[6] On 10 May, however, a declaration by the Azhar sheikhs was published in both *al-Ahrām* and *al-Akhbār,* summarizing the arguments of this *fatwā.*[7] Eight days later it was followed by an elucidation by the minister of *Awqāf,* ʿAbd al-Munʿim Nimr, in response to criticism by ulema in other Arab countries.[8] Much later, on 16 November 1979, the state mufti *(Muftī l-Diyār al-Miṣriyya)* issued a *fatwā* on the subject.[9] The discussion here is based on the declarations of the Azhar sheikhs and the minister of *Awqāf* published on 10 and 18 May 1979.

The official ulema's arguments in support of the agreement derive from the classical doctrine which teaches that the head of an Islamic state *(al-imām)* may conclude an armistice with the enemy whenever he deems one to be in the interest of Muslims. However, they do not refer to the duration of the armistice, which, according to most legal schools, must be limited in order to keep the jihad obligation alive. This omission may have been merely political, but could also be a consequence of the ulema's modernist position that peaceful co-existence is the normal state of affairs between *Dār al-Islām* and *Dār al-Ḥarb,* a view different from the classical doctrine that holds that war, jihad, is the natural relationship between the Islamic and non-Islamic worlds. In the latter doctrine, a peace treaty between an Islamic and a non-Islamic state is allowed only in case of necessity, as a temporary suspension of hostilities.

The evidence the ulema adduce for the general permissibility of treaties with the enemy is similar to that found in the standard texts on *fiqh:*[10] they cite K 8:61 *('And if they incline to peace, do thou incline to it')* and the examples of the Prophet in concluding a treaty with the Meccans at Ḥudaybiyya and in planning to conclude an agreement with the Ghaṭafān tribe to the effect that, for a consideration, they would abandon the confederacy of tribes then laying siege to Medina.

The ulema's point of view was severely criticized in *al-Daʿwa*[11] by ʿAbd al-ʿAẓīm al-Maṭāʿnī, who defends the view that in the present circumstances a peace treaty with Israel is not allowed according to Islam.[12] The circumstances under which the Prophet concluded the treaty of Ḥudaybiyya were so different from the present situation, he argues, that this comparison cannot be offered as evidence for the lawfulness of the treaty with Israel. And what is more, the treaty of Ḥudaybiyya was to last only ten years. The intended pact with Ghaṭafān was never made and cannot, therefore, in al-Maṭāʿnī's view, count as evidence. As for K 8:61, he argues that this verse has no general validity, and must be read in combination with K 47:35 *('So do not faint and call for peace; you shall be the upper ones').* The former verse is applicable when the enemy recognizes all Muslim rights, whereas the second verse obtains when this is not the case—as in the present situation according to al-Maṭāʿnī. Moreover, many jurists have taught that K 8:61 has been abrogated by the Verses of Fighting, such as K 9:5 *('Then, when the sacred months are drawn away, slay the idolaters wherever you find them, and take them, and confine them, and lie in wait for them at every place of ambush').* But even if K 8:61 has not been abrogated, al-Maṭāʿnī maintains, the Koran makes fighting incumbent in a number of specific instances—as in the situation of an oppressed Muslim people asking for help—on the strength of K 4:75 *('How is it with you, that you do not fight in the way of God, and for the men, women and children who, being abased, say, "Our Lord, bring us forth from this city whose people are evildoers, and appoint to us a protector from Thee, and appoint to us from Thee a helper"?'*).

Interestingly, al-Maṭāʿnī does not mention the role of the head of the state in deciding when to wage war and when to accept peace, something which is an essential and realistic element in the classical theory. He was therefore an easy prey for the official ulema. The main thrust of the Al-Azhar's counter-attack was directed against this politically sensitive issue, and in his reply al-Maṭāʿnī was forced to recognize the head of state's authority in these matters.[13] His criticism consequently emasculated, he tried to present it as counsel to the ruler, similar to advice offered by the Companions to the Prophet. The Al-Azhar scholars also charged that al-Maṭāʿnī had misunderstood why the examples of the treaty of Ḥudaybiyya and the intended pact with Ghaṭafān were cited. It was not in order to prove by analogy that the conclusion of the Camp David Agreement was permitted, but in evidence of the principle that peace treaties between Islamic and other states are permissible.

It is not surprising that the attack against the Camp David Agreement should come from the *al-Daʿwa* group. They had criticized the Egyptian-Israeli *rapprochement* from the very beginning. This was consistent with their close ties to the conservative Arab oil states and an ideology that ascribed all evils in Egyptian society to four external enemies: Judaism, the Crusades, Communism, and Secularism.[14] As peace with Israel thus would mean surrender to one of the main enemies of Islam, it is intolerable. Moreover, depicting Jews as intrinsically untrustworthy and wicked, *al-Daʿwa* reasons that any pact with them would be precarious.

Occasionally *al-Daʿwa* refers to the effort of introducing Islamic law and Islamicizing society as jihad. From the context, however, it is clear that no armed struggle is meant: 'Our country is an Islamic country and Islam must return to it through *our* jihad. He who claims that it is *dār ḥarb* only wants to surrender it as an easy prey to the enemies of Islam.'[15] The contributors often mention that jihad signified much more than fighting and that spreading the message of Islam by peaceful means is also a form of jihad. Obedience to the ruler is regarded as a natural necessity: 'Obedience is following orders . . . if there is no obedience, civil war will break out . . . Obedience then is obligatory as long as it does not constitute disobedience to God's commands.'[16] These attitudes clearly reflect the social background of the *al-Daʿwa* group, whose economic position is linked to the Open Door Policy and who are not committed to radical political and socio-economic change in Egyptian society.

If the word jihad is used in *al-Daʿwa* to mean fighting, this is (apart from occasional references to the freedom struggle of oppressed Muslim peoples like the Afghans, the Muslims of the Soviet Union, or those of the South Philippines) always done in the context of the Arab–Israeli conflict. But anyone joining this struggle must await the orders of the head of state, as is clearly shown in the following words of the editor-in-chief, ʿUmar al-Tilimsānī, written in October 1978, with reference to the Camp David talks:

> If asked for an alternative I would say that I am ready, and, I believe, all Muslims and non-Muslims of Egypt are ready to place themselves to-day and tomorrow under the command of the president of the state. If he appeals to God's Book, demands from us the austerity required by the nature of the situation, and prepares us dogmatically, morally and militarily for the decisive stand, we shall not bargain or demand a price. Because then we shall enlist ourselves for jihad in the way of God, because jihad in the way of God is the only way to reduce every aggressor to his natural proportions.[17]

There is nothing here that reminds us of the zeal of the Muslim Brothers in 1948, when they sent guerrilla bands to Palestine to aid the Palestinian people before the war between Israel and the Arab states had broken out. On the contrary, jihad against Israel is not envisaged as something immediate or pressing:

> We shall seek its [the Jewish occupation of Jerusalem] remedy only in devotedness and sacrifice, and in the training for the holy jihad *(al-jihād al-muqaddas),* which we must promote with the youth of the present generation, so that they can teach it to those who come after them. We shall be victorious through

> God's favour and power: *'And they will say, "When will it be?" Say: "It is possible that it may be nigh"'.* (K 17:51.)[18]

For the other Islamic political groups war against Israel is of only secondary importance. Foremost on their agenda is the struggle in their own country to establish an Islamic government or society. The issue is lucidly dealt with in *al-Farīḍa al-Ghā'iba* (The Absent Duty), a booklet written by Muḥammad ʿAbd al-Salām Faraj, the ideologue of the Jihad Organization and our main source for the discussion on internal jihad.[19] The author adduces three arguments in order to refute the view that the jihad duty requires that Jerusalem be liberated before anything else. In the first place, he argues, the Jews are in the present situation the further enemy, whereas the rulers of Egypt are the nearer one. According to the prescriptions of the Koran the nearer enemy ought to be attacked first (cf. K 9:123: *'O believers, fight the unbelievers who are near to you and let them find in you a harshness').* His second point is that the struggle for the liberation of Jerusalem can only be waged under the banner of Islam, not under the leadership of impious rulers. Finally he maintains that the colonial presence of Israel in the Islamic world is completely the fault of the rulers of the Muslims. These must therefore be replaced before Jerusalem can be set free.

The standpoint of the Association of Muslims *(al-Takfīr wa-l-Hijra)* is similar on this score, except that, as we shall presently see, they not only abominate the rulers, but Egyptian society at large, with all its institutions. They therefore keep aloof from the struggle between Israel and Egypt in its present state and are not inclined to fight in order to rescue Egypt and Egyptian society. Their leader, Muṣṭafā Shukrī, expressed himself as follows on this point: 'If the Jews or others would arrive here, the movement should not participate in combat within the framework of the Egyptian army, but, on the contrary, go to a safe place. In general our line is to flee from both the external and the internal enemy and not to offer resistance.'[20]

The well-known fundamentalist thinker and militant, Sayyid Quṭb (hanged in 1966), used to elucidate the concept of jihad by saying that it is the permanent revolution of the Islamic Movement. This is an indication of the centrality of the concept in

Islamic activist thought. This notion of jihad, that is internal jihad, the struggle within one's own society in order to change it according to the Islamic ideals, has also been the subject of heated discussions. The analysis here concentrates on the definition of the enemy and the permissibility of the immediate use of violence, and draws on two texts: the booklet 'The Absent Duty' *(al-Farīḍa al-Gā'iba)* by Muḥammad ʿAbd al-Salām Faraj, which expresses the views of the Jihad Organization and also expounds the ideas of other groups and organizations in order to rebut them, and its refutation by the Sheikh al-Azhar, Jād al-Ḥaqq ʿAlī Jād al-Ḥaqq.[21] The booklet consists of an introduction and three parts. Part One deals with the definition of the enemy and tries to demonstrate that the present rulers of Egypt are unbelievers and must therefore be fought. In Part Two, a number of contrary positions, which actually represent the points of view of the whole spectrum of Islamic organizations and groups, are systematically refuted. The last part is of less interest to us; it mentions a number of instances of the Prophet's and the Companions' use of tactics and enumerates the rules of warfare.

The title of the book refers to the jihad duty. According to the author, the command to take part in jihad is no longer observed and is even denied by some. In his introduction the author stresses that jihad is the method by which to establish an Islamic government, a duty for all Muslims because God orders men to judge and govern according to His revelation: *'So judge between them according to what God has sent down, and do not follow their caprices.'* (K 5:48.) Finally, the author cites traditions, some of which are clearly millenarian and connected with the coming of the Mahdi, in order to demonstrate that after a period of tyranny an Islamic state, encompassing the whole earth, will soon be established.

Jihad is basically a struggle of Muslims against unbelievers who are not protected by a treaty of *dhimma* or an armistice. An appeal to the doctrine of jihad to justify a struggle waged against people who are to all appearances Muslims and consider themselves so, requires some reasoning. This is done in the first part of 'The Absent Duty.' The props of the author's disquisition are two *fatwās* by the well-known fundamentalist scholar Ibn Taymiyya (1263–1328) dealing with the consequences of Mongol or, as he calls it, Tartar rule in the Middle East.[22] The first *fatwā* addresses itself to the question of whether these rulers are Muslims as they claim to be, and the second explains the position of Muslims under their rule.

In spite of their profession of faith *(shahāda),* it is beyond dispute for Ibn Taymiyya that these Mongol rulers must be fought because they are unbelievers. For they venerate and obey Genghis Khan and consider him of the same rank as the Prophet Mohammed; they take unbelievers as allies against Muslims; and, what is of the utmost importance, they do not apply the *Sharīʿa,* but judge according to their own law *(yasaq* or *yasa).* Even if it is held that they are not unbelievers, this last charge justifies that they be fought on the strength of K 2:278 *('O believers, fear you God; and give up the usury that is outstanding, if you are believers. But if you do not, then take notice that God shall war with you, and His Messenger'),* which was directed against the inhabitants of Taif, who first refused to abide by the *Sharīʿa* and abandon their usurious practices. Territory under their rule where Muslims live is, according to Ibn Taymiyya, neither *dār ḥarb* nor *dār silm* [*dār islām*]. It is a category of its own, 'where both Muslims and those who deviate from the *Shariʿa* must be treated each according to what they deserve.' Muslims are certainly not allowed to help such rulers.

For ʿAbd al-Salām Faraj it is not difficult to find parallels between the Middle East under Mongol rule and present-day Egypt: the Egyptian rulers apply laws made by unbelievers instead of the *Sharīʿa,* they take unbelievers as their allies, and they are venerated even more than their Creator: 'Therefore the rulers of these days are apostates. They have been brought up at the tables of colonialism, no matter whether of the crusading, the communist, or the zionist variety. They are Muslims only in name, even if they pray, fast, and pretend that they are Muslims.'[23] He then continues and expounds in detail that apostasy is much more serious than just unbelief, because the *Sharīʿa* prescribes that the apostate must be killed unless he repents, whereas unbelievers may escape this fate by, for example, accepting *dhimma* or an armistice.

Having thus established that jihad against the government is incumbent immediately, the author devotes Part Two to refuting alternative arguments. He first tackles those who maintain that an Islamic society and an Islamic state can be brought about through individual piety, obedience to God, and by establishment of pious associations *(jamᶜiyyāt khayriyya).* Piety and obedience, he argues, can only mean jihad under the present circumstances, and founding pious associations is out of the question because they perforce must collaborate with the infidel state.

Next he addresses the *Jamāᶜāt Islāmiyya,* without, however, mentioning their name. That they want to realize their ideals simply by propaganda *(daᶜwa)* and by creating a broad base is only a consequence of their cowardice, because populism cannot be a substitute for jihad. Moreover, the Koran teaches that the establishment of an Islamic regime is the work of only a very small group: '*For few indeed are those that are thankful among My servants*' (K 34:11); '*If thou obeyest the most part of those on earth they will lead thee astray from the path of God*' (K 6:116); and '*Yet, be thou ever so eager, the most part of men believe not*' (K 12:103). This minority, the author goes on, must first try to get control of the mass media by force, and the rest will then follow automatically: 'The effort that is really useful is the one for the sake of setting free these mass media from the hands of these . . . It is well known that as soon as we are victorious and have command, there will be a response, for He Who must be praised and is exalted says: "*When comes the help of God, and victory, and thou seest men entering God's religion in throngs*"' (K 110:2).[24] As can be imagined, Faraj makes short shrift of the view that was sometimes brought forward by the *Jamāᶜāt Islāmiyya,* according to which a real Islamic state could eventually be founded by the pious and devoted after having won positions of influence in society. From such people, he asserts, nothing can be expected, as they will have had to collaborate with the existing state in order to establish themselves, and will have been corrupted in the process.

Another target of his attacks is the Association of Muslims *(al-Takfīr wa-l-Hijra).* This group considers not only the rulers as unbelievers, but also the entire Egyptian society *(takfīr).* However, being well aware of the balance of power between their small band and the rest of society, their tactics differ from those of the Jihad Organization. Their solution is to withdraw or emigrate from society *(hijra),* either geographically by going to live in small settlements along the edge of the desert, or socially by founding a community within, but totally separated from, society at large. They compare their lack of power with that of Mohammed and the first Muslims during the earliest Meccan period, when Mohammed only preached in secret to friends and relatives. Their strategy is a long-term one. They want to create a counter-society which, once it has acquired power, would proclaim jihad and take over the country.

After a short exposé of the theory of *hijra* in Islam and under what conditions emigration is compulsory, Faraj ridicules their notions: 'There are also those who say: The way to establish the Islamic state is by emigrating to another place, establishing the state there and coming back again victoriously. But in order to save effort, they should establish the Islamic state in their own place and then leave victoriously.'[25] Neither does he approve of their view that jihad is not (yet) obligatory since, as *al-Takfīr wa-l-Hijra* maintain, their position is to be compared with that of the first Muslims in Mecca. The consequence would be, he argues, that all other prescriptions, for example fasting, that were revealed after this Meccan period, would not be applicable either. This is obviously not the case. Moreover God has said: *'Today I have perfected your religion for you'* (K 5:3).

The jihad obligation can take different forms. In general it is a collective duty *(farḍ kifāya),* for example a duty of which the fulfillment by a sufficient number of believers is the responsibility of the whole community. Only under special circumstances can the jihad duty become an individual obligation *(farḍ ʿayn)* for everybody who is capable of going to war. One such case occurs, however, when enemies attack and occupy Islamic territory. Thus, in the concluding sections of Part Two the author demonstrates that under the present circumstances jihad has indeed become an individual duty, as the enemies, the infidel rulers, have taken over the country and are occupying it. He further deals with some modernist positions on jihad, now held by many official ulema. The first view he attacks is that jihad is only defensive warfare:

> This is a false opinion . . . The correct point of view is to be found in the answer given by the Messenger of God—may God bless him and preserve him—to the question: 'What is jihad in the path of God?' He said: 'Who fights in order that God's word be uppermost [cf. K 9:40], is on the path of God.' The aim of fighting in Islam is therefore raising God's word on earth, both by attacking and by defence . . . Islam was spread by the sword, against the leaders of unbelief who tried to keep it [Islam] away from humanity, and therefore nobody is forced [to accept Islam] . . . Therefore it is obligatory for the Muslims to raise their swords against the leaders who hide what is true and divulge what is false. Otherwise the truth will not reach the hearts of the people.[26]

In addition, he argues, quoting a host of classical texts, that the Sword Verses or the Verses of Fighting (K 9:5 and 2:216) have abrogated all other verses concerning relations with unbelievers. Modernist writings often emphasize that jihad covers a much wider set of meanings than merely fighting. They explain that there are spiritual and moral forms of jihad which are more important than fighting and that the jihad duty can also be performed by the tongue or the pen *(jihād al-daʿwa)* or by financial support. Faraj rejects all this. God has said: *'Prescribed to you is fighting [qitāl,* not: *jihād*]' (K 2:216); just as He has said: *'Prescribed for you is the Fast'* (K 2:183). This proves that fighting is obligatory and that one cannot just discharge one's duty by preaching or propaganda, or by any other means apart from combat.

The Sheikh al-Azhar's *fatwā* against *al-Farīḍa al-Gāʾiba* is long and detailed. Much of it is taken up by discussion of the authenticity of certain Traditions or interpretation of particular words and expressions in the Koran and the Hadith in order to sap the foundations of his adversary's positions. Occasionally there are interesting remarks that show how close ulema thought is to the official political ideology. The ruler in Islam is described as 'the representative of the nation *(wakīl al-umma),*' which has the right to choose its rulers and to depose them.[27] With regard to our interest here, the *fatwā* deals with two issues: the question of when and under what conditions a Muslim, and especially a Muslim ruler, becomes an unbeliever, and second, the jihad doctrine and its application.

The first debate is a very old one in Islam. It goes back to the first century when the Kharijites justified their revolt by pointing out that the caliph had committed grave sins and could therefore no longer be considered a Muslim. This, however, was not the generally accepted position, which held that a Muslim would be regarded as an apostate only when he expressly abjured Islam or denied axiomatic articles of faith *(ma ʿulim min al-din ḍarūratan)* in act or speech.[28] Non-observance of the *Shariʿa* is not enough. There must be an explicit act or utterance which denies the obligatory character of certain prescriptions. There is, of course, much room for interpretation, and one might argue that a ruler who does not apply parts of the *Sharīʿa* denies its binding character and is therefore an apostate. Jād al-Haqq, however, does not go into this question. Instead, he formulates a totally new principle in this matter, namely that one becomes an apostate only by renouncing the *Sharīʿa* in its entirety and he toils mightily to explain in this sense the verse: *'Whosoever judges not according to what God has set down—they are the unbelievers'* (K 5:44). Finally he asserts that judging a Muslim's belief or unbelief is not the task of a layman, but exclusively the task of the ulema. His conclusion is that 'accusing a ruler of unbelief because he does not enforce some of God's prescriptions and ordinances, is founded on no text in the Koran nor on the Sunna.'[29]

Having argued that under these circumstances a ruler is not an unbeliever, he then tackles the question of whether a rebellion against him might be allowed on other grounds. After quoting a host of Traditions, he declares:

> On the strength of these and other authentic Traditions we must conclude that Islam does not allow rebellion against nor the assassination of a Muslim ruler as long as he sticks to Islam and acts according to it, even if this is only by performing prayer. If the ruler acts contrary to Islam, the Muslims must take care of him by counsel and sound and sincere appeal . . . Whenever a ruler does not administer God's ordinances nor enforce His law in any way, he loses the right to demand obedience with regard to such commands as are sinful or blameworthy.[30]

Jād al-Ḥaqq's treatment of the jihad doctrine conforms completely with the writings of the Modernists. He states clearly that there are many forms of jihad apart from fighting and that, if combat is necessary in order to protect Islamic territory or the religion of Islam, the jihad duty can also be performed by financial support, by the tongue, or by the heart. Islam, he argues, has not been spread by the sword, Orientalist slander notwithstanding. This would be contrary to verses like: '*No compulsion is there in religion*' (K 16:25); '*Call thou to the way of thy Lord with wisdom and good admonition, and dispute with them in the better way*' (K 16:125); and '*Wouldst thou then constrain the people, until they are believers?*' (K 10:99). As for the Sword Verse, he asserts that it has not abrogated all other verses regarding the relationship between Muslims and unbelievers, which are all applicable under specific circumstances. Jihad is, then, essentially defensive warfare, and when the need for jihad exists, it is to be carried out by the regular army to which the nation has entrusted this task.

The discussions summed up above demonstrate that the jihad doctrine is still very much alive and the subject of fierce controversies. This, however, does not tell us anything about the actual impact of jihad doctrine on Egyptian politics. In order to clarify this issue we shall first have a look at Egypt's foreign policy and, more specifically, her relations with Israel. Even without going deeply into the motives underlying the change in Egyptian policy towards Israel, it is evident that they were not religious. However, in order to confer greater legitimacy on the Camp David Agreements, especially in the face of the Islamic opposition, the government invited a number of religious institutions and religious dignitaries to pronounce on the matter from the point of view of the *Sharīʿa*. Not surprisingly these *fatwās* and declarations lent full support to Sadat's policy, stating that termination of jihad on the strength of a peace treaty was under the present circumstances permitted. As for the Islamic opposition to the new relationship with Israel, represented by the *al-Daʿwa* group, their stance was not based on the jihad doctrine. Going through the editorials of *al-Daʿwa*, it becomes clear that their main motives for opposing the Camp David Agreement were Islamic solidarity with the Muslim

Palestinians and aversion to and mistrust of the Jews. References to jihad are rare, and the jihad doctrine is only invoked to counter the legal arguments of the official ulema and to demonstrate that a peace treaty is not allowed under the given circumstances and war continues to be obligatory. From the foregoing, it appears that in Egyptian foreign policy the jihad doctrine does not play an independent role, not for the government, as could be expected, and not for the Islamic opposition. Its role is only marginal or complementary; and it is interpreted in different ways in order to justify political stances that have already been taken for other reasons, religious or otherwise.

In national politics there is more room for Islamic discourse, which by increasingly employing Islamic symbols and idioms the state has tried to dominate and even to monopolize. For obvious reasons the doctrine of internal, revolutionary jihad is not mentioned except to refute its legitimacy; this form of jihad is an essential part of the ideology of the opposition Islamic movements. To them it is identical with revolution, which like jihad, is an instrumental or tactical concept, covering all kinds of activities conducive to the ultimate objective: the overthrow of the established order and the restructuring of the state and society.

Only for the most radical organizations does internal jihad require actual fighting and the use of violence, themselves calling for considerable doctrinal acrobatics, as the enemies to be fought are to all appearances Muslims. However, by applying a very strict definition of Islam, the radicals' enemies are excluded and regarded as unbelievers. Differences among the various groups with regard to the application of this definition are related to differences in strategy. Some organizations see only the rulers and their supporters as being beyond the pale of Islam. They are in favour of an immediate struggle to topple the government, and count on popular support for their cause once they have seized power. Others see only themselves as true Muslims and regard anybody not belonging to their organization as an unbeliever. For them, being only a small minority in society, immediate jihad is out of the question; by conversion and recruitment they hope to create a position of power which will ultimately enable them to wage a successful jihad against their adversaries.

Thus it is clear that jihad is a concept with a wide semantic spectrum, and its actual meaning differs from organization to organization. Even if there is agreement among some groups that jihad signifies armed struggle only, these groups disagree on strategy and the immediacy of the struggle. The concept and doctrine of jihad, it appears, do not give clear and unambiguous directives; their interpretation and application depend very much on the political and strategical positions taken by the Islamic opposition groups. Jihad, therefore, cannot be considered as an independent driving force in Egyptian national politics. But like the notion of revolution, it can be used to justify positions that have already been taken and, what is perhaps more important, to enhance the loyalty and devotion of an organization's followers.

Notes

Notes to Preface (pp. vii–ix)

1. A. J. Arberry, *The Koran Interpreted.* Oxford: Oxford University Press, 1964.

Notes to Chapter 2 (pp. 9–17)

1. According to Imām Nawawī, this ḥadīth shows that those unbelievers who have received the message of Islam can be attacked unawares if the need so arises. The correct view is that for those who have not received the message of Islam, it is essential to give them the Divine Message before giving them the ultimatum of war, but for those who have received this message, it is desirable to inform them before entering into the battle. Exception can, however, be made in this case, when there is a dire necessity (Vol. II, p. 81).
2. *Jaish* is an army and *Sariyya* is a detachment of army.
3. The idea behind it is to provide them opportunity to live in Medina, the stronghold of Islam, so that they may acquire the knowledge of Islam and learn its practices.
4. *Al-Ghanīma* means spoils of war, which fall to the lot of the Muslims after an encounter, whereas *Fai*ʾ is that wealth which the non-Muslims surrender without armed conflict. Four-fifth of the total spoils coming in the hand of the Muslim army under Ghanīma is distributed amongst those who participate in war, whereas Faiʾ is given to the non-soldiers also as the Amīr deems fit. It is in fact the common possession of the whole Muslim society.
5. This word *jizya* is derived from the verb *jazā*ʾ, which means "he rendered (something) as a satisfaction" or "as a compensation (in lieu of something else)." This tax is a sort of compensation to the Muslim society on the part of unbelievers, living in the protection of the Islamic State for not participating in the military service and enjoying the "covenant of protection" *(dhimma).* No fixed rate has been set either by the Qurʾān or by the Holy Prophet (may peace be upon him) for this tax, but from all available aḥādīth, it is evident that it is considerably lower than Zakāt to which Muslims are liable. It should also be borne in mind that only such of non-Muslim citi-

zens, who, if they were Muslim, would be expected to serve in the armed forces of the State, are liable to the payment of Jizya, provided they can easily afford it.

6. "They are from them" does not mean that they are to be treated like the non-believing combatants and thus killed. What it means is that since the children and women of the unbelievers live in their houses and in case of the night raid it is difficult to distinguish them from the nonbelieving combatants, so there is every likelihood of their being killed though quite unintentionally. It should be clearly borne in mind that this is an exception rather than the rule. The explicit injunction of Islam is that women, children, the sick and the religious devotees are not to be killed. Only the combatants are to be killed.
7. This verse has a very close relationship with the aḥādīth recorded above. When the Muslims besieged the tribe of Naḍīr, they found great difficulty in prevailing upon that tribe as it found protection within the fort surrounded by a thick cluster of trees. In order to make the siege more effective and force the Jews to yield, there was no other way but to cut the trees. Upon this the hypocrites of Medina and Banū Quraiẓa and Banū Naḍīr said that the Holy Prophet (may peace be upon him) did not observe the principles which he himself preached, for example, Allah has clearly condemned those persons who destroy tilth:

   > "When he holds authority, he makes effort in the land to cause mischief in it and destroy tilth and offspring; and Allah loves not mischief" (ii. 205).

   The Muslims were themselves very much perturbed over what they had been forced to do by cutting down trees. It was upon this that the above-mentioned verse (lix. 5) was revealed, which tells that both the parties which cut down the trees and those who left them standing on their trunks are right in the eye of Allah. The instructions which were given to the army by the righteous Caliphs proved beyond any shadow of doubt that unnecessary cutting down of fruit trees or destruction of crops, or any wanton act of destruction in war is forbidden in Islam. Here in the case of Banū Naḍīr if the Muslims had cut down the trees, it was a dire necessity.

   It should also be borne in mind that the trees which had been cut down by the Muslims were *Līna* and not those trees the fruits of which had been used by the Jews for food. They were accustomed to the use of other fruits which the other trees like Ujwa and Barnī had yielded (*Faṭh-ul-Bāri,* Vol. VII, p. 495)

8. Badr is situated at some distance from Medina. The date of this battle is 17 Ramadān, the second year of Hijra. The Holy Qur'ān has described the day on which the Battle of Badr was fought as a day of distinction *(Yaum-ul-Furqān),* because it was decisive in the history of mankind in the sense that the truth, in spite of its meagre material resources, gained clear victory over falsehood with all its material strength and glory. A different result would perhaps have changed the entire course of human history. On the one side were arrayed the forces of evil with all their might and on the other side the servants of Allah had appeared on the stage of history to stem their rising tide and shatter their power. The Holy Prophet (may peace be upon him) was fully conscious of the gravity of the situation and, therefore, spent most of his time in beseeching the Lord to intervene in the affair and ensure a decisive victory for truth and thus prove that He is not a silent spectator in the long-drawn conflict between good and evil, and when He feels that the standard-bearers of truth, despite their earnest endeavours, are too feeble to stand the onslaughts of evil, He strengthens the forces of truth and helps them defeat the forces of evil, and thus impresses upon the heart of people a truth which becomes the first step towards the acknowledgment of one Omnipotent Lord.
9. The complete verse is: "And recall that time ye implored your Lord and He answered you. Verily, I will succour you with one thousand angels, rank on rank. And Allah made not this save as a glad tidings and that your hearts might thereby be set at rest: and succour cometh not but from Allah. Verily Allah is Mighty, Wise" (viii. 10).
10. The complete verse is: "It does not behove a prophet to take captives unless he has battled strenously on earth. You may desire the fleeting good of this world—but God desires (for you the good of) the Hereafter, God is Almighty. Wise. Had it not been for a decree from God that had already gone forth, there would indeed have fallen great on you a chastisement on account of all (the captives) that you took. Enjoy that, all that is lawful and good, which you have gained in war, and remain conscious of God. Verily God is much-forgiving, a Dispenser of grace" (vii. 68).

Notes to Chapter 4 (pp. 27–41)

1. Only the first chapter has been translated here.

2. ʿAbdallāh Ibn al-Ḥasan (d. 145/762), a traditionist.
3. As in most Islamic writings, the author assumes that the reader knows the Koran by heart, so that it was often sufficient to quote only a few words of the Koran texts. The reader was capable of completing them for himself. Here, the full text of each quotation will be given in the notes. Full text of [2:216]: *"Prescribed for you is fighting, though it be hateful to you. Yet it may happen that you will hate a thing which is better for you; and it may happen that you will love a thing which is worse for you. God knows and you know not."*
4. Full text of [9:122]: *"It is not for the believers to go forth totally; but why should not a party of every section of them go forth, to become learned in religion, and to warn their people when they return to them, that haply they may beware."* For the original meaning of this verse, which almost certainly is not referring to going to war, cf. R. Paret. *Sure 9, 122 und der Ǧihād. Welt des Islam*, n.s. II (1953), pp. 232ff.
5. Full text of [4:95]: *"Such believers as sit at home—unless they have an injury—are not the equals of those who struggle in the path of God with their possessions and their selves. God has preferred in rank those who struggle in the path of God with their possessions and their selves over the ones who sit at home; yet to each God has promised the reward most fair."*
6. Full text of [48:17]: *"There is no fault in the blind, and there is no fault in the lame, and there is no fault in the sick. . ."*
7. Full text of [9:91]: *"There is no fault in the weak and the sick and those who find nothing to expend, if they are true to God and His Messenger. There is no way against the good-doers—God is All-forgiving, All-compassionate—."*
8. The most important occurrence when the jihad becomes a personal obligation is an attack by the enemy on Islamic territory. All inhabitants of the area under attack—including women and slaves—are then obliged to expel the enemy.
9. Jibrīl is the Arabic name for the archangel Gabriel. According to the Islamic doctrine, God's words were revealed to Mohammed through Djibrīl.
10. Full text of [8:39]: *"Fight them until there is no persecution and the religion is God's entirely; then, if they give over, surely God sees the things they do."*
11. Mālik Ibn Anas (d. 179/795), famous lawyer. The Traditions related by him were collected by his pupils in the compilation *al-Muwaṭṭaʾ*. The school founded on his doctrines, the Malikite, is still extant and counts its adherents chiefly in North Africa.
12. This Tradition can be found in *al-Muwaṭṭaʾ*: jihad 10. However, Av-

erroes' suggestion that we are dealing here with words of the Prophet must be a *lapsus.* The Tradition in question goes back to Abū Bakr. Cf. *al-Muwaṭṭa*ʾ: jihad 10.

13. Abū Bakr (d. 13/634), personal friend of Mohammed and after his death in the year 11/632, his successor (caliph). During his short reign, he subdued once more the revolting tribes of the Arabian Peninsula and made a beginning with the conquest of Syria and Iraq.
14. Al-Ḥasan Ibn Muḥammad al-Tamīmī, a non-identified traditionist.
15. Full text of [47:4]: *"When you meet the unbelievers, smite their necks, then, when you have made wide slaughter among them, tie fast the bonds; then set them free, either by grace or ransom, till the war lays down its loads. So it shall be; and if God had willed, He would have avenged Himself upon them; but that He may try some of you by means of the others. And those who are slain in the way of God, He will not send their works astray."*
16. Full text of [8:67]: *"It is not for any Prophet to have prisoners until he make wide slaughter in the land. You desire the chance-goods of the present world, and God desires the world to come; and God is All-mighty, All-wise."* This verse is generally taken to have been a reproof at the address of Mohammed for his releasing on ransom most of the captives after the Battle of Badr. The phrase *"make wide slaughter in the land"* goes to point out the danger that these released captives may, when occasion arises, attack the Muslims afresh.
17. Abū ʿUbayd Saʿd Ibn ʿUbayd al-Zuhrī (d. 98/716), famous traditionist.
18. ʿAbd al-Mālik Ibn ʿAbd al-ʿAzīz Ibn al-Mājishūn (d. ca 213/827), Malikite lawyer.
19. ʿAbd al-Salām Ibn Saʿīd Ibn Ḥabīb al-Tanūkhī, known as Saḥnūn (d. 240/854), one of the best known early Malikite lawyers.
20. Abū Ḥanīfa al-Nuʿmān (d. 150/767), well-known lawyer. The School founded on his doctrines is called the Hanafite School and counts its adherents chiefly in the regions formerly belonging to the Ottoman empire and in Central Asia.
21. He is only allowed to do this with the permission of his owner.
22. This remark is not entirely correct. In view of its singular position in the context, it is possibly an interpolation.
23. For the full text of this Tradition, cf. p. 35.
24. Sufyān al-Thawrī (d. 161/778), famous traditionist and lawyer. A School founded on his doctrines existed for several centuries.
25. Al-Awzāʿī (d. 157/774), famous lawyer. Like the School of Thawrī, his School was superseded after a few centuries by other, still extant Schools.

26. Al-Shāfiʿī (d. 204/820), famous lawyer. He was the first to systematize the study of original sources (*ʿilm al-uṣūl*). The Shafiʿite School derives its name from him and obtains its widest recognition along the borders of the Arabian Peninsula, in East Africa and in the Indian Archipelago. Occasionally, he is related to have given two different solutions for one and the same problem. Later generations of scholars decided which interpretation was the most authoritative.
27. For the full text of this Tradition, see p. 41.
28. Full text of [9:5]: "*Then, when the sacred months are drawn away, slay the idolaters wherever you find them, and take them, and confine them, and lie in wait for them at every place of ambush. But if they repent, and perform the prayer, and pay the alms, then let them go their way; God is All-forgiving, All-compassionate*".
29. Dāwūd Ibn al-Haṣīn (d. 135/752–3), well-known traditionist.
30. ʿIkrima (d. 105/723–4), well-known traditionist. He was the slave of Ibn ʿAbbās and many Traditions were related on his athority.
31. ʿAbdallāh Ibn al-ʿAbbās (d. 68/686–7). One of the Companions of the Prophet and one of the most important scholars among the first generation of Muslims.
32. Anas Ibn Mālik (d. ca. 92/710), well-known traditionist. In his youth, he was the Prophet's servant.
33. Abū Dāwūd (d. 275/888), author of one of the authoritative compilations of Traditions.
34. For the full text of K 9:5, see note 28.
35. During Mohammed's life, his relations with the unbelievers manifested a gradual escalation. This escalation is reflected in the Koran. In his Meccan period, he attempted to win the unbelievers by persuasion and arguments. When this failed, it was revealed that the believers should leave the unbelievers alone. The verse determining that polytheists may only be fought if they make the first move (K 2:190) dates from the beginning of his Medinese period. At last the verses were revealed which gave the absolute command to fight the unbelievers (K 2:216, K 9:5—the verse of the Sword—and K 9:29). According to most scholars, this command cancelled all previous verses with regard to the relations with unbelievers.
36. Sumra Ibn Jundub al-Fazāri (d. 59/678–9), well-known traditionist.
37. Zayd Ibn Wahb (d. 96/714–5), well known traditionist.
38. ʿUmar Ibn al-Khaṭṭāb (d. 23/644), second caliph of the Islam and successor of Abū Bakr (see note 13). During his reign, which lasted for ten years (13/634–23/644), Syria, Iraq and Egypt were conquered. He is regarded as the founder of the organization of the Islamic state.

39. This Tradition has not been included in any of the authoritative compilations.
40. For the full text, see note 28.
41. Al-Layth Ibn Saʿd (d. 175/791–2), well-known lawyer and traditionist.
42. Full text of [48:25]: *"They are the ones who disbelieve and have barred you from the Holy Mosque and the offering, detained so as not to reach its place of sacrifice. If it had not been for certain men believers and certain women believers whom you knew not, lest you should trample them, and there befall you guilt unwittingly on their account (that God may admit into His mercy whom He will), had they been separated clearly, then We would have chastised the unbelievers among them with a painful chastisement."*
43. Full text of [17:15]: *"Whosoever is guided, is only guided to his own gain, and whosoever goes astray, it is only to his own loss; no soul laden bears the load of another. We never chastise, until We send forth a Messenger."*
44. After the Emigration *(Hijra)* in the year 622 it became obligatory for fresh converts to Islam to emigrate to Medina and to join the other Muslims. After the conquest of Mecca in 630 this obligation fell into abeyance according to most scholars.
45. Sometimes there is controversy about the qualification of a certain act. It may, for instance, be obligatory according to some, and a matter of indifference according to others. In order to reconcile these opinions, it is often assumed that the act in question is recommendable.
46. Full text of [8:66]: *"Now God has lightened it for you, knowing that there is weakness in you. If there be a hundred of you, patient men, they will overcome two hundred; if there be of you a thousand, they will overcome two thousand by the leave of God; God is with the patient."* This verse has abrogated the previous one, 8:65: *"O Prophet, urge on the believers to fight. If there be twenty of you, patient men, they will overcome two hundred; if there be a hundred of you, they will overcome a thousand unbelievers, for they are a people who understand not."*
47. In the year 628, Mohammed concluded a peace treaty with the Meccans for a period of ten years. However, when the Meccans began to incite to rebellion some troops that were allied to Mohammed, he broke off the treaty and attacked Mecca, which he conquered in the year 630.
48. For the full text, see note 28.
49. Full text of [9:29]: *"Fight those who believe not in God and the Last Day and do not forbid what God and His Messenger have forbidden—such men as practise not the religion of truth, being of those who have been given the Book—until they pay the tribute out of hand and have been humbled."*

50. Full text of [8:61]: *"And if they incline to peace, do thou incline to it; and put thy trust in God; He is the All-hearing, the All-knowing."*
51. In the year 627, the Meccans besieged Medina with the assistance of some Bedouin tribes, the Confederates. These tribes had come along with the Meccans in prospect of financial reward. Mohammed attempted to bribe one of these tribes into moving away. At first, this tribe, Ghaṭafān, demanded half of the Medinese date-harvest, but when after some negotiating they had agreed on a third, the citizens of Medina remonstrated. However, before matters had been settled, Mohammed had succeeded in expelling the Meccans and their allied tribes in the Battle of the Trench.
52. Abū Thawr (d. 240/854), well-known lawyer. A school founded on his doctrines existed for a few centuries only.
53. Full text of [8:39]: *"Fight them until there is no persecution and the religion is God's entirely; then, if they give over, surely God sees the things they do."*
54. See p. 37.
55. The ninth chapter of the Koran, called *Sūrat Barāʾa* or *Sūrat al-Tawba,* is considered as the last chapter revealed.
56. In the year 8/630.
57. For the full text, see note 44.
58. For the full text, see note 49.

Notes to Chapter 5 (pp. 43–54)

1. Different from Arberry, who has: ". . . to those who fight . . .."
2. Died 870. Famous compiler of *ḥadīth* and editor of the *ṣaḥīḥ al-Bukhārī,* one of the six canonical *ḥadīth* collection.
3. Died 875. Famous compiler of *ḥadīth* and editor of the *ṣaḥīḥ Muslim,* one of the six canonical *ḥadīth* collection.
4. *Ribāṭ* is a verbal noun meaning remaining at the frontiers of Islam with the intention of defending Islamic territory against the enemies. Later it began to mean fortification and sufi establishment.
5. One of the Islamic beliefs regarding Afterlife is that someone who has died will be hard-handedly interrogated with regard to his deeds by the Angels of the Grave.
6. Died ca. 890. Famous compiler of *ḥadīth* and editor of the *Sunan al-Tirmidhī* one of the six canonical *ḥadīth* collection.

7. Which means that the Tradition is widely accepted although among its transmitters there is one who is not entirely reliable.
8. Died 855. Famous jurist and traditionist, compiler of a voluminous collection of Traditions with the title *al-Musnad.*
9. Cf. K. 2:189 and 8:39.
10. Cf. K. 9:40.
11. Cf. K. 9:29.
12. Cf. K. 2:189 and 8:39.
13. First caliph after Mohammed's death. Ruled from 632–634.
14. Second caliph after Mohammed's death. Ruled from 634–644.
15. An early Islamic sect that held, among other things, that the caliph is to be elected by the community of the Muslims from among the pious believers, regardless of descent and tribal affiliation, and that a Muslim ceases to be a believer if he commits a grave sin.
16. Cousin and son-in-law of Mohammed and fourth Caliph after his death. Ruled from 656–661.
17. A legendary ancient Arabian tribe, mentioned in several places in the Koran. They refused to accept the message of the Prophet Hūd, whom God had sent to them, and were then destroyed by a violent gale.
18. Another name for the Kharijites.
19. Part of the ritual of *ṣalāt,* consisting of a bow followed by two prostrations.
20. In the year 627 the Meccans and allied tribes attacked Medina. In order to defend the town, the Prophet had a trench dug which prevented the enemy from entering. After a siege of a few months, the enemy withdrew.
21. In 630 Muhammad led a large expeditionary force to Tabūk, located in the North, near the Gulf of ʿAqaba. This can be regarded as the beginning of the great conquests.
22. Also called the pillars, *arkān,* of Islam, to wit: pronouncing the profession of faith, the five daily prayers, the *zakāt,* fasting during the month of Ramadān and pilgrimage to Mecca for those who are capable of it.

Notes to Chapter 6 (pp. 55–58)

1. See C. Snouck Hurgronje, "The Holy War 'made in Germany,'" in *Verspreide Geschriften* (Bonn/Leiden: 1923–1927), vol. 3, pp. 257–285,

and "Deutschland und der heilige Krieg," ibid., pp. 285–293, and C. H. Becker, "Die Kriegsdiskussion über den heiligen Krieg," in *Vom Wesen und Werden des islamischen Welt: Islamstudien* (Leipzig: 1932), vol. 2, pp. 281–310.

Notes to Chapter 7 (pp. 59–102)

1. In K 7:157–8, Mohammed is called *"al-nabī al-ummī."* According to traditional Islamic Koran interpretation these words mean: "the illiterate prophet." Mohammed being illiterate enhances the miracle of the Koran. Modern research, however, has demonstrated that in this verse the word *ummī* means "non-Jewish" or "heathen."
2. The *textus receptus* of this verse reads *"to those who are being fought" (li-alladhīn yuqātalūn).* A critical examination of the historical facts supports the alternative reading: *"to those who are fighting" (li-alladhīn yuqātilūn).* According to the first reading permission is granted to fight back against attacks from the enemy, whereas, according to the latter reading, permission to fight is granted to those who were already fighting against oppression.
3. In the Koran, the words: *"in the way of God" (fī sabīl Allāh)* are often added to the word for fighting in order to emphasize its religious sanction and to distinguish it from other forms of fighting that are not allowed.
4. Abū Yūsuf Yaʿqūb (d. 182/798), a well known lawyer and pupil of Abū Ḥanīfa.
5. Abū ʿUbayda (d. 18/639), army commander during the reign of ʿUmar.
6. For the full text of this Tradition, see p. 41.
7. This is the opinion of the Hanafite School. For the opinions of the other Schools, consult pp. 41–43.
8. Fakhr al-Dīn Abū ʿAbd Allāh Muḥammad al-Rāzī (d. 606/1209), famous theologian and philosopher.
9. Abū al-Thanāʾ Maḥmūd Shihāb al-Dīn al-Ālūsī (d. 1270/1854), Islamic scholar and author of a Koran commentary.
10. After Mohammed's death in 632, many tribes of the Arabian Peninsula revolted. During the reign of Abū Bakr (632–4) they were again subdued by Abū Bakr's army commander Khālid ibn al-Walīd. In one of the battles, the Battle of Yamāma, the Muslims suffered heavy losses. According to the traditional story, there were many Koran reciters among those who were killed. As the Koran, at that time,

had not yet been put down in writing, this incident induced Abū Bakr to give orders to compile the Koran in writing. Contemporary research has shown that this story is probably a later invention.

11. The Tabūk campaign took place in the year 9/630.
12. Full text of K 33:12–20: "*And when the hypocrites, and those in whose hearts is sickness, said, 'God and His Messenger promised us only delusion.' And when a party of them said, 'O people of Yathrib, there is no abiding here for you, therefore return!' And a part of them were asking leave of the Prophet, saying, 'Our houses are exposed'; yet they were not exposed; they desired only to flee. And if entrance had been forced against them from those quarters, and then they had been asked to apostatise, they would have done so, and but tarried about it briefly. Yet they had made covenant with God before that, that they would not turn their backs; and covenants with God shall be questioned of. Say: 'Flight will not profit you, if you flee from death of slaying; you will be given enjoyment of days then but little.' Say: 'Who is he that shall defend you from God, if He desires evil for you, or desires mercy for you?' They shall find for themselves, apart from God, neither protector nor helper. God would surely know those of you who hinder, and those who say to their brothers, 'Come to us,' and come to battle but little, being niggard towards you. When fear comes upon them, thou seest them looking at thee, their eyes rolling like one who swoons of death; but when the fear departs, they flay you with sharp tongues, being niggardly to possess the good things. Those have never believed; God has made their works to fail; and that is easy for God. They think the Confederates have not departed; and if the Confederates come, they will wish they were desert-dwellers among the Bedouins asking for news of you. If they were among you, they would fight but little.*"
13. For the original meaning of this verse, see Chapter 4, note 4.
14. One of the clans of the Quraysh tribe. Mohammed's family belonged to this clan.
15. Mohammed's uncle, who took care of him after his father and grandfather had died.
16. The tribe that inhabited the town of al-Ṭāʾif, situated ca. 45 miles southeast of Mecca.
17. The names of the Jewish tribes in Medina.
18. With the Muʾta-affair the author refers to the military expedition sent by Mohammed in the year 629 in order to punish Shuraḥbīl.
19. Kisrā is the Arabic name of the Persian emperor Chosroes.
20. For the full text of this Tradition, see p. 37–38.
21. The first four successors of Mohammed are usually called the "Rightly Guided Caliphs."

Notes to Chapter 8 (pp. 103–148)

1. *Kitāb al-jihād* (ed. by Nazīh al-Ḥammād. Beyrut: Dār al-Nūr, 1391/1971), 122 pp.
2. Cf. Sivan (1968); Hadia Dajani-Shakeel, 'Jihad in twelfth-century Arabic poetry: a moral and religious force to counter the Crusades,' *MW* 66 (1976), pp. 96–113. For more details, v. the title-indices of GAL and GAS s.v. *jihād, kitāb al-jihād, risālat al-jihād, faḍl al-jihād, faḍā'il al-jihād* e.t.q. Some of these works have been printed, e.g.: 'Imād al-Din Ismā'il ibn 'Umar *al-ma'rūf bi*-Ibn Kathir (d. 774/1372–73), *Al-ijtihād fī ṭalab al-jihād* (Cairo: Jam'iyyat al-nashr wa-l-ta'lif al-Azhariyya, 1347/1928–29), 24 pp. (GAL, Vol. II, p. 49); Shams al-Din Aḥmad ibn Ibrāhim ibn Muḥammad ibn al-Naḥḥās al-Dimashqi al-Dumyāṭi, *Mashāri' al-ashwāq ilā maṣāri' al-'ushshāq wa-muthir al-gharām ilā dār al-Islām*. Publ. in an abridged version by Maḥmūd al-'Ālim (d. 1311/1893) under the title: *Fukāhat al-adhwāq min mashāri' al-ashwāq*, 1st ed. (Cairo: al-Maṭba'a al-Saniyya al-Kubrā, 1290 H.) 76 pp.; 2nd ed. (Cairo: Maktabat al-Qāhira, 1390/1970), 144 pp. (GAL S, Vol. II, p. 83).
3. *Al-jihād fī l-Islām* (Cairo: Jāmi'at al-Azhar/al-Hay'a al-'Amma li-Shu'ūn al-Maṭābi' al-Amīriyya, 1967), 82 pp.
4. *Fatāwā khaṭira fī wujūb al-jihād al-dīnī al-muqaddas li-inqādh Filasṭin wa-ṣiyānat al-Masjid al-Aqṣā wa-sā'ir al-muqaddasāt* (Cairo: al-Maṭba'ah al-Salafiyyah [1948]), p. 8.
5. *Kitāb al-Mu'tamar al-Rābi' li-Majma' al-Buḥūth al-Islāmiyya* (Cairo: 1388/1968), p. 301.
6. *Le Monde*, 24-11-1977.
7. E.g. the *fatwā* isued by the *muftī* of Egypt in June 1948, publ. in: *Fatāwā khaṭira*, pp. 29–31.
8. For India and Algeria during the nineteenth century, cf. Rudolph Peters, 'Dār al-Ḥarb, Dār al-Islām und der Kolonialismus.' In: *XIX. Deutscher Orientalistentag (Freiburg, Sept.-Okt. 1975). Vorträge* (Wiesbaden: 1977), pp. 579–587 and the literature quoted there. For the Arab-Israeli conflict, cf. 'Abdallāh al-Qalqīli, *Al-fatāwā l-Urdunniyya. Qism al-ta'āmul ma' al-'aduww wa-aḥkām al-jihād* ([Beyrut:] al-Maktab al-Islāmi, 1389/1969), 110 pp.
9. W. W. Hunter, *Our Indian Musalmans: Are they Bound in Conscience to Rebel Against the Queen?* 2nd ed. Lahore, Premier Book House, pp. 185–186; Ahmad Khan, *Review on Dr. Hunter's Indian Musalmans: Are they Bound in Conscience to Rebel Against the Queen?* Benares: Medical Hall Press, 1972, pp. i–ii; C. Snouck Hurgronje, *De*

Atjehers. Batavia and Leiden: Landsdrukkerij, 1894, vol. 2, pp. 387–388; Muḥammad ibn ᶜAbd al-Qādir al-Jazāʾirī, *Tuḥfat al-zāʾir fīr tārīkh al-Jazāʾir wa-l-amīr ᶜAbd al-Qādir*. Ed. Mamdūḥ Ḥaqqī. Beyrut: Dār al-Yaqaẓa al-ᶜArabiyya, 1964, p. 316; L. Mercier, *'Aly ben ᶜAbderrahman ben Hodeïl el Andalusy. L'ornement des āmes et la devise des habitants d' el Andalus. Traité de guerre sainte*. Paris, Geuthner, 1939, pp. 76–83; O. Depont and X. Coppolani, *Les confréries religieuses musulmanes*. Algiers: Jourdan, 1897, pp. 33–37.

10. Faraj Muḥammad Ghayth, *Ghāyat al-irshād ilā aḥkām al-jihād* (Cairo: Muṣṭafā l-Bābī al-Ḥalabī, 1955), p. 27.
11. Maḥmūd Shit Khaṭṭāb, *Irādat al-qitāl fī l-jihād al-Islāmī* (Beyrut: Dār al-Irshād, 1968), p. 34.
12. Khaṭṭāb (1968), p. 39; ᶜUthmān al-Saᶜīd al-Sharqāwī, *Sharīᶜat al-qitāl fī l-Islām* (Cairo: Maktabat al-Azhar, 1392/1972), pp. 244–248.
13. Abū l-A ᶜlā l-Mawdūdī, *Al-jihad fī sabīl Allāh* (Beyrut: Dār al-Fikr, n.d.), pp. 27–29; in the same strain: Sayyid Quṭb in: Abū l-Aᶜlā l-Mawdūdī, Ḥasan al-Bannā and Sayyid Quṭb, *Al-jihād fī sabīl Allāh* (Beyrut: Al-Ittiḥād al-Islāmī al-ᶜĀlamī li-l-munaẓẓamāt al-ṭullābiyya, 1969), pp. 105–109; and ᶜAbd al-Ḥāfiẓ ᶜAbd Rabbih, *Falsafat al-jihād fī l-Islām* (Beyrut: Dār al-Kitāb al-Lubnāni, 1972), pp. 56–57.
14. Kāmil Salāma al-Daqs, *Āyāt al-jihād fī l-qur'ān al-karīm* (Kuwait: Dār al-Bayān, 1392/1972), pp. 98–99.
15. Wahba Zuḥaylī, *Āthār al-ḥarb fī al-fiqh al-Islāmī. Dirāsa muqārina*. Beyrut: Dār al-Fikr, 1965, pp. 18–19. To the same effect: ᶜAbd Rabbih (1972), p. 15; Daqs (1972), p. 6; Muḥammad ᶜIzzat Darwaza, *Al-jihād fī sabīl Allāh fī l-Qur'ān wa-l-ḥadīth* (Dimashq: Dār al-Yaqaẓah al-ᶜArabiyya, 1395/1975), p. 64; Muḥammad Ismāᶜ-īl Ibrāhīm, *Al-jihād rukn al-Islām al-sādis* (Cairo: Dār al-Fikr al-ᶜArabi, 1970), p. 136; Muḥammad Faraj, *Al-madrasa al-ᶜaskariyya al-Islāmiyya* (Cairo: Dār al-Fikr al-ᶜArabi, n.d. [*c*. 1969]), pp. 71–89; ᶜAli ᶜAli Manṣūr, *Al-sharīᶜ-a al-Islāmiyya wa-l-qānūn al-dawlī al-ᶜāmm* (Cairo: al-Majlis al-Aᶜlā li-l-Shuʾūn al-Islāmiyya, 1390/1971), p. 237; ᶜUthmān al-Saᶜīd al-Sharqāwī, *Sharīᶜat al-qitāl fī l-Islām*. Cairo: Maktabat al-Azhar, 1972, pp. 19–20.
16. Jamāl al-Din ᶜAyyād, *Nuẓum al-ḥarb fī l-Islām* (Cairo: Maktabat al-Khānjī, 1370 [*c*. 1951]), pp. 26–28; ᶜAbd Rabbih (1972), p. 341; Muḥammad ᶜAbdallāh Darāz, 'Mabādiʾ al-qānūn al-dawli al-ᶜāmm li-l-Islām,' *Risālat al-Islām* 2 (1950), pp. 148–164; p. 159; Muḥammad ᶜAbdallāh al-Sammān, *Al Islām wa-l-amn al-dawli* (Cairo: Dār al-Kitāb al-ᶜArabī), 1952, p. 7; Manṣūr (1971), p. 319.
17. The classical authors held either that these verses had been abro-

gated by the Verses of Fighting that give a general command to fight the unbelievers, or they interpreted these verses in accordance with classical theory. Thus, the word *'peace-greeting' (al-salām)* in K 4:90 is understood as *'conversion to Islam' (al-Islām)*, whereas the command of K 8:61 is taken to be restricted by [47:35]: *("So do not faint and call for peace; you shall be the upper ones.")* so that the order obtains only when the Muslims are weak and it is in their interest to conclude peace. Cf. Ibn ʿArabī, *Aḥkām al-Qur'ān*, Cairo: 1967, Vol. I, p. 481, Vol. II, p. 864; Jaṣṣāṣ, *Aḥkām al-Qur'ān*. Cairo: n.d. Vol. IV, pp. 254–255.

18. Maḥmūd Shaltūt, *Al-qur'ān wa-l-qitāl* (Cairo: Maṭbaʿat al-Naṣr wa-Maktab al-Ittiḥād al-Sharqī, 1367/1948), pp. 60–61.
19. E.g. Maḥmūd Shit Khaṭṭāb, *Al-rasūl al-qā'id* (2nd rev. ed., Cairo: Dār al-Qalam, 1964), 499 pp.; Faraj (*c.* 1969).
20. ʿAbdallāh Muṣṭafā l-Marāghī, *Al-jihād* (Cairo: Maṭbaʿat al-Sunna al-Muḥammadiyya, 1369/1950), p. 14.
21. Faraj (*c.* 1969), p. 231.
22. For the opinion of classical authors on this topic, cf. Morabia (1975), p. 343.
23. J. J. G. Jansen, *The Interpretation of the Koran in Modern Egypt.* (Leyden: E. J. Brill, 1974), pp. 35–54.
24. Shaltūt (1948), p. 39.
25. ʿAbdallāh Ghawsha, 'Al-djihād ṭarīq al-naṣr.' In: *Kitāb al-Mu'tamar al-Rābiʿ li-Madjmaʿ al-Buḥūth al-Islāmiyya* ([Cairo:] 1388/1968), p. 263. Evidently, this part of the interpretation of K 8:60 indirectly criticizes the Egyptian government for its heavy reliance on Soviet military and technological aid.
26. Jamāl al-Din al-Afghānī, 'Al-Ḥarb al-ʿādila wa-l-ḥarb ghayr al-ʿādila.' In: *Al-Aʿmāl al-Kāmila* (ed. by Muḥammad al-ʿAmāra. Cairo: Dār al-Kātib al-ʿArabī, n.d.), p. 439; Muḥammad ʿAbduh & Muḥammad Rashīd Riḍā, *Tafsīr al-Manār* (2nd ed., Cairo: Dār al-Manār), Vol. 10, pp. 69–72, 168; Daqs (1972), pp. 113–114; Ghawsha (1968), pp. 261–263; Shaltūt (1948), pp. 44–45; Khaṭṭāb (1964), p. 29.
27. Shaltūt (1948), p. 53; Mohammad Talaat Al Ghunaimi, *The Muslim Conception of International Law and the Western Approach* (The Hague: Martinus Nijhoff, 1968), pp. 177–178; Zuḥayli (1965), p. 119.
28. Rashīd Riḍā (1912), p. 36.
29. Mawdūdī (n.d.), p. 10; Aḥmad Muḥammad Jamāl, *Muftarayāt ʿalā l-Islām* (Beyrut: Dār al-Fikr, 1392/1972), pp. 268–269.
30. Morabia (1975), pp. 480–563.
31. Ibrāhīm (1964), p. 56.

32. Muḥammad Shadid, *Al-jihād fī l-Islām* (Cairo: Mu'assasat al-Maṭbūʿāt al-Ḥadītha, n.d.), pp. 7, 90; Niʿmat Ṣidqī, *Al-jihād fī sabīl Allāh* (Cairo: Dār al-Iʿtiṣām, 1975), pp. 22–31.
33. *Al-bayān al-usbūʿī li-l-ra'īs al-Ḥabīb Būrqība,* 5-2-1960 (Tūnus: Kitābat al-Dawla li-l-akhbār wa-l-irshād).
34. For the ensuing discussion, cf. Rudolph Peters, 'Recente discussies rond de Islamitische vastenmaand, Ramadan,' *Internationale Spectator* (The Hague), 23 (1969), pp. 1812–1825.
35. Muḥammad al-Ḥabīb ibn al-Khūdja, 'Al-jihād fī l-Islām.' In: *Min Waḥy* Laylat al-Qadr. Dirāsāt Islāmiyya (Tūnus: al-Dār al-Tūnusiyya li-l-Nashr, 1971), p. 130.
36. Sobhi Mahmassani, 'The principles of international law in the light of the Islamic doctrine.' In: *Académie de droit international. Recueil des courses* 117 (1966), Vol. I, p. 321; Darwazah (1975), p. 7; Shadid (n.d.), p. 153.
37. A. Sanhoury, *Le califat. Son évolution vers une Société des Nations orientale* (Paris: Geuthner, 1926), pp. 148–50.
38. Muḥammad Abū Zahra, 'Al-jihād.' In: *Kitāb al-Muʾtamar al-Rābiʿ li-Majmaʿ al-Buḥūth al-Islāmiyya* ([Cairo:] 1388/1968), p. 67.
39. Ḥasan al-Bannā, 'Risālat al-jihād.' In: *Majmūʿat rasā'il al-Imām al-shahīd Ḥasan al-Bannā* (Beyrut: Dār al-Nūr, n.d.), p. 58; Mawdūdī (n.d.), p. 29.
40. *Tafsīr al-Manār,* Vol. 2, p. 254.
41. Ibid., p. 460.
42. Muḥammad Rajāʾ Ḥanafī ʿAbd al-Mutajallī, *Ramaḍān shahr al-jihād* (Cairo: al-Majlis al-Aʿlā li-l-Shu'ūn al-Islāmiyya, 1973), p. 23.
43. ʿAbd al-Ḥalīm Maḥmūd, 'Al-jihād'. In: *Kitāb al-Muʾtamar al-Rābīʿ li-Majmaʿ al-Buḥūth al-Islāmiyya* ([Cairo:] 1388/1968), p. 43; ʿAbd al-Fattāḥ Ḥasan, *Mīthāq al-umam wa-l-shuʿūb fī l-Islām* (Cairo: al-Idāra al-ʿĀmma li-l-Thaqāfa al-Islāmiyya bi-l-Jāmiʿ al-Azhar, 1959), p. 1.
44. E.g. Manṣūr (1971), p. 216; Mahmassani (1966), p. 282; Majid Khadduri, *War and Peace in the law of Islam.* Baltimore: The Johns Hopkins Press, 1955, pp. 70–71.
45. ʿAbd al-Raḥmān ibn Muḥammad ibn Khaldūn, *Muqaddima* (ed. by ʿAlī ʿAbd al-Wāḥid Wāfī. 2nd ed., Cairo: Ladjnat al-Bayān al-ʿArabī, 1384/1965), Vol. 2, p. 823.
46. In accordance with his theory that state and religion are to be separated in Islam, ʿAlī ʿAbd al-Rāziq maintained that jihad in Islam only served state interests and had nothing to do with religion: 'At first sight it is clear that the aim of jihad is not only missionary and that it does not serve the purpose of bringing people to believe

in God and His Prophet. Its aim is only the corroboration of power and the expansion of authority.' (ʿAli ʿAbd al-Rāziq, *Al-Islām wa-uṣūl al-ḥukm*. Ed. and ann. by Muḥammad ʿAmāra. Beyrut: Al-Muʾassasa al-ʿArabiyya li-l-Dirāsāt wa-l-Nashr, 1972, pp. 147–148.) Elsewhere in his book, however, he contradicts this statement by saying: 'No wonder that jihad is one of these means [i.e. means of corroborating religion and supporting the mission]. It is a violent and harsh means, but how can one know, maybe something evil is sometimes required to attain something good and destruction may be necessary to achieve civilization.' (Ibid., p. 166). For criticisms on this point, raised by the orthodox *ʿulamāʾ*, see: ʿAbdelhamid Muhammad Ahmad, *Die Auseinandersetzung zwischen al-Azhar und der modernistischen Bewegung Ägypten* (Hamburg, 1963), pp. 88–89, 96–99.

47. By freedom of religion Muslim authors refer to the freedom of *dhimmis* to exercise their religion under certain conditions, the freedom of Muslims to exercise their religion outside the Territory of Islam and the freedom of non-Muslims to be converted to Islam. This freedom does not include the right of Muslims to abandon their religion. Cf. Rudolph Peters & Gert J. J. de Vries, 'Apostasy in Islam.' *WI*, n.s. 17 (1976–77), pp. 1–25.
48. In classical Islam, there existed various interpretations of this verse. According to some, it has been abrogated by the unconditional command to fight the unbelievers. Others hold that it refers to a certain custom amongst the women of the *Anṣār*, according to which these women, when a baby died, would vow that the next one, if it remained alive, would be converted to Judaism. In general, however, this verse was taken as a prohibition to force those who could become *dhimmis* to embrace Islam. This implies that it was allowed to compel pagan Arabs and apostates to conversion. Being aware of the impossibility of forcing a conviction upon somebody, they professed that outward behaviour in conformity with Islamic prescriptions was sufficient. In most cases conviction would follow automatically. Others saw this not as a compulsion to be converted but rather as a punishment for obstinacy: By the time Mohammed began to fight, he had adduced so much evidence and so many arguments for the truth of his mission, that not believing in it ought to be regarded as sheer obstinacy. Ibn al-ʿArabī, Vol. I, pp. 232–234; Abū ʿAbd Allāh Muḥammad b. Aḥmad al-Ansārī al-Qurṭubī, *Al-jāmiʿ li-aḥkām al-qur'ān* (Cairo: Dār al-Kutub al-Miṣriyya, 1354/1935), Vol. 3, pp. 279–81; Ibn Ḥazm, *Al-Muḥallā*. Beyrut: n.d. Vol. 7, p. 346.

49. Shaltūt (1948), p. 13. This opinion is similar to Paret's interpretation of K 2:256, according to which *'there is no compulsion in religion'* means *'there can be no compulsion in religion'* and not *'there* should *be no compulsion in religion.'* Cf. R. Paret, 'Lā ikrāha fi-d-dīn. Toleranz oder Resignation,' *Der Islam* 45 (1969), pp. 299–301.
50. *Tafsīr al-Manār,* Vol. 2, p. 211.
51. Ghayth (1955), p. 62; to the same effect, Zuḥaylī (1965), p. 99.
52. Although the exclusively defensive character of jihad was only recently put forward by the modernists, there are indications that this concept is much older. The classical rule that the *Imām* is obliged to raid enemy territory once a year in order to keep the idea of jihad alive must have been a dead letter during long periods of Islamic history. Morabia (1975, pp. 480–563) describes the effects of the stagnation of the Islamic expansion on the doctrine of jihad, and calls it the 'internalizing' *(intériorisation)* of the jihad-doctrine. In his view this consists of three elements: the application of the concept of jihad to the struggle for the protection of Islam against internal dangers like rebellions and heresies, the development of the notion of jihad as moral struggle *(al-amr bi-l-maʿrūf wa-l-nahy ʿan al-munkar)* and, finally, the development of the notion of jihad as a spiritual struggle against one's own evil inclinations. To these elements a fourth one might be added: the conviction amongst the common people that jihad is only a defensive war, obligatory in case the enemy attacks Islamic territory. The collection of *Thousand and One Nights* contains the didactic story of Tawaddud, a slave girl that astonishes the *ʿulamāʾ* by her extensive knowledge of Islam. With regard to jihad, we read: 'He said: "What is the jihad and what are its essential elements *(arkān)*?" She answered: "As for its essential elements, they are: an attack on us by the unbelievers, the presence of an *Imām,* preparedness and constance when one meets the enemy."' *(Alf layla wa-layla,* 4 vols. Cairo: Maṭbaʿat Muḥammad ʿAli Ṣubayḥ wa-Awlādih, n.d., Vol. 2, p. 309.) These phrases cannot be traced back to the works on *fiqh.* My assumption is that they reflect popular ideas on jihad. Admittedly, this assusmption is based upon scant evidence and the topic deserves, therefore, further research.
53. Ahmad Khan (1872), pp. xviii–xix. The original article had appeared in *The Pioneer* of the 23rd November, 1871.
54. Cf. Moulavi Cheragh Ali, *A Critical Exposition of the Popular 'jihād,' showing that all the Wars of Mohammad were Defensive; and that Aggressive War, or Compulsory Conversion, is not allowed in the Koran* (Cal-

cutta: Thacker, Spink and Co., 1885), civ + 249 pp.; Moulvi Abu Said Mohammed Husain, *A Treatise on Jihad* [*Iqtisad fī masail il-jihad*] (Lahore: Victoria Press, 1887), 32 pp.; Syed Ameer Ali, *A Critical Examination of the Life and Teachings of Mohammed* (London, etc.: Williams & Norgate, 1873), pp. 147–216; J. M. S. Baljon, *The Reforms and Religious Ideas of Sir Sayyid Ahmad Khan* (Leyden: Brill, 1949), pp. 30–31; Smith (1946), pp. 14–47; Aziz Ahmad & G. E. von Grunebaum, *Muslim Self-statement in India and Pakistan, 1857–1968* (Wiesbaden: Harrassowitz, 1970), pp. 3–5.

55. Husain (1887), p. 2.
56. Muḥammad ᶜAbduh, *Al-Islām wa-l-Naṣrāniyya maᶜ al-ᶜilm wa-l-madaniyya* (8th ed., Cairo: Dār al-Manār, 1373 [*c. 1954*]), pp. 62–67; *Tafsīr al-Manār,* Vol. 2, pp. 103–104, 208–213, 312–318, Vol. 3, p. 39, Vol. 10, pp. 167–173, 360–377, Vol. 11, pp. 123–126; J. Jomier, *Le Commentaire coranique du Manar.* (Paris: Maisonneuve, 1954), pp. 251–281; Rashīd Riḍā (1912); Id. *Al-waḥy al-Muḥammadī* (5th ed., Cairo: *Dār al-Manār,* 1375 [*c.* 1955]), pp. 126–136; Id. *Fatāwā* (ed. by Ṣalāḥ al-Din al-Munajjid & Yūsuf Q. Khūri. Beyrut: Dār al-Kitāb al-Jadīd, 1390/1970), Vol. 2, pp. 575–576, Vol. 3, pp. 1152–1157.
57. Olivier Carré, *Enseignement islamique et idéal socialiste* (Beyrut: Dar el-Machreq, 1974), pp. 206–211.
58. Rashīd Riḍā (1912), p. 35.
59. Shaltūt (1948), p. 30.
60. Fundamentalist literature on jihad: Mawdūdi (n.d.); Aᵓbū ᵓl-Aᶜlā l-Mawdūdi, Ḥasan al-Bannā & Sayyid Quṭb, *Al-jihād fī sabīl Allāh* (Beyrut: Al-Ittiḥād al-Islāmī al-ᶜĀlamī li-Munaẓẓamāt Ṭullābiyya, 1969), 135 pp.; Ḥasan al-Bannā (n.d.); Sayyid Quṭb, *Fi ẓilāl al-qur'ān* (5th ed., Beyrut: Dār al-turāth al-ᶜArabī, 1386/1967), Vol. 1, part 2, pp. 159–167, Vol. 3, part 9, pp. 174–201, Vol. 4, part 10, pp. 9–11, 103–110, 218–220, Vol. 5, part 17, pp. 17, 94–100; Id. *Ṭarīq al-daᶜwa fī ẓilāl al-qur'ān* (ed. by Aḥmad Fā'iz. 2nd ed., Beyrut: Dār al-Arqam, 1394/1974), 386 pp.; Id. *Al-salām al-ᶜālamī wa-l-Islām* (5th ed., Cairo: Maktabat Wahba, 1386/1966), 199 pp.; Aḥmad Nār, *Al-qitāl fī l-Islām* (Djudda: Al-Dār al-Suᶜūdiyya li-l-nashr wa-l-tawziᶜ, 1389/1969), 264 pp.; Daqs (1972).
61. Mawdūdī (n.d.), pp. 12–13.
62. Quṭb (1974), pp. 310–311.
63. Quṭb (1967), Vol. 3, part 9, pp. 166–167; id. in: Mawdūdī, a.o. (1969), p. 101; Nār (1969), pp. 18–21.
64. *Tafsīr al-Manār,* Vol. 2, p. 211; Darwaza (1975), p. 47; Shaltūt (1948), pp. 27–28; Abū Zahra (1968), p. 92.

65. Mawdūdi (n.d.), pp. 30–31; Quṭb in: Mawdūdī, a.o. (1969), p. 110; Daqs (1972), p. 87.
66. Daqs (1972), p. 105. To the same effect and with attacks especially directed against Ahmad Khān and the Ahmadiyya-movement: Muḥammad al-Bahī, *Al-fīkr al-Islāmī al-ḥadīth wa-ṣilatuh bi-l-istiᶜmār al-gharbī* (6th ed., Beyrut: Dār al-Fikr, 1973), pp. 44, 47–49; Zuḥaylī (1965), pp. 94–95.
67. Quṭb (1967), Vol. 3, part 9, p. 174.
68. Nār (1969), p. 42.
69. In classical Islam, some held that this verse had been abrogated by the sword-verses, whereas others were of the opinion that the Muslims only had to accept such a peace-offer if they had an interest in doing so. Ibn al-ᶜArabī, Vol. 2, pp. 864–865.
70. Shadīd (n.d.), p. 127.
71. Ibrāhīm (1964), pp. 56, 87, 139–140; Aḥmad Mūsā Sālim, *Al-Islām wa-qaḍāyānā l-muᶜāṣira (Cairo: Maktabat al-Qāhira al-Ḥadītha, n.d.* [*c.* 1970]), p. 260; Aḥmad Muḥammad al-Ḥawfī, *Al-jihād* (Cairo: Al-Majlis al-Aᶜlā li-l-Shu'ūn al-Islāmiyya, 1970), pp. 10–11; see also the discussion between a number of leading *ᶜulamā᾿* on the duty of Muslims to defend their fatherland in *Liwā᾿ al-Islām* 10 (1956), nr. 6, pp. 378–384.
72. To the best of my knowledge the word *waṭan* was first used in combination with jihad during the ᶜUrābī revolt. Many preachers that backed ᶜUrābī's cause, coupled the concept of defence of the fatherland with that of defense of religion. Cf. Naqqāsh (1884), Vol. 5, p. 150, 196.
73. *Al-Muṣawwar* (Cairo), 12-10-1973. Dr. U. Haarmann of Freiburg (FRG) kindly sent me a copy of this text. See also U. Haarmann, 'Die Pflichten des Muslims—Dogma und geschichtliche Wirklichkeit,' *Saeculum* 26 (1975), p. 109.
74. Cf. Shameem Akhtar, 'An inquiry into the nature, origin and source of Islamic law of nations,' *IS*, 10 (1971), pp. 23–37; Najib Armanazi, *L'Islam et le droit international* (thèse) (Paris: Librairie Picart, 1929) 162 pp. (Ar. transl.: *Al-sharᶜ al-dawlī fī l-Islām*. Damascus: Maṭbaᶜat Ibn Zaydūn, 1930, 184 pp.); Muḥammad ᶜAbd Allāh Darāz, 'Mabādi᾿ al-qānūn al-dawlī al-ᶜamm li-l-Islām,' *Risālat al-Islām* 2 (1950), pp. 148–164; M. A. Draz, 'Le droit international public et l'Islam,' *Revue Égyptienne de Droit International Public* (1947), pp. 17–27; Al Ghunaimi (1968); Muhammad Hamidullah, *Muslim Conduct of State*. 3rd ed. Lahore: Sh. Muhammad Ashraf, 1953; ᶜAbd al-Fattāḥ Hasan, *Mīthāq al-umam wa-l-shuᶜūb fī l-Islām*. Cairo: 1959; Za-

frullah Khan, 'Islam and international relations,' *Internationale Spectator* (The Hague), 10 (1956), 11, pp. 308–323; Mahmassani (1966); Manṣūr (1390/1971); Ahmed Rechid, 'L'Islam et le droit des gens.' In: *Académie de Droit International. Recueil des Cours* 60 (1937), II, pp. 375–504; Hāmid Sulṭān, *Aḥkām al-qānūn al-dawlī fī l-sharīʿa al-Islāmiyya* (Cairo: Dār al-Nahda al-ʿArabiyya, 1970), 269 pp.; Muḥammad Kāmil Yāqūt, *Al-shakhṣiyya al-dawliyya fī l-qānūn al-dawlī al-ʿamm wa-l-sharīʿa al-Islāmiyya* (Cairo: ʿĀlam al-Kutub, 1970–71), 785 + 14 pp.; There are also a few Arabic authors on international law that mention in passing some of the Islamic prescriptions. E.g.: ʿAbd al-ʿAzīz ʿAlī Jāmiʿ, ʿAbd al-Fattāḥ ʿAbd al-ʿAzīz and Ḥasan Darwish, *Qānūn al-ḥarb* (Cairo: Maktabat al-Anglo-Miṣriyya, 1952), pp. 37–39; Khālid Farrāj and Ḥasan Darwish, *Al-mūjaz fī l-qānūn al-dawlī al-ʿāmm* (Cairo: Maktabat al-Anglo-Miṣriyya, 1967), pp. 119–123; Sumūḥī Fawq al-ʿĀda, *Al-qānūn al-dawlī al-ʿāmm* (Damascus: Maṭbaʿat al-Inshāʾ, 1960), 1073 pp., *passim;* Muḥammad Ḥāfiẓ Ghānim, *Al-uṣūl al-jadida li-l-qānūn al-dawli al-ʿāmm* (Cairo: Maṭbaʿat Nahḍat Miṣr, 1952), pp. 423–424; Id. *Mabādiʾ al-qānūn al-dawlī al-ʿāmm* (Cairo: Dār al-Nahḍa al-Miṣriyya, 1967), pp. 714–715; Muḥammad Ṭalʿat al-Ghunaymi, *Al-Aḥkām al-ʿāmma fī qānūn al-umam. Dirāsa fī kull min al-fikr al-gharbī wa-l-ishtirākī wa-l-Islāmi. Qānūn al-salām* (Alexandria: Munshaʾat al-Maʿārif, 1970), 1237 pp., *passim;* Muḥammad Saʿd al-Dīn Zakī, *Al-ḥarb wa-l-salām* (Cairo: 1965), pp. 25–28, 179–218.

75. E.g.: K.Th. Pütter, *Beiträge zur Völkerrechts-Geschichte und Wissenschaft* (Leipzig: Adolph Wienbrack, 1843), 219 pp.; E. Nys, 'Le droit des gens dans les rapports des Arabes et des Byzantins.' In: E. Nys. *Études de droit international public et droit politique* (Brussels: Alfred Castaigne, 1896), pp. 46–74.
76. Only according to Shafiʿite opinion can the relatives of an unbeliever, killed by Muslims in defiance of the rules that forbid to kill certain categories of unbelievers, like women, children, etc., or to wage war without previous warning, claim *diya* (bloodmoney).
77. 'Law of nations or international law is the name for the body of customary or treaty rules which are considered legally binding by States in their intercourse with each other.' L. Oppenheim, *Internatioal Law. A Treatise* (ed. by H. Lauterpacht. London, etc.: Longman, Green & Co., 1955), Vol. I, pp. 4–5.
78. H. Kruse, *Islamische Völkerrechtslehre. Der Staatsvertrag bei den Hanafiten des 5./6. Jahrhunderts d, H. (11./12. Jahrh. n. Chr.).* Göttingen: 1953, p. 5.
79. Hermann Janson, *Die rechtlichen und ideologischen Beziehungen des*

islamischen Staatenkreises zum Abendländischen Völkerrecht (Diss.) (Bern, 1955), p. 35.

80. Armanazi (1929), p. 40.
81. Hamidullah (1953), pp. 3–4.
82. Al Ghunaimi (1968), p. 96.
83. Al Ghunaimi (1968), p. 195; Yāqūt (1970–71), p. 486.
84. Hamidullah (1953), p. 3.
85. Ibid., p. 38.
86. Ibid., p. 62.
87. Ibid., pp. 231–232.
88. One author works the other way round as he tries 'to show that the main principles of international law are in conformity with the basic doctrine or philosophy of Islam and perhaps may even be said to be part of that doctrine or philosophy.' Mahmassani (1966), p. 205.
89. Art. 38—not 30—of the Statute of the International Court of Justice says: 'The Court, whose function is to decide in accordance with international law such disputes as are submitted to it, shall apply: (a) . . .; (b) . . .; (c) . . .; (d) Subject to the provisions of Article 59, judicial decisions and the teachings of the most highly qualified publicists of the various nations, as subsidiary means for the determination of rules of law.'
90. Akhtar (1971), p. 33.
91. Al Ghunaimi (1968), p. 223.
92. Ezzeldin Foda, *The Protected Arab Court of Justice. A Study in Regional Jurisdiction with Specific Reference to the Muslim Law of Nations* (The Hague: Martinus Nijhoff, 1957), pp. 124–139.
93. This attitude can also be observed in writings on other branches of Islamic law. Often, the same arguments are used. Cf. J. Brugman, *De betekenis van het Mohammedaanse recht in het hedendaagse Egypte* (Diss. Leiden) (The Hague: 1960), pp. 131–150.
94. E. Nys, *Les Origines de droit international* (Brussels, 1894).
95. M. de Taube, 'Le monde de l'Islam et son influence sur l'Europe orientale.' In: *Académie de Droit International. Recueil des Cours* (1926), I, pp. 380–397.
96. Armanazi (1929), pp. 50–52; Hamidullah (1953), pp. 66–68; Manṣūr (1971), pp. 28–30; Al Ghunaimi (1968), pp. 82–86; Daqs (1972), p. 88.
97. J. Brugman (1960), p. 140.
98. Cf. Hamidullah (1953), pp. 43–44; Ḥasan (1959), p. 7; Mahmassani (1966), pp. 242–244; Sulṭān (1970), pp. 72–73, 157; Darāz (1950),

p. 149; Muḥammad Abū Zahra, *Al-ʿalāqāt al-dawliyya fī l-Islām* (Cairo: al-Dār al-Qawmiyya li-l-Ṭibāʿa wa-l-Nashr, 1384/1964), pp. 20–25.
99. Al Ghunaimi (1968), pp. 196–197.
100. Ibid., p. 198.
101. Ibid., p. 129.
102. To this category belong: Al Ghunaimi (1968), Sulṭān (1970), Manṣūr (1971) and Yāqūt (1970–71).
103. Descriptions of this kind are to be found in: Armanazi (1929), Rechid (1937), Darāz (1947), Hamidullah (1953), and Mahmassani (1966).
104. Contrary to Bell's translation which reads: *'and.'*
105. Al Ghunaimi (1968), pp. 69–70, 124–128; Sulṭān (1970), pp. 18–19, 178–185; Akhtar (1971), p. 28.
106. Yāqūt (1970–71), pp. 481–490.
107. Darāz (1950), p. 161; Mahmassani (1966), pp. 234–235; Al Ghunaimi (1968), pp. 91, 96–103; Sulṭān (1970), pp. 46, 201–207; Yāqūt (1970–71), pp. 746–747, note 1. One must doubt, however, whether these Muslim authors have really found the philosophers' stone in connection with this problem. The crux of international law is the absence of an authority that can enforce the observance of international legal rules by *all* legal subjects. Even if we assume that religious sanction can to a certain extent replace a law-enforcing authority, then this would still affect only the Muslim legal subjects.
108. Brugman (1960), p. 137.
109. Armanazi (1929), pp. 38–42; Rechid (1937), pp. 421–433; Abū Zahra (1964), pp. 72–73; Mahmassani (1966), pp. 264–267; Zuḥaylī (1965), pp. 328–345; Sulṭān (1970), pp. 199–201; Manṣūr (1971), pp. 327–329.
110. Whether this treaty, mentioned by Wāqidī and Ibn Isḥāq, has really existed is open to doubt. Cf. W. Montgomery Watt, *Muhammad in Medina* (London, etc.: Oxford University Press, 1956), pp. 196–197.
111. Cf. Chapter 2, par. 14.
112. Al Ghunaimi (1968), p. 211; Sulṭān (1970), p. 209.
113. Abū Zahra (1964), pp. 74–83; Zuḥaylī (1965), pp. 362–367; Al Ghunaimi (1968), pp. 184–185; Sulṭān (1970), p. 210.
114. Cf. Wensinck (1936–69), Vol. III, p. 98.
115. Muḥammad al-Bishbīshī, *Al-ʿalāqāt al-dawliyya al-islāmiyya* (Cairo: Al-Majlis al-Aʿlā li-l-Shu'ūn al-Islāmiyya, 1965), pp. 53–54; Aḥmad Shalabī, *Al-jihād fī l-tafkir al-Islāmi* (Cairo: Maktabat al-Nahḍa al-Miṣriyya, 1968), p. 114; Sulṭān (1970), pp. 208–209.

116. Cf. Chapter 2, par. 5.
117. Armanazi (1929), pp. 73–75; Rechid (1937), pp. 464–466; Ḥasan (1950), pp. 20–21; Hamidullah (1953), pp. 190–194; Abū Zahra (1964), pp. 94–95; Zuḥaylī (1965), pp. 150–161; Mahmassani (1966), p. 289; Sulṭān (1970), p. 248; Manṣūr (1971), pp. 296–303; Daqs (1972), p. 91.
118. Cf. pp. 33–37.
119. Manṣūr (1971), p. 320.
120. ʿAbd al-Mutaʿālī al-Ṣaʿidī, *Fī maydān al-ijtihād* (Helwan: Jamʿiyyat al-thaqāfa al-Islāmiyya, n.d.), pp. 133–139.
121. Hamidullah (1953), pp. 231–232.
122. Amin al-Khawlī, *Al-djundiyya wa-Il-silm. Wāqiʿ wa-mithāl* (Cairo: Dār al-Maʿārif, 1960), p. 106; Zaki (1965), p. 203; Hamidullah (1953), p. 283.
123. Cf. pp. 31–32.
124. The most detailed statement of the modernist position is to be found in Zuḥayli (1965), pp. 403–474, and Daqs (1972), pp. 550–569.
125. Hamidullah (1953), pp. 269–271; Zuḥayli (1965), p. 637; Mahmassani (1966), pp. 295–297.
126. Cf. pp. 38–40.
127. Rechid (1937), pp. 500–502; Ḥasan (1950), pp. 22–23; Zuḥaylī (1965), pp. 356–357; Bishbīshī (1965), pp. 53–58; Mahmassani (1966), pp. 53–58.
128. Abū Zahra (1964), pp. 78–79; Al Ghunaimi (1968), pp. 184–185; Manṣūr (1971), pp. 281–286, 370–379; Sharqāwī (1972), p. 40.

Notes to Chapter 9 (pp. 149–170)

1. Elie Kedourie, *The Chatham House Version and Other Middle Eastern Studies* (London, 1970), p. 177.
2. See Rudolph Peters, *Islam and Colonialism: The Doctrine of Jihad in Modern History* (The Hague, 1979), ch. 4.
3. This survey is based on the following literature: Nabīl ʿAbd al-Fattāḥ, *al-Muṣḥaf wa-l-Sayf: Ṣirāʿ al-Dīn wa-l-Dawla fī Miṣr, Ruʾya Awwaliyya* (Cairo, 1984); Hamied N. Ansari, 'The Islamic Militants in Egyptian Politics,' *International Journal of Middle East Studies*, xvi (1984), 123–44; Fouad Ajami, 'In the Pharaoh's Shadow: Religion and Authority in Egypt,' in *Islam in the Political Process*, ed. J. P. Piscatori (Cambridge, 1983), pp. 12–36; Nazih N. M. Ayubi, 'The Political Revival

of Islam: The Case of Egypt,' *International Journal of Middle East Studies,* xii (1980) 481–90; O. Carré and M. Seurat, 'L'utopie islamiste au Moyen-Orient arabe et particulièrement en Egypte et Syrie,' in *L'Islam et l'état dans le monde d'aujourd'hui,* ed. O. Carré (Paris, 1982), ch. 1; R. Hrair Dekmejian, 'The Anatomy of Islamic Revival: Legitimacy Crisis, Ethnic Conflict and the Search for an Islamic Alternative,' *Middle East Journal,* xxxiv (1980), 1–12; Ali E. Hillal Dessouki, 'Islamic Organizations in Egypt,' in *Islam and Power,* ed. Alexander S. Cudsi and Ali E. Hillal Dessouki (London, 1981), pp. 107–18; Saad Eddin Ibrahim, 'Anatomy of Egypt's Militant Islamic Groups: Methodological Note and Preliminary Findings,' *International Journal of Middle East Studies,* xii (1980), 423–53; *idem,* 'Islamic Militancy as a Social Movement: The Case of Two Groups in Egypt,' in *Islamic Resurgence in the Arab World,* ed. Ali E. Hillal Dessouki (New York, 1982) pp. 117–37; *idem,* 'Egypt's Islamic Militants,' *MERIP Reports,* ciii (1982), 5–14; Gilles Képel, *Le Prophète et le Pharaon: Les mouvements islamistes dans l'Egypte contemporaine* (Paris, 1984).

4. *Takfīr* or accusing of unbelief is a practice going back to the early Islamic sects like the Kharijites. More recently the Wahabi and the Sudanese Mahdi movement used it in order to justify war against their Muslim adversaries. In the Egyptian context the discussion goes back to the prison terms of the Muslim Brethren under Nasser. For a survey of the various answers to the question of who exactly were to be regarded as unbelievers, see Sālim ʿAlī al-Bahtasāwī, *al-Ḥukm wa-qadiyyat takfīr al-Muslim* (Cairo, 1397/1977).
5. See Sabine Hartert, 'Ein Aegyptisches *Fatwa* zu Camp David,' *Die Welt des Islams,* xxii (1982), 139–42; Peters, *Islam and Colonialism,* pp. 106–8.
6. A German translation was published by Sabine Hartert in the above mentioned article.
7. Italian translation in I. Camera d'Afflitto, 'Traduzione e commento del communicato emesso dagli ʿulama di al-Azhar, relativo all' accordo di pace tra Egitto e Israele,' *Oriente Moderno,* lx (1980), 79–84.
8. *al-Ahrām,* 18 May 1979.
9. *al-Fatāwā l-Islāmiyya min Dār al-Iftā al-Miṣriyya,* x (Cairo, 1403/1983), 3621–36.
10. See Peters, *Islam and Colonialism,* p. 33.
11. *Al-Daʿwa,* July 1979, pp. 58–9.
12. ʿAbd al-ʿAẓīm al-Maṭāʿnī is a professor in the faculty of Arabic Linguistics of al-Azhar University and the editor of the *fatwā* section of *al-Daʿwa.*

13. The reaction of al-Azhar, written by Muḥammad Ḥusām al-Dīn at the instruction of the Sheikh al-Azhar, ʿAbd al-Raḥmān Bayṣār, was published in *al-Daʿwa* of Sept. 1979, pp. 30–3, followed by al-Mataʿni's reply.
14. See Képel, *Prophète et Pharaon*, p. 108.
15. *Al-Daʿwa*, Jan. 1977, p. 47 (a recation against radical Islamic movements).
16. *Ibid*, May 1978, p. 41.
17. *Ibid.*, Oct. 1978, p. 3.
18. *Ibid.*, May 1980, p. 7.
19. Text published in *al-Aḥrār*, 14 Dec. 1981, and in *al-Fatāwā l-Islāmiyya min Dār al-Iftā al Miṣriyya*, x (Cairo, 1403/1983), 3762–92; Parts of the text (about one third) published in *Jamāl al-Bannā, al-Farīda al-Ghāʾiba: Jihād al-Sayf . . . am Jihād al-ʿAql. . . ? Maʿ fuṣūl kamīla min kitāb "al-Farīḍa al-Ghāʾiba" al-Mansūb li-l-muhandis Muḥammad ʿAbd al-Salām Faraj* (Cairo, 1984). I quote from the text published in *al-Fatāwā l-Islāmiyya*.
20. Képel, *Prophète et Pharaon*, p. 83.
21. Text in *al-Fatāwā l-Islāmiyya*, x. 3726–61; French tr. in G. C. Anawati, 'Une résurgence du Kharijisme au XXe siècle: L'Obligation absente,' *Mélanges de l'Institut dominicain d'Etudes orientales*, xvi (1983), 191–228.
22. For the texts of these *fatwās* see Ibn Taymiyya, *al-Fatāwā l-Kubrā* (Repr. Beirut, 1397/1978), iv. 331–58.
23. *al-Fatāwā l-Islāmiyya*, x. 3766.
24. *Ibid.*, p. 3773.
25. *Ibid.*, p. 3774.
26. *Ibid.*, pp. 3776–7.
27. *Ibid.*, p. 3750.
28. See R. Peters and Gert J. J. de Vries, 'Apostasy in Islam,' *Die Welt des Islams*, xvii (1976–7), 1–25, and the *fiqh* literature quoted there.
29. *al-Fatāwā l-Islāmiyya*, x. 3743.
30. *Ibid.*, p. 3745.

Bibliography

GENERAL WORKS ON JIHAD IN WESTERN LANGUAGES

Cross, Crescent and Sword: The Justification and Limitation of War in Western and Islamic Tradition. Edited by J. T. Johnson and J. Kelsay. New York: Greenwood Press, 1990.

Ghunaimi, Mohammad Talaat Al. *The Muslim Conception of International Law and the Western approach.* The Hague, 1968. An attempt to present the doctrine of jihad as a form of Islamic international law.

Hamidullah, Muhammad. *Muslim Conduct of State.* 6th rev. ed. Lahore, 1973. A survey of the classical jihad doctrine based on an extensive reading of the classical sources, but somewhat marred by the author's apologetic approach.

Just War and Jihad: Historical and Theoretical Perspectives on War and Peace in Western and Islamic Traditions. Edited by J. Kelsay and J. T. Johnson. New York, 1991.

Jansen, Johannes J. G. *The Neglected Duty: The Creed of Sadat's Assassins and Islamic Resurgence in the Middle East.* New York and London, 1986. An analysis and translation of *al-Farida al-Gha'iba*. The translation, especially of the numerous quotations of the classical works on Islamic law and the *hadith,* is not always reliable.

Khadduri, Majid. *War and Peace in the Law of Islam.* Baltimore, 1955. A reliable survey of the classical doctrine of jihad.

Krüger, Hilmar. *Fetwa und Siyar: zur internationalrechtlichen Gutachtenpraxis der osmanischen Şeyh ül-Islām vom 17. bis 19. Jahrhundert unter besonderen Berücksichtigung des "Behcet ül-Fetāvā."* Wiesbaden, 1968. Examines the role of the jihad doctrine in Ottoman foreign relations from the 17th to the 19th century.

Kruse, Hans. *Islamische Völkerrechtslehre.* Bochum, 1979. Deals especially with treaties between the Islamic and other states according to classical Hanafite law.

Morabia, A. *Le ǧihād dans l'islam médiéval: le "combat sacré" des origines au XIIe siècle.* Paris: Albin Michel, 1993. A careful and detailed analysis of the origins of the jihad doctrine and its historical development until the 12th century.

Noth, Albrecht. *Heiliger Krieg und heiliger Kampf in Islam und Christentum.* Bonn, 1966. A comparison of jihad with similar notions in Christianity against the historical background of the Crusades.

Peters, Rudolph. *Islam and Colonialism: The Doctrine of Jihad in Modern History.* The Hague, 1979. Deals with jihad as a means of mobilization in anti-colonial struggles and with new interpretations of the jihad doctrine.

Peters, Rudolph. "The Political Relevance of the Jihad Doctrine in Sadat's Egypt." In *National and International Politics in the Middle East: Essays in Honour of Elie Kedourie.* Edited by E. Ingram, pp. 252–273. London, 1986.

Salem, I.K., *Islam und Völkerrecht: das Völkerrecht in der islamischen Weltanschauung.* Berlin: Express Edition, 1984.

Shaybānī, Muhammad al-. *The Islamic Law of Nations: Shaybani's Siyar.* Tr. and intr. by M. Khadduri. Baltimore, 1966. A translation of one of the earliest works on jihad.

Sivan, Emmanuel. *L'islam et la Croisade: Idéologie et propagande dans les réactions musulmanes aux Croisades.* Paris, 1968.

TRANSLATIONS OF CLASSICAL SOURCES ON JIHAD

Hanafite School

Abū Yusūf (d. 182/798), *Kitāb al-Kharāj.*

E. Fagnan, *Le livre de l'impôt foncier.* Paris: Paul Geuthner, 1921, p. 27–36, 290–320.

Muḥammad Ibn al-Ḥasan al-Shaybānī (d. 189/804), *Kitāb al-Siyar.*

Majid Khadduri, *The Islamic Law of Nations. Shaybani's Siyar.* Baltimore: The Johns Hopkins Press, 1966. 311 p.

Aḥmad al-Qudūri (d. 428/1037), *al-Mukhtaṣar.*

L. Bercher, *Le Livre de la guerre sainte. Revue Tunisienne de Droit,* 2 (1954), p. 123–49.

Ch. Solvet, *Institut du droit mahométan sur la guerre avec les infidèles.* Paris: 1829.

Burhān al-Dīn Maḥmud al-Maḥbūbī (d. 7th/13th century), *Wiqāyat al-Riwāya.*

B. Haneberg, *Das Muslimische Kriegsrecht.* Abh. d. bayer. Ak. d. Wissensch., Philos.-Philol. Cl. 12 Bd, 2. Abth. München: 1870. p. 276–290.

Muḥammad Ibn ʿAlī al-Ḥaṣkafī (d. 1088/1677), *al-Durr al-Mukhtār sharḥ Tanwīr al-Abṣār.*

Brij Mohan Dayal, *The Durr al-Mukhtār, being the well-known commentary of the Tanwīr al-Absār of Muḥammad ibn ʿAbdallah al-Tamartashi.* Lucknow: 1913.

Malikite School

Ibn Abī Zayd al-Qayrawānī (d. 386/996), *al-Risāla.*

L. Bercher, *La risāla ou Epître sur les éléments du dogme et la loi de l'Islam selon le rite Mālikite.* Algiers: Jules Carbonel, 1949, p. 162–7, 291.

E. Fagnan, *Risala ou traité abrégé de droit malékite et morale musulmane.* Paris: Paul Geuthner, 1914, p. 107–10, 231.

ʿAlī Ibn ʿAbd al-Raḥmān Ibn Hudhayl al-Andalusī (d. end of the 8th/14th century). *Tuḥfat al-anfus wa-shiʿār sukkān al-Andalus.*

Louis Mercier, *L'Ornement des âmes et la devise de habitants d'el Andalus. Traité de Guerre Sainte Islamique.* Paris: Paul Geuthner, 1939. 349 p.

Khalīl Ibn Isḥāq (d. 767/1365), *al-Mukhtaṣar.*

J. Guidi and D. Santillana, *Il Muḥtaṣar, sommario del diritto malechita di Ḫalil.* 2 vols. Milan: Ulrico Hoepli, 1919. Vol. 1, p. 385-424.

E. Fagnan, *Le Djihad ou guerre sainte.* Algiers: 1908.

A. Perron, *Précis de jurisprudence musulmane.* Exploration scientifique de l'Algérie pendant les années 1840–42. Paris: 1844–54, vols. 10–15.

Shafiᶜite School

ᶜAlī Ibn Muḥammad al-Māwardī (d. 450/1058). *Kitāb al-Aḥkām al-Sulṭāniyya.*

E. Fagnan, *Les statuts governementaux ou règles du droit public et administratif.* Algiers: Adolphe Jourdan, 1915. p. 71–131, 267–99.

Abū Isḥāq Ibrāhīm al-Shirāzī (d. 476/1083), *Kitāb al-Tanbīh.*

G. H. Bousquet, *Kitāb at-Tanbīh ou le Livre de l'Admonition.* 4 vols. Algiers: La Maison des Livres, 1949–52. Vol. 4, p. 35–51.

Abū Shudjāᶜ (d. 593/1196), *al-Taqrīb fī al-Fiqh.*

S. Keyzer, *Précis de jurisprudence musulmane selon le rite Chaféite.* Leyden: E. J. Brill, 1859. P. 52–4.

G. H. Bousquet, *Abrégé de la loi musulmane selon le rite de l'Imam El-Chafi. Revue Algérienne,* 1935. I, p. 193–207; 1936, I, 1–16, 48–52, 66–72, 78–86.

Abū Zakarīyā Yaḥyā al-Nawawī (d. 676/1278), *Minhāj al-Ṭālibīn.*

L. W. C. van den Berg, *Le Guide des Zélés Croyants. Manuel de jurisprudence selon le rite de Chāfiᶜi.* 3 vols. Batavia: Imprimerie du Gouvernement, 1882–4. Vol. 3, p. 255–88 (see, however, the corrections in Bousquet's translation of Shīrāzī).

Badr al-Dīn Ibn Djāmāᶜa (d. 733/1333), *Taḥrīr al-Aḥkām fī Tadbīr Millat al-Islām.*

Hans Kofler, *Ibn Ǧamāᶜa's Handbuch des islamischen Staats-und Verwaltungsrecht. Islamica* VII (1935), p. 35–64, Schlussheft (1938), p. 18–130.

Ibn Qāsim al-Ghazzī (d. 918/1522), *Fatḥ al-Qarīb* (cmt. on *al-Taqrīb fī al-Fiqh* by Abū Shudjāᶜ).

L. W. C. van den Berg, *La Révélation de l'Omniprésent.* Leyden: E. J. Brill, 1894. P. 604–31 (see, however, the corrections in Bousquet's transl. of Shīrāzī).

Ahmad ibn Naqib al-Misri (d. 1368), ᶜUmdat al-Sālik

Noah Ha Mim Keller (ed. and tr.), *The Reliance of the Traveller: a Classical Manual of Islamic Sacred Law.* Evanston, IL: Sunna Books, 1991, pp. 599–611.

Hanbalite School

ʿAbdallāh Ibn Aḥmad Ibn Qudāma (d. 620/1223), *al-ʿUmda fī Aḥkām al-Fiqh.*

H. Laoust, *Le précis de droit d'Ibn Qudāma.* Beirut: Institut Français de Damas, 1950. P. 271–81.

Taqī al-Dīn Ibn Taymiyyah (d. 728/1238), *al-Siyāsa al-Sharʿiyya.*

H. Laoust, *Le traité de droit public d'Ibn Taimiyah. Tr. ann. de la Siyāsah Šarʿiyyah.* Beirut: Institut Français de Damas, 1948. P. 122–36.

Omar A. Farrukh, *On public and Private Law in Islam, or Public Policy in Islamic Jurisprudcence.* Beirut: Khayat's, 1966. P. 135–63.

Shiʿite works

Al-Muḥaqqiq al-Ḥillī (d. 676/1277), *Sharāʾiʿ al-Islām fī Masāʾil al-Ḥalāl wa-al-Ḥarām.*

A. Querry, *Droit Musulman. Recueil de lois concernant les Musulmans schyites.* 2 vols. Paris: Imprimerie Nationale, 1871–2. Vol. 1, p. 321–5.

RECENT ISLAMIC WRITINGS ON JIHAD IN WESTERN LANGUAGES

Khalifa Abd al-Hakim, *War and Peace.* In: Aziz Ahmad and G. E. von Grunebaum, *Muslim Self-statement in India and Pakistan, 1858–1968.* Wiesbaden: Harrassowitz, 1970. P. 182–9.

Muhammad Abu Zahra, *Begriff des Krieges im Islam.* Aus dem Ar. übers. v. Prof. Dr. Omar Amin von Leers, revidiert v. Dr. Ezz El-Din Ismail. Cairo: Der Oberste Rat für Islamische Angelegenheiten, n.d. 73 p.

Mohamed Abu Zahra, *International Relations in Islam.* In: *The first Conference of the Academy of Islamic Research.* Cairo: S.O.P.-Press, 1383/1964, p. 187–236.

Mawlawi Cheragh Ali, *A Critical Exposition of Popular Jihad:* Calcutta: Thecker, Spink & Co., 1885, civ + 227 + 249 p.
Najib Armanazi, *L'Islam et le droit international.* Thèse. Paris: 1929. 162 p.
Mohamed Aly Bechebichy, *Les relations internationales islamiques.* Tr. p. Ibrahim el-Mouwelhy, rev. p. Ahmed Rachad. Cairo: Conseil Supérieur des Affairs Islamiques, 1966. 56 p.
Mohammed Talaat al-Ghunaimi, *The Muslim Conception of International Law and the Western Approach.* The Hague: Martinus Nijhoff, 1968. 228 p.
Abu Said Mohammad Husain, *A Treatise on jihad.* Tr. fr. Urdu. 2nd impr. Lahore: Victoria Press, 1887, 32 p.
J. Jomier, *Le Commentaire Coranique du Manar.* Paris: Maisonneuve, 1954. P. 251–81 (summarizes the ideas of Muḥammad ʿAbduh and Muḥammad Rashīd Riḍā).
Zafrullah Khan, *Islam and International Relations. Internationale Spectator* (The Hague) 10 (1956), nr. 11, pp. 308–22.
Ahmed Rechid, *l'Islam et le droit des gens.* In: *Recueil des Cours. Académie de droit international,* 1937 (Paris: 1938). Vol. II, pp. 375–504.
Aslam Siddiqi, *Djihad, an Instrument of Islamic Revolution. Islamic Studies* 2 (1963), pp. 383–98.

Acknowledgements

The author has adapted his own previously published material for this book. Texts by other authors are reprinted in their original forms.

Throughout the book, the author has replaced Bell's translation[1] of quotations from the Koran, which he used in earlier works, with Arberry's translation.[2] The author gratefully acknowledges the original publishers of the following material:

Chapter 1: Copyright © 1995 by Oxford University Press, Inc. for *The Oxford Encyclopedia of the Modern Islamic World,* edited by John L. Esposito. Reprinted by permission.

Chapter 2: Copyright © 1973 by Sh. Muhammad Ashraf, Lahore, for *Ṣaḥīḥ Muslim,* rendered into English by ʿAbdul Ḥamīd Ṣiddīqī. Reprinted by permission.

Chapter 3: Copyright © 1989 by Kegan Paul International, London and New York, for Malik ibn Anas, *Al-Muwaṭṭaʾ of Imam Mālik ibn Anas: The First Formulation of Islamic Law.* Translated by Aisha Abdurrahman Bewley. Reprinted by permission.

Chapter 4 and 7: Copyright © 1977 by E. J. Brill, Leiden, for *Jihad in Mediaeval and Modern Islam: The Chapter on Jihad from Averroes' Legal Handbook 'Bidāyat al-Mudjtahid' and the Treatise 'Koran and Fighting' by the Late Shaykh al-Azhar, Maḥmūd Shaltūt.* Translated and annotated by Rudolph Peters. Reprinted by permission.

Chapters 6 and 8: Copyright © 1979 by Mouton-de Gruyter, Ber-

[1]Edinburgh, 1939.
[2]A. J. Arberry, *The Koran Interpreted.* Oxford: Oxford University Press, 1964.

Illustrations in the text were reproduced courtesy of the British Museum and Rudolph Peters.